Psychology & Crime

Key Approaches to Criminology

Psychology and Crime

When this book series was first conceived one of its key rationales came from my experience of working in a department where students studied Criminology as one half of a Joint Honours degree. By far the most popular combination was Criminology and Psychology, yet students frequently were unable to make any theoretical or empirical links between the two subjects. Little wonder, really, given that the two subjects were housed in separate buildings, on different parts of the campus, and taught by teams who operated independently. The ambition of the book, then, is to help academics and students make appropriate intellectual connections between these related disciplines, integrating the two subject 'halves' of a Joint Honours degree or team-taught modules.

It is, of course, not just Joint Honours students who sometimes struggle to see the relevance of studying crime and criminal justice within a broader context. It is virtually impossible to study, teach or research in Criminology without dipping into scholarship from Psychology, yet there is often a lack of understanding of psychological and psychoanalytical approaches, and sometimes downright resistance to the contribution of psychologists to our understandings of offending, victimization, governance, control, and so on. Here is a book that challenges such antipathy; though not before itself subjecting both the discipline and the common myths perpetuated about criminological psychology to critical analysis. Craig Webber provides a lively, erudite and hugely relevant overview of *Psychology and Crime*, not only introducing readers to the historical contours that have shaped what we know (and what we think we know) about psychological approaches to studying crime and deviance, but also tackling head-on some of the most contentious, contested and urgent issues facing criminologists and criminal justice practitioners in the current epoch. Combining theoretical rigour with practical, familiar examples, students and other readers finally have a resource that will invigorate their understanding of the synergies between the two fields. Not only does *Psychology and Crime* fulfil the ambitions of the *Key Approaches to Criminology* series but it is, quite simply, a terrific read.

Yvonne Jewkes
Series Editor

Psychology & Crime

Craig Webber

Los Angeles | London | New Delhi
Singapore | Washington DC

First published 2010

SAGE Publications Ltd
1 Oliver's Yard
55 City Road
London EC1Y 1SP

SAGE Publications Inc.
2455 Teller Road
Thousand Oaks, California 91320

SAGE Publications India Pvt Ltd
B 1/I 1 Mohan Cooperative Industrial Area
Mathura Road
New Delhi 110 044

SAGE Publications Asia-Pacific Pte Ltd
33 Pekin Street #02-01
Far East Square
Singapore 048763

Library of Congress Control Number Available

British Library Cataloguing in Publication data

A catalogue record for this book is available
from the British Library

ISBN 978-1-4129-1941-8
ISBN 978-1-4129-1942-5

Typeset by C&M Digitals (P) Ltd, Chennai, India
Printed by MPG Books Group, Bodmin, Cornwall
Printed on paper from sustainable resources

Mixed Sources
Product group from well-managed
forests and other controlled sources
www.fsc.org Cert no. SA-COC-1565
© 1996 Forest Stewardship Council
FSC

For Sarah and Maia

What gets into you all? We've studied the problem. We've been studying it for damn well near a century, yes, but we get no further with our studies. You've got a good home here, good loving parents, you've got not too bad a brain. Is it some devil that crawls inside of you?

Stanley Kubrick's *A Clockwork Orange*, 1971.

Contents

Preface

The interest in crime and psychology is often referred to as if it were a new phenomenon. New textbooks, university courses and journals devoted to the subject appear daily. There is both academic and popular fascination with the 'criminal mind' and violent individuals. The oft-mentioned rationale for students wishing to study psychological approaches to crime is the desire to find out what makes criminals tick. By attending to what is new about the subject, the background and historical continuities are rendered opaque. This has led to the subject being seen as separate to sociological criminology and divorced from the rich theoretical history that has accrued in this field. This book aims to restore these links. One of the themes of this volume, therefore, is to highlight the already existing, albeit often implicit, psychological elements of criminology. Similarly, I wish to point out the similarities between arguments that emanate from within psychology and sociology and where integration would lead to more robust analysis.

Despite the title, the book will refer to this field as criminological psychology, following Clive Hollin's recommendation in an early textbook (Hollin 1989), and more recently in 2002 in the *Oxford Handbook of Criminology*. The reason for this is to more fully embed psychological research within the rich tradition of criminology. Psychological criminology tends to be a more narrowly delimited field which eschews sociological traditions. Moreover, this is also in accord with the description of the field in the British Psychological Society's journal, *Legal and Criminological Psychology*. Other terms have developed to describe psychologists working in this field, notably **forensic psychology**. Many of the studies mentioned are written by academics who would more fully associate themselves with this term. Work in the area of eyewitness testimony, risk assessment of offenders and treatment strategies are all part of the work of forensic psychologists. However, forensic psychology is often even more divorced from the rich heritage of sociological criminology and so the term criminological psychology will be used instead to better describe this field and promote the direction that the psychological study of crime should follow.

A further issue that the book will seek to redress is the often uncritical approach to crime of much psychology. Seemingly unaware of critical criminology's critique of definitions of crime or the postmodern challenges to orthodox social science, psychological approaches are turned into systems of risk control with little understanding of the wider social implications of this enterprise (Hudson 2003). Consequently, this book will aim to demystify some of the myths of psychological criminology through situating the subject within its historical and theoretical foundations, whilst maintaining a critical awareness of the field's advantages and limitations. The book does not aim to provide an exhaustive overview of every aspect of the study of crime. Rather the aim is to stimulate debate as to the role of psychology in the study of crime. A key theme that will be traced throughout each chapter will be how criminology and psychology has shifted from finding cures for the causes of crime to attempts to control it. The main point is that the sheen of scientific rationality brought by contemporary psychology can lead to short-cuts in police investigations.

Organisation of the book

Chapter 1 presents an overview of the history of the study of crime and notes how sociology and psychology were once more closely linked than they are now and that theory reflects the historical period in which it is created.

Chapter 2 is the first of two chapters that explore crime that is committed predominantly by individuals. A critical analysis is presented of this form of investigation. The American F-B-I. approach, in particular, is unable to account for wider structural issues in its attempt to get into the mind of the serial killer. This is contrasted with the work of David Canter.

Chapter 3 explores the investigation of sex crimes. Following the theme of the book, it is argued that only through combining different forms of analysis can we begin to understand this crime.

Chapter 4 begins the process of widening the book's focus to include the social psychology of crime. The topic of this chapter is crime in groups. The discussion focuses on youth crime, but also explores the way that psychology and sociology can be combined fruitfully to enable a more robust analysis that draws on the strengths of each discipline.

Chapter 5 investigates research into mass murder. Contrasting this phenomenon with serial murder, the discussion begins with crimes committed by individuals or small groups such as the recent massacres at schools and universities, and then widens out to look at killings during a war or conflict. This is a topic that has not been explored by sociological criminology to the extent that might be expected. A contrast is made to the greater interest that psychologists have shown for this topic.

Chapter 6 looks at the contemporary interest in terrorism and argues this topic needs to be understood through a combination of historical, psychological and sociological methods of research.

Chapter 7 is a discussion of the role of psychology in the investigation of crime. In particular, there is a discussion of research into eyewitness memory, the detection of deception, the decision making of juries and police interviewing techniques.

The final chapter presents an overview of the main themes of the book. It is argued that psychology needs to become more fully aware of the social, historical and political aspects of its research in order to avoid becoming an uncritical system of governance. The book ends by exploring themes presented in the first chapter and raised throughout to do with **risk**, surveillance and the promotion of order over justice in the twenty-first century. A glossary of some key terms is provided at the end of the book. When a term is further defined in the glossary it will appear in bold in the text.

Acknowledgements

I would like to thank Caroline Porter at Sage for being ever so patient. The best commissioning editor a first-time author could have. The students at the University of Southampton for their lively contributions in seminars on the topics in this book. The constructive comments from the reviewers provided some useful suggestions for making the book better. The errors and omissions are, of course, still mine. I must thank the newest addition to the Webber clan, my beautiful daughter Maia, who provided too many distractions during the last few months of this project. Some distractions are worth it. And my fantastic wife Sarah for her love and support during the writing, thinking and worrying.

1

Psychology, Sociology and Crime: Mapping the Historical Terrain

Chapter Contents

OVERVIEW

The opening chapter sets the study of crime in a historical context, arguing that the psychology of crime is context dependent and what we choose to study is as much a cultural phenomenon as it is one directed by social scientific concerns. Historical fashions direct the gaze of the psychologist, and learning historical lessons on the uses and abuses of psychology are essential requirements of contemporary psychology.

KEY TERMS

determinism late modernity modernity postmodernity

This opening chapter will discuss the changing fortunes of psychological and sociological accounts of crime and criminals. It will chart the emergence of different theories both in terms of how they fit together and their growth from engagement, and critique, of other theories. The chapter will not seek to reiterate the history of the subject, but to focus on how theories gained resonance and were reflected in the society and culture in which they were expressed, and how in turn they had an impact on social policy and popular images of crimes and criminals. The key theme is that there are many overlaps between sociology and psychology that need to be recognised and that drawing on the findings of each discipline can be a very powerful way to create more robust theories. This is not to say that these overlaps are in any way deliberate or that the authors were even aware of each other's arguments, although that may be the case on occasion. The point is to highlight the fruitless disciplinary boundary forming that results in academics only referring to research cited in 'their' journals, such as psychologists only citing 'psychological' research and similarly for sociological criminologists.

The sociologist Nikolas Rose, who has written extensively on the role of psychology in society, referred to this as the 'baneful disciplinization of the human sciences' (Rose 1999: xvi). This chapter is a reminder, followed through in the rest of the book, that disciplinary insularity is an outmoded position to take when the ease with which one can conduct research across academic boundaries allows, and encourages, theoretical synthesis. A criticism of this type of theory synthesis is that logical contradictions between one approach and another can become blurred. Certainly, it is accepted that an uncritical synthesis is open to this problem.

However, what is being argued here is that this critique should not close off critical theoretical synthesis and wider research beyond academic boundaries. This chapter aims to foster a historical imagination that remembers that such synthesis was once commonplace. What this book represents is a form of what the criminologist Gregg Barak terms 'integrative criminology'. He defines this as an 'interdisciplinary approach to understanding crime and crime control which incorporates at least two disciplinary (or non-disciplinary) bodies of knowledge' (Barak 2001: 153; Barak 1998). Although Barak suggests that this is a relatively new approach, this book will highlight the moments when integration has already occurred.

One example is Taylor, Walton and Young's (1973) *The New Criminology* that sought to combine Marxist and symbolic interactionist accounts of crime as well as social psychology to provide a fully social theory of crime. This book was written at a time when questioning the legitimacy of those in authority was commonplace, consequently, it will also be noted that theory reflects the concerns of the time (Danziger 1990). The chapter will conclude by noting that the textbook is critical not of psychology *per se*, but rather the way myths have developed around what criminological psychologists do. Popular representations or 'shadow criminology' to use Paul Rock's term (1978) of serious criminals as pathological monsters different from ourselves are not borne out by the evidence. The thought that serious criminals may be just like you, live next door to you, live with you, is more frightening and unsettling than believing that criminals are monsters.

It is an obvious place to start a book on psychology and crime with an overview of some of the major psychological approaches to studying human behaviour (see Table 1.1). This is not meant to be an exhaustive overview, merely a reminder for those who have already studied psychology, and an introduction for those who have not. All psychological approaches share the common focus of studying internal mental processes. Psychology can be distinguished from psychiatry through the latter's focus on the study and treatment of mental illness and emotional disturbance. Psychiatry is a branch of medicine that, for the most part, focuses on illness and derivations from 'normal'[1] behaviour. Psychology is interested in a broader range of human behaviour that includes mental functions such as perception (e.g. taste, colour or object sizes), the capacity and ability of memory, as well as behaviour that some might describe as 'abnormal' such as aggression. The manner of doing this varies according to the tradition.

The rise of the science of crime and the challenge of the 'risk society'

This section charts the rise of a science of crime and ends with a discussion of the risk society thesis. It is possible to talk about one science of crime because until

Table 1.1 *Perspectives in psychology*

Perspectives in psychology	Key idea	Research method	Criticism
Biological	Psychological principles derived from biological mechanisms. Evolutionary theory is also sometimes used within this approach.	Invasive techniques to monitor brain activity has given way to techniques such as Magnetic Resonance Imaging, a non-invasive brain scan.	Reductionist. Biology cannot account for all psychological principles. Evolutionary ideas are powerful. However, unlike animals, humans create meaning.
Behavioural	*Tabula rasa:* The Blank slate. Humans learn their behaviour.	Stimulus–response research.	Neglects the meaning that humans afford behaviour. Neglects the role of human agency in choosing to act in certain ways.
Cognitive	Brain a computer. Behaviour is more complex than the stimulus–response psychology that preceded it.	Experiments that seek to find out how people think about their behaviour.	Little scope for humans to make sense of the world. We are more than just an information processor.
Psychoanalytic	Unconscious impulses direct behaviour.	Psychoanalysis, combination of free association in dialogue with a therapist.	Main ideas such as the existence of an ego, superego etc. have not been proven to exist.
Social Psychology	Humans construct the world and what it means to them.	Observation and experimentation.	Different approaches, can be non-scientific where observations are carried out in a non-systematic way. Can also be scientific through the use of tools such as surveys and questionnaires.

recently there were significant overlaps in the main aims of those interested in the study of crime; namely the search for the cause of crime. All vibrant disciplines are beset by controversies and heated debates, however, criminology is somewhat different, not least because, as will be argued below, it is not a discipline at all. The tensions that exist within criminology tend to be split between the two dominant subjects that form its core ideas, sociology and psychology. Recently, these two subjects have viewed each other with suspicion and occasional contempt. Where sociology tends to place its emphasis on society and environment, psychology situates its main focus within the individual. This often leads to diametrically opposed explanations for phenomena and is sometimes referred to as the **structure/agency debate**. Taking poverty as an example, sociologists tend to see this phenomenon as having an external effect on people, it is an economic phenomena that individuals can have relatively marginal control over. For some psychologists, poverty is the result of individual failure due to low IQ, personality or lack of positive motivation such as might be caused by depression. When these two approaches are contained within criminology not only are there the usual heated discussions but there is the added frisson of distrust in another discipline's methods and theoretical foundations. Yet, fundamentally, the concern is with what causes crime.

To a certain extent this is a stereotype of the differences between sociology and psychology, but it is one held by many academics. However, this chapter will seek to remind those who hold this opinion that a certain amount of historical amnesia (Pearson 1983, 1994) has set in that leads to forgetfulness of the significant overlaps between the two approaches. For those students not yet tainted by the animosity, the chapter merely seeks to show that there are useful theoretical and empirical overlaps between sociological and psychological approaches to crime and deviance. The following demonstrates the interconnectivity of sociology and psychology when both are brought together in criminology by looking at the way that the study of crime became increasingly 'scientific'. Moreover, the bipolarity of the structure/agency debate has developed into a more complex argument that posits an integration between the two extremes of structural **determinism** and the free choice of the agent. By way of setting out the argument early, W.I. Thomas in the first edition of the *American Journal of Sociology* in 1894 noted that sociology and social psychology were inseparable (Strauss 1964). As will be noted, social psychology is a distinct branch of psychology that perhaps more than any other fits with the sociological approach. But, none the less, such is the widening gap between the two disciplines that psychology is more likely to be seen in its own department rather than sharing one with sociology.

According to Garland (2002) criminology as a 'science of crime' has been in existence for about 120 years. The term 'criminology' was created in the 1890s as a broader term than others such as criminal sociology or criminal psychology. The latter two terms are too specific and separately based within disciplinary boundaries peculiar to their own traditions. Consequently, the discipline of criminology from the outset subsumed the concerns of other, more established traditions within its intellectual remit. As Lea has noted (1998), criminology can be seen not as a subject in its own right, but as a field that academics from other disciplines can enter, such as economists, historians, geographers, psychologists and sociologists. The only thing distinct about this field is that those who enter it study crime first and foremost, and the focus tends to be on the question of what causes crime. How academics from different subjects do that is, to a large degree, based upon the traditions of their 'master' disciplines. Hence, Garland has argued that '[i]ts **epistemological** threshold is a low one, making it susceptible to pressures and interests generated elsewhere' (2002: 17). Garland also criticises the argument that criminological questions were being asked by many people before the term itself became widespread from the 1890s. Eighteenth-century philosophers such as Jeremy Bentham and Cesare Beccaria may have discussed crime, but they were not asking distinctive 'criminological' questions that were concerned with what makes the criminal different from the non-criminal and what causes this differentiation. Instead, their concerns were with the nature of the responses to crime by society. Criminals were, by and large, rational actors choosing to commit crime and therefore should be punished in proportion to the seriousness of the offence.

Punishment should take the form of attempting to change the moral failures of the offender in prisons. The discipline of psychology, as a science of human behaviour distinct from philosophy or medicine, can be traced to the later nineteenth century. No precise dates are possible, but certainly from about 1875 a new series of questions were asked that may be called psychological with the creation of the first psychology laboratory by Wilhelm Wundt in 1879 being a major factor in psychology's further development (Rose 1985; Janz 2004).

The early history of psychology in Britain shows only a slow growth with about 30 lecturing staff in English universities and six chairs in psychology (which means there were only six professors of psychology) up until the Second World War. At this time, the main task of psychology was to measure the mental attributes of humans. This process of categorisation, measurement and comparison lead to the creation of the 'normal' range of attributes that a human should have against which people could be compared. However, it was not the psychologists who sought out the problems to which this new science could be directed. Instead, it was those for whom effective and controllable humans were useful. Early psychology was directed towards industry, education, the military and the courts. These institutions, when run efficiently, maintained and reproduced a set of practices that, by their very efficiency, would reveal someone who deviated from these norms. Thus, the norms of the institution were what psychologists had to use as the yardstick with which to measure deviations. As Rose has argued (1985), psychology is a science that aims to regulate social life, it is a science that evolved to maintain the functional efficiency of the social world. One could add a Marxist analysis to this and argue that such functional efficiency is an integral feature of a capitalist world where to question too much the way things are is to potentially cause anarchy and rebellion. Behaviour that does not follow the functional efficiency necessary for the smooth running of business needs to be held in check and psychology is best placed to do that. However, psychology has recently been confronted by a new challenge that some see as indicative of a move to a late or postmodern society. It has been argued that there has been a shift away from individual causes of crime towards the statistical analysis of a group's risk factors. This has impacted on the way that crime and justice research is carried out.

It has been argued that the search for individual causes of crime fell out of fashion between the 1970s and 2000 (Garland 2001; Hudson 2003). David Garland argued that the:

> new policy advice is to concentrate on substituting prevention for cure, reducing the supply of opportunities, increasing situational and social controls, and modifying everyday routines. The welfare of deprived social groups, or the needs of maladjusted individuals, are much less central to this way of thinking. (2001: 16)

Criminologists have drawn on the risk society thesis in literature by sociologists such as Anthony Giddens (1990) and Ulrich Beck (1992), to analyse changes in the way that the apparatus of social control and justice has changed. Rather than focus on the risk factors of an individual, criminal justice has increasingly moved towards making judgements that are collective in focus and based on prediction (O'Malley 2001). This is a form of actuarialism, the kind of risk assessment undertaken by insurance companies to determine how likely it is that a car might be stolen. For example, rather than looking at the risk posed by an individual sex offender, statistical judgements based on all sex offenders are applied to the individual to categorise their potential risk, such as after release from prison (Feeley and Simon 1994). This is based on the belief that treating sex offenders is impossible, too difficult or too expensive (Hudson 2003). Moreover, in the risk society we are increasingly challenging the expertise of experts, such as psychologists or criminologists (Giddens 1990). Essentially experts cannot offer what society wants, security. This has clearly impacted on the work of psychologists, but how profoundly it has undermined the core philosophy of the focus on individual differences is unclear. In many ways, there is a contradiction within psychology anyway, since many theories attempt to categorise individuals into groups. Moreover, there are many criticisms of the risk society thesis, some point out that the perceived shift to a focus on risk is nothing new. Fears over terrorism, as Chapter 6 will show, are not exclusive to those living after '9/11'. Moreover, since New Labour were elected in the UK in 1997 the much quoted phrase 'tough on crime, tough on the causes of crime' has had a tentative, patchy but nevertheless significant effect. After the credit crunch and world-wide recession, the part-nationalisation of the banks and other parts of industry and the election of the Democrat Barack Obama as American President, we may yet see a return to welfarism and away from the sense of risk so pervasive under President George Bush and Prime Minister Tony Blair.

Historical developments in the theory of crime

Historians have tended to split the history of western development into various eras, although academics disagree on the terminology. For the purposes of this discussion they will be referred to as the pre-modern, the modern, the late modern and the postmodern. Each era overlaps in significant ways, and there are many arguments as to when one era ends and another begins. The short answer is that there is no agreed moment, and neither can there be. Even use of the term postmodernism, for example, does not signify the start of this era, because naming something does not mean that prior thinking was not postmodern, it merely provides a term that may be better than one that went before. Moreover, it equally does not mean that the previous era has come to a definitive conclusion. Many ideas that could be regarded as belonging to a previous era are still evident long after that era has come to an end. For example, putting faith in the supernatural or the spiritual tend to be seen as belonging to the pre-modern era, yet anyone who reads their horoscopes, crosses their fingers or touches wood for luck are engaging in activities that are not 'scientifically' proven to work, and could, therefore, be regarded as belonging to the pre-modern era. Consequently, readers will need to be aware that this is only meant to serve as an initial guide to help comprehension of historical trends in the understanding of crime and criminals. For example, some of the theories of crime presented in Table 1.2 overlap with previous or later eras. Not only that, but the choice of which theories to place within each section is a highly subjective enterprise. Readers can use it as a resource, but as suggested in the study questions at the end of this chapter, it can be critically analysed and readers are encouraged to do so. Three key thinkers can be associated with the modern, late modern and postmodern eras, yet despite each of these eras taking us from the middle eighteenth century to contemporary theories their major contributions were all written by the early twentieth century. Karl Marx (1818–83), Emile Durkheim (1858–1917), and Max Weber (1864–1920) form a trinity of key thinkers about society whose influence still resonates today. The detail of their theories and ideas are not the point of this book, readers are directed in the further reading at the end of the chapter to other sources. What is important to point out is that their ideas formed the central concerns of later scholars and helped shape new ways to see the world, often long after they had died.

Pre-modern views of criminology

In general terms, during the pre-modern era those who engaged in deviant activities were not regarded as a distinct group of people different from those who did not offend, but rather they were seen as being in some way affected by outside influences. Significantly, however, these outside influences were not of the making of humans. Superstition, religion and the supernatural were the causes of deviancy. Particular humans could act upon such forces to identify the reasons for the aberration, but humans were not the cause of the problem. For example, the search for witches in Britain where 'tests' were carried out on those suspected of witchcraft. Unlike in later modernist theories, where

Table 1.2 Historical shifts in understanding crime

Epoch	Social structure (following Durkheim 1893/1984)	Dominant ideology	Cause of crime	Key theories
Pre-modern. Pre-1750: Pre-**Enlightenment**	Mechanistic (simple division of labour).	Religion/faith.	Unearthly Forces beyond a person's control. Against God, e.g. witchcraft. 'The devil makes work for idle hands.'	Superstition and Religion; demonology.
Modern. 1750–1920 Post-Enlightenment	Organic (complex division of labour), but consensus in values.	Science will lead to continual progress in Human activities.	Individual and social forces beyond person's control.	Individual and sociological Classicism; individual and sociological positivism: Durkheim, Gall. Spurtzheim's phrenology, Lombroso's *La Scuola Positiva*.
Late modern. 1920–1979	Organic, consensus threatened.	Science important but fallible.	Crime is meaningful, but also the result of inequalities.	Weber, Merton's SS&A, Cloward and Ohlin and A.K. Cohen, The Chicago School, Sykes and Matza, Drift, National Deviancy Conferences, The New Criminology, The Birmingham School.
Postmodern. 1979–present	Organic, plurality of values.	Loss of faith in science and progress, search for underlying causes superseded by 'what works' and risk assessment.	The practical criminology of government such as Rational Choice Theory and Routine Activities Theory is contrasted firstly with left and right realism and then in the 1990s with the boredom and search for excitement as expressed in cultural criminology.	Cornish and Clark's Rational Choice Theory. Cohen and Felson's Routine Activity Theory. Charles Murray, J.Q. Wilson, described as right realism by the left realists. Lea and Young's left realism. Jack Katz, Jeff Ferrell, Cultural Criminology. Tony Jefferson, David Gadd and Psychosocial Criminology.
The Futures of Criminology. Present plus.	The end of history a myth, the rise of the neo-conservatives and religious fundamentalism are ideologies that were thought to be concluded. New bipolar geopolitical tensions, especially since 9/11. Postmodernity, as historical epoch, is a premature proposition.	Realisation that ideology is up for grabs. Public can still be manipulated despite widespread cynicism. Religiosity dominant in America and Middle East politics. Search for pre-crime symptoms for early intervention.	The search for cause becomes hypergenetic, Magnetic Resonance Imaging to see inside the brain as it thinks about crime. Crime prevention occurs mostly before crime has been committed. At the non-technological end, ASBOs are pre-crime sanctions; at the high end of technology DNA samples could be taken earlier.	Psychology will be at the forefront of this new direction, although the emphasis will be more on medical and risk assessment research. Psychology is here seen as being a part of a wider programme of value-for-money managerialism where any research needs to show a tangible outcome in crime reduction. Humanistic and social psychology and the greater synthesis of psychology and sociology may help to balance some of the more extreme threats to civil liberties. Similarly, the election of American President Barack Obama and the world recession that lead to many banks becoming part-nationalised may usher in a new, more liberal form of governance.

outside forces are thought to compel people to commit crime, such as the role of Capitalism in creating inequality, poverty and hence crime, in the pre-modern era the outside influences were not the *creation* of humans. Contemporary scholars would not regard the types of activities employed to determine the cause of a problem, such as witchcraft, as scientific. Although the methods had a logic to those practising them, modern scholars would regard as pre-scientific the dunking of supposed witches in water until death proved they were innocent. Similar distinctions can be made with regard to the way medicine was practised with medieval writers such as Galen believing the body to be made of four humours, or substances, excessive quantities of one or the other corresponding to illness and changes in personality. According to Hans J. Eysenck, a psychologist whose work on personality types and crime is highly influential, Galen is thus responsible for an early form of personality typology made up of the Melancholic (sad), Choleric (aggressive), Sanguine (sociable) and Phlegmatic (calm) (Eysenck 1977/1964). As an example of the way that outdated and discredited ideas can influence later scholars, Eysenck's personality types are strongly influenced by the medieval writings of Galen, about which more later. So the pre-modern era can be said to be dominated by ideas that are pre-scientific, in that they are not based on a vigorous scientific methodology to determine if they are valid or not.

Crime and Modernity

Criminology and psychology are generally regarded as disciplines that developed out of the modern period. The major historical event that characterises this period is the move from an agricultural to an industrial economy. This economy was not based on the changing seasons that previously organised when work was done in the agricultural economy. In moving away from nature, the industrial economy required a socially constructed routine to control working patterns. With the inevitability of spring, summer, autumn and winter gone, behaviour could now be manipulated directly and the various nascent branches of science sought to find the best ways to do this from increasing the efficiency of the machines in the factories to the humans who worked alongside them. Modernism is characterised by the greater faith in objectivity, rationality and the application of the scientific method. In sociology the application of the scientific method is termed **positivism** after the term coined by one of the earliest sociologists Auguste Comte whose most influential book *Cours de philosophie positive* (written in several volumes from 1830–1842) set out the argument for a scientific form of sociology that provided a positive agenda for political change.

Positivism can be split into two main forms, individual and sociological positivism. Individual positivism describes that form of social science that takes as its main focus the individual. Individual positivism has an assumption that behaviour is the result of individual, internal factors to the neglect of social factors. For example, individual positivists would not be concerned with issues like poverty in explaining why there is a higher rate of crime in groups who are poor. Instead, they might argue that the cause is lower intelligence based on Intelligence Quotient (IQ) scores in groups of people who are poor (see e.g Hernnstein and Murray 1994). The research methods are wide-ranging but tend to be those which can be verified by other researchers using the same procedure so are likely to result in data that is statistical. Psychology, in general, has been regarded as being individual positivism, although there are some theories, such as some areas of social psychology, which focus to a greater extent on environmental factors. However, most approaches are still mainly interested in internal mental processes. The point that needs to be borne in mind is that, despite their difference, at this stage of social science both sociological and psychological theories sought to apply scientific principles to the study of human behaviour.

Forms of individual positivism

Individual positivism takes on different forms and has changed across time, although all forms share certain characteristics in common. A brief overview of some of the more widely cited studies follows beginning with a key moment that took the individual positivist tradition into a new sphere of scientific credibility.

Darwin and the evolution of the species

It is perhaps pertinent to start with one of the key influences on the positivist tradition in criminology: Darwin's theory of evolution. Charles Darwin's *On the Origin of the Species* (1859) was a contentious theory. Nothing really has changed here as there is still controversy over what some groups have argued is a contradiction of the Christian belief in the creation of humans by God, through the story of Adam and Eve. In the nineteenth century the debate was still based around this specific difference in viewpoint, only then there was not as much scientific evidence in support of Darwin's theory. Over time organisms adapt to their environment, with those best able to do so passing on their genetic blueprint for the next generation. Darwin's theory that humans have evolved from earlier species began some people to speculate that maybe there were different types of human, differing from each other in such areas as intelligence and race. It was also argued that maybe criminals were also different to non-criminals. The initial research into this idea began with phrenology.

Phrenology, mental insanity and the psychopath

Phrenology is the study of the association between bumps on the skull and behaviour, with a raised area on the skull being thought to be indicative of more or less of a particular character trait. Phrenology is often seen as an unscientific precursor to more sophisticated research into the identification of criminals. Ceramic phrenology heads are often seen for sale alongside ceramic hands used in palmistry. Just such an association has rendered phrenology an unworthy topic for study in the history of criminology. However, Rafter has argued that phrenology should not be ignored because it is discredited (2005). There are many discredited scientific ideas that criminology has studied. Phrenology is important because it helped shape the scientific study of crime and influenced the work of the leading nineteenth-century positivist Cesare Lombroso. As a progenitor of positivist explanations for crime it can be credited with moving the debate in a radical direction, away from treating crime as a rational choice requiring the punishment of the offender towards seeing crime as a pathology to be treated. Phrenology's most influential exponent was Franz Joseph Gall, a physician from Vienna who outlined the basic propositions below in 1800, with the final one being proposed by Gall's main follower, the German physician Johann Gaspar Spurzheim. The main propositions were as follows:

1   The brain is the organ of the mind.
2   The brain is the aggregation of about 30 separate organs or faculties, such as Combativeness, Covetiveness and Destructiveness, that function independently.
3   The more active an organ, the larger its size.
4   The relative size of the organs can be estimated by inspecting contours of the skull.
5   The relative size of the organs can be increased or decreased through exercise and self-discipline. (Rafter 2005: 66)

From 1800 to 1830 phrenology was developed by psychiatrists and physicians into a 'scientific' system based on measurement and observation, but within 20 years there occurred a popularising of phrenology. It is this latter development that has caused most criminologists to avoid the topic. By the 1850s the interest in phrenology was on the wane. However, the categorisation of crimes into different causes opened up an area of research into the possibility of multiple and varied causations and in the idea of desistance from crime, particularly in relation to the fifth assumption above. Rafter's argument also raises an important issue about the unwillingness of contemporary criminologists to study areas related to criminology but which are regarded as embarrassing. For many sociological criminologists the study of psychology is itself regarded as embarrassing and to be avoided. But, Rafter points to the need to study areas that may be outside of one's theoretical worldview because they can still add to our understanding.

Another branch of research that began during the middle of the nineteenth century was into the idea of psychopathy. It was necessary to explain why some people could commit heinous crimes, but not appear to be intellectually damaged. Before the term psychopath was coined, however, the term 'moral insanity' described someone whose behaviour lacks moral awareness of right and wrong but where their intellect had not been impaired. This term was replaced by Rush (1786, cited Rafter 1997) with micronomia and anomia. This links into the sociological concept of **anomie** used most famously in the work of Emile Durkheim, to be discussed below. All of these terms are precursors to the term psychopath, familiar to contemporary readers. With the decline in phrenology, so psychiatry, particularly in prisons and asylums began to take over the study of criminals. The term psychopath first appears, according to Rafter, in 1845 in an Austrian psychiatric textbook (Rafter 1997), and was elaborated by two German psychiatrists Krafft-Ebing (1886/1965) and Kraepelin (1917), before becoming a popular concept in the American Psychiatric literature between 1915 and 1925. The definition of the term is very vague, the American authors misunderstood significant aspects of the concept from the German tradition, and the three main authors, Bernard Glueck (1917a, 1917b, 1918a, 1918b, 1919), William Healy (1915) and Edith R. Spaulding (1923/1969), each defined the term differently and sometimes contradicted each other. However, as Rafter has argued the term served a metaphorical purpose to describe almost anyone who did not fit what was then regarded as the norms to which people should be measured. Consequently, heterosexual masculinity was the norm and any man not exhibiting behaviour regarded as an instance of this was seen as inferior and a psychopath.

This set of ideas, that those who commit crime may look different, or be made differently, began the process of creating a science of the criminal. The criminal started to be seen as different to the non-criminal in biological ways. As the cities developed around the world and began to get crowded during the nineteenth and early twentieth centuries, so middle class fears of crime and disorder began to find their answer in the newly emerging sciences of psychiatry, psychology and now criminology.

An example of how ideas that developed in one century are developed and elaborated in another, and in consequence, cut across historical moments is the continued research into psychopathy. Contemporary definitions of psychopathy developed from the description provided by Cleckley (1941) in his book *The*

Mask of Sanity. He suggested 16 criteria for a diagnosis of psychopathy, which included lack of insight into the effect of one's behaviour on others, superficial charm, lack of anxiety and failure to plan ahead. Using these as a starting point Hare developed the Psychopathy Checklist (PCL) (Hare 1980), which has since been revised and developed to include a diagnostic tool for children and adolescents called the Antisocial Process Screening Device (APSD) (Frick and Hare 2001). In America the diagnostic tool for all behavioural disorders is the *Diagnostic and Statistical Manual* (DSM IV) (APA 1994), however it has been criticised for a number of arbitrary categories that do not sufficiently delineate between behaviours. Such an example is its inability to distinguish a psychopathic disorder from conduct disorders (CD) and antisocial personality disorder (ASPD) (Blair, Mitchell and Blair 2005). Essentially, psychopathy is distinguished from CD and ASPD by an emotional dysfunction that leads to a greater use of instrumental aggression, as opposed to reactive aggression. Instrumental aggression is characterised by the use of aggression for the purpose of achieving a goal, either financial or emotional, whereas reactive aggression refers to aggression that is caused by something. Therefore, psychopathy is not adequately described in the American system of diagnosis and so its use as an explanation for why some types of crime are committed is problematic.

Lombroso (1836–1909), the Positivist School and the inheritability of crime

As Rafter has argued, the avoidance of engagement with phrenology has meant that its impact has been overlooked. Whereas Rafter argues that phrenology formed a radical new idea that sought to show that humans were capable of change, Lombroso's criminal anthropology was, initially, based upon an idea of the criminal being born into their behavioural pattern. Garland has noted that the ideas of Lombroso are nothing new and an extension of racial anthropology in the 1870s and the creation of categories such as genius or insane (Garland 2002). That Lombroso's approach became one of the dominant ideas set the new science of criminology on a route that was to be dominant for the best part of 80 years. Whereas phrenology was an idea that suggested that people could change, and that there were finely tuned gradations in severity of behaviour, Lombroso presented a human as a *fait accompli*, ready made and without much hope of change, except long-term policies to prevent those identified as criminal from reproducing.

Lombroso was an Italian physician who used craniometry and anthropometry to study and categorise different racial attributes of Italian soldiers. Essentially, Lombroso measured the bodies of different subjects and categorised them into types. These body types were then linked to behaviour, so that if several subjects with large earlobes had been involved in a certain crime, Lombroso noted this down and collected such observations into his first book, *L'Uomo Delinquente* (1876). Lombroso argued that the criminal was an **atavism**, a throwback to an earlier stage of evolution. Lombroso, like many of his contemporaries such as A.M. Guerry and A. Quetelet, was interested in the emerging use of statistics. His work was about measuring the body to see if the body would give away any indication of criminality. Although there is an indebtedness to Darwin, the use of statistics was the most important element of this approach (Horn 2003), and in this there is a link to the work of Durkheim and the sociological positivists, to be discussed below.

Much research during the late nineteenth and early twentieth century is essentially a variation on the same theme: crime is a stable trait that can be measured and which is either largely inherited or conditioned in early life and remains a constant influence. Crime is caused by internal mechanisms gone wrong. Crucially, this has little effect on the underlying rationality of humans. Crime is not caused by humans acting irrationally since their underlying physiology or upbringing compels them to act in the only way they can. The legal system in the UK was set up, albeit unsystematically, to account for both those who rationally chose to commit crime and to take into account extenuating circumstances for those whose background suggested a social or psychological pathology. The originator of psychoanalysis Sigmund Freud represents a conduit, or link between the constitutional[2] theories of Lombroso and the later approaches of psychology to social learning and upbringing. His work also marks the beginning of a questioning of this rationality, at the same time as critics suggested that psychoanalysis was not scientific (Frosh 1999). Chaos and disorder were thought to be under the control of humans, and yet humans were about to embark on a global war.

The First World War, psychiatry and psychoanalysis

The First World War marked a unique moment of global reflection on the progress of humans. The seemingly inexorable rise to ever greater moments of human progress faltered at the start of the 1914–18 war. However, as the historian Eric Hobsbawm argues, there was effectively 31 years of conflict and war between 1914 and the Japanese surrender in 1945. These wars seemed to mark the end of the march to civilisation. As Hobsbawm writes: 'Mankind survived. Nevertheless, the great edifice of nineteenth century civilisation crumpled in the flames of world war, as its pillars collapsed' (1994: 22). Hobsbawm points out that in many scientific disciplines there was a sense of unease about the achievements that could be made through positing a purely rational human actor or trying to understand the world solely through the application of scientific methods (Hobsbawm 1987).

In the field of psychology, Sigmund Freud represents this unease with the idea that human behaviour is directed not by reason but by underlying unconscious impulses and instincts. Freud (1856–1939) began his career as a surgeon, before moving into general medicine as a house physician at the main hospital in Vienna where he took a course in psychiatry which lead to his role as a lecturer at the University of Vienna (Fadiman and Frager 2004). Consequently, Freud would have been aware of the Phrenology and Psychopathy literature, as well as Lombroso. Whereas phrenology posited an external manifestation of internal brain mechanisms presenting as bumps on the scalp, and Lombroso believed that criminals were manifestations of earlier stages of evolution, Freud was concerned to find causes for behaviour where no physical or chemical reason could be determined. For example, people might present with symptoms of hysteria that might manifest in loss of sensation in the hand, but where there was no sign of damage or disease from the wrist to the body. This suggested to Freud a psychological basis for the disorder. Freud argued that every mental process, every thought or emotion had a meaning, even if that meaning was not consciously intelligible to the individual. Apparently unintentional behaviour, for Freud, had a reason. The drives or impulses that propel these actions compel the individual to do things to satisfy the impulse. As we develop and grow the means of satisfying these impulses change. From our basic needs as a newborn for food, warmth and shelter, to our developing needs for sexual gratification, our means of satisfying them become more sophisticated and socially acceptable. From the baby screaming for food, to the adult feeding themselves. Most human needs are developed by the time we reach puberty. However, we can get fixated on a particular need and the means for satisfying it can become central to the needs of the individual. Early upbringing created the propensity to become 'stuck' at a particular personality type.

Psychoanalysis can be split between two main areas, the Freudian tradition posited a relatively stable individual once they had emerged from the first three years of their lives and a more flexible version advocated by followers of Erik Erikson (1902–94) where change was possible throughout the life course. (See Table 1.3 on page 23 for an outline of Freud's psychosexual stages and Erikson's psychosocial stages.) Indeed, as Stephen Frosh (1999) maintains, to speak of 'psychoanalysis' as if it were a unified approach is a misnomer since individual psychoanalysts can disagree on the same point. Nevertheless, psychoanalysis begins to challenge the positivistic quest of psychology to identify single causes for crime and in their place presents a more complex theory of humans. We can see in this, arguably, the first signs of the retreat from the aetiology of crime towards the more pragmatic attempts of contemporary psychology, and all other forms of governance, to attend to the risk and not cause of crime.

Forms of sociological positivism

Just as there are a variety of different forms of individual positivism characterised by psychological and biological research, so there are also a variety of
sociological forms of positivism that seek to apply a scientific method to studying the social influence of crime and deviance.

Durkheim and sociological positivism

The main focus of Durkheim's work is the structure of society and its institutions such as religion, education and the division of labour. They are deemed
to have structural properties, to be long lasting, and to pre-date, and post-date
the individuals who live within them. As already noted, beginning with the
work of Comte, and then the French sociologist Emile Durkheim, sociological
positivism has a long tradition in sociology. Two books by Durkheim stand out
as examples of this form of social science: *Suicide* (1897/1951) and *Rules of
Sociological Method* (1895/1938). Durkheim's argument is that the social world
can be studied in the same way as the natural world, utilising similar methods
to study it. Social facts, Durkheim argued, should be treated as things, they are
external to the individual and shape them. That is, the individual is born into
a society that is already created and this shapes the individual. An example is
language that is already in existence when we are born and which we must
learn to use if we wish to function in society. When changes occur in the social
environment they impact upon human behaviour. Behaviour is moulded by the
environment. For example, a key idea in Durkheim's work is **anomie**. This literally means without norms. Anomie develops when social systems go through
major changes. A norm is the usual way of behaving. Durkheim termed this the
conscience collective, or collective consciousness. For example, it is assumed we
all share certain beliefs as to what constitutes a crime. But, when the social
environment goes through significant changes, such as an economic boom or
depression, then our connection to the norms of society start to break down, a
state of anomie. In other words, the relationships we have with other people
normally keep our behaviour in check. But, significant social change disrupts
those relationships.

Using scientific methods, the social world can be studied, catalogued and
classified in the same way as the natural world. Therefore, when there is a state
of anomie, a situation external to the individual, it should be possible to measure
changes in behaviour. Durkheim's famous study of suicide demonstrates this.
Taking one's own life is often seen as the most personal behaviour that an
individual can take. However, Durkheim argued that rates of suicide, how many
there were per population, varied between different countries, but remained
fairly stable within a country across time. Because different people were involved

in each year's statistics this suggested that the rate of suicide was not related to an individual predisposition but was related to the social environment in each country. Durkheim argued that the important factor was the different religions that dominated in the countries he studied. Protestant countries had a higher rate of suicide than Catholic countries because the conventions of the Catholic belief system encouraged a more cohesive support network. There were more people to comfort, protect and deter those wishing to commit suicide. So, for Durkheim, the difference was social, not individual as the psychologists were suggesting:

> There is between psychology and sociology the same break in continuity as between biology and the physiochemical sciences. Consequently, every time a social phenomenon is directly explained by a psychological phenomenon, we may be sure that the explanation is false. (Durkheim 1895/1938: 104)

However, it is often forgotten that Durkheim was aware of the emerging research in psychology and the way that it was quickly developing into a respected science (Giddens 1978). Psychology was valuable to the sociologist and complimented their training, even if for Durkheim it was inferior. In *Suicide*, the sociologist was concerned with the collective nature of the subject, the trends and consistencies across time, not with the specific aspects of individual cases; this was the task of psychology. In an interview the sociologist Robert K. Merton noted why there was an animosity towards psychology in the work of Durkheim, and the way that the two disciplines tend to be in opposition:

> I have ... never taken ... the polar position that if you're a sociologist, you dare not slip into considering questions of psychological process ... Now there is a great tendency, of course, in the Durkheimian tradition to do just that, because Durkheim ... was fighting entrenched groups of psychologists and social psychologists who were questioning the intellectual legitimacy of sociology. (Cullen and Messner 2007: 21)

Both the individual and sociological positivist approaches share certain issues in common. Both assume that there is a consensus in society as to what are agreed norms and values. Emphasis tends to be placed on the official statistics as a useful guide to the rate of crime in society. Research tends to be quantitative and experimental. Crime is deemed to be a deviation from the norm. There is an altruistic, welfare-oriented element to these approaches in that deviations from the norm are not held to be in the control of the individual, but instead outside their rational control. This is either as a consequence of internal mental deficits of some kind in individual positivism, or else the consequence of social structural factors such as the economy, religion or poverty in the sociological variant. Since the causes are not in the control of the individual, or group, and that crime is therefore not seen as being a rational choice, then punishment is not deemed to be appropriate. After all, you would not punish someone for having the flu when there is little they can do about it. Indeed, this medical model is one that tends to be associated with positivism. Crime tends to be regarded as **pathological**, as an illness to be treated rather than a moral failure to be punished. Moreover, such approaches tend to posit causes which are regarded as necessary for the activity to take place. Without the cause, the activity would not occur.

Merton, Chicago and their influence

Durkheim's concept of anomie was used in Robert K. Merton's sociology and the lessons that human behaviour can be understood at a social and structural level was central to the Chicago School of Sociology. Also influential on American sociology in the early to mid-twentieth century was psychology. The work of Merton (1938) and the many authors who formed the Chicago School of Sociology during its most fertile period from 1915 to 1935 (Bulmer 1984) drew on an exciting range of different ideas that would render more vivid the insularity of contemporary sociology, criminology and psychology. The work of the sociologist Robert K. Merton will be discussed in Chapter 4, however it is worth pointing out his use of ideas such as reference group theory that derived from his colleague Herbert Hyman at Columbia University (Runciman 1966) and which have been much discussed within psychology (Webber 2007a). However, it was at the University of Chicago where the interdisciplinary nature of the department allowed for much cross-fertilisation of ideas (Bulmer 1984). The sociologists drew from natural scientific models such as Burgess and Park's use of an ecological model to explain the way that the city of Chicago developed. Believing that the city does not grow in a random way, a theory of social ecology suggested that the city grew by a natural process where humans adapted to their environment and moved to areas most suited to their social position. As their situation changed they moved out of the area. This was compared to how plants adapt to their environment. The concentric zone model is the best known example of this where the city grows in rings around a central business district. Each ring is an area within which different people live. So the first ring outside the central zone was where the new immigrants to the city first settled since this was the cheapest accommodation. But, people moved out as their social and financial situations became better, meaning that this area was in a constant state of flux. This, in turn, meant that social networks between people were never able to become established (Park 1952). This lack of association, or social disorganisation, was thought to be a major cause of crime.

However, by way of critique of social disorganisation theory, the work of Edwin Sutherland drew on social psychological research into social learning theory to argue that rather than social disorganisation causing crime, instead many forms of crime required people to work with each other. Moreover, many forms of crime needed to be learned in the same way as non-deviant activities. Sutherland, therefore presented a theory of differential association (1949). An example might be someone who chooses to steal a car. Before that can be carried out the person needs to learn how to hotwire a car, drive it and get away from the scene. A high level of learning needs to take place before that can be achieved. Such learning takes place within a social setting; the skills that need to be learned clearly need to be passed on by someone else.

These approaches have been characterised as sociological positivism, but it needs to be noted that this over-emphasises a certain aspect of the research. Although the Chicago sociologists drew on social psychological ideas and utilised statistical methods, they also used qualitative **ethnographic** methods and were influenced by the social psychologist George Herbert Mead (1934) whose work formed the core of symbolic interactionism. This approach influenced writers such as Howard Becker (1963) and Erving Goffman (1959). Becker and Goffman's ideas sensitised social scientists to the symbolic quality of the actions of humans and accelerated the questioning of the modernist concern with science, rationality and causation after the Second World War.

Late modern approaches to the theory of crime

The period after the Second World War initially lead to a social and moral consensus as people retained the deference to authority that they had needed during the conflict. Politicians, police officers, teachers and the rule of law were rarely questioned. The world had moved from actual conflict to a tense stand-off between the capitalist 'West' and the Union of Soviet Socialist Republics (USSR) and its socialist allies. The Cold War was as much ideological as it was territorial or military. The world was effectively split between those who pursued capitalism and those who pursued communism. The Vietnam War was a kind of proxy war between the USA and the USSR, an attempt to stop the spread of communism from the USSR-sponsored North to the American-sponsored South. The result was a 10 year conflict that America effectively lost in 1975. Yet, the pictures that came back to America were startling and deeply disturbing. More explosive was used in Vietnam than in the whole of the Second World War (Hobsbawm 1994). Around the country people started to question the legitimacy of the war and to question authority. Much of the questioning came from young people, and their culture became ever more confrontational. The post-Second World War consensus started to break down into more and more factions. It was the era of feminism, anti-racism and the civil rights movement. This anti-authoritarianism spread to the academic world and many disciplines began to be more critical.

In criminology, the way law developed over time and reflected different moral debates lead to a contrast between those who believe there is a reality to crime that can be counted and classified, the positivist tradition discussed above, and those who believe that crime is socially constructed, changeable and not real, the labelling, symbolic interactionist or social constructivist tradition. For example, crimes that are newly created, or alternatively activities that were once illegal, can become decriminalised or regarded in law as less dangerous. The recent reclassification of marijuana in England and Wales from a class B to a class C drug, and then back again, is an example of this. Crime can be created through changes in law (Lemert 1967). Similarly, the lowering of the age of homosexual sexual intercourse, firstly from being illegal at any age, to being legal at 21, then 18, and now 16 to bring the age of consent in line with the law as applied to heterosexual sexual intercourse.

It is often thought that there are some crimes that are so serious that their enactment has always been a crime no matter when in history they were committed. Murder or rape tend to be the commonest offences mentioned. However, some sociologists such as Howard Becker (1963) argue that all crime is socially constructed. This idea is part of the symbolic interactionist perspective, where humans actively create meaning out of the world. An example would be the taking of someone's life, which can be differentially defined depending upon the circumstances. An ordinary member of the public deliberately taking a life tends to be termed murder, but that same person killing someone defined as an enemy during war is doing their patriotic duty. A car company that knowingly produces a car that may be faulty and could lead to an accident that could kill is rarely prosecuted for murder. Such arguments moved theory in a new direction during the 1960s and 1970s, into what some have termed a late modern direction. Late modernity is characterised by challenges to the scientific principles of rationality that was deemed to be dominant during the preceding period. It was essentially a challenge to positivism's orthodoxy during the majority of the twentieth century. Rather than seeing the criminal as different to the non-criminal and seeking an explanation for that difference, some researchers began to question the concreteness of this distinction. Were all criminals devoted to crime? All of the time? The answer according to Gresham Sykes and David Matza (1957) was that people 'drifted' between different identities and found ways to justify their behaviour, termed 'techniques of neutralization'. Again, it needs to be remembered that such ideas were not new, merely that the conditions were right for there to be a sufficiently large critical mass of academics who shared the same approach. Theory and social upheaval became fused in the later 1950s and accelerated into the 1960s as people increasingly questioned official versions of events which led to a breakdown in consensus.

The 1960s, the social construction of crime
and the challenge to dominant ideologies

Although not as widespread, psychology and its related disciplines of psychiatry and psychoanalysis, also had its moment of questioning the authority of those in power, including psychologists. For example, Sykes and Matza's techniques of neutralisation has its counterpart within psychology and psychiatry. For example, Judith Herman (1992), one of the advocates of recovered memory syndrome, notes that the more powerful the person the more likely they are to want to define reality in their favour. They do this by positing:

> an impressive array of arguments, from the most blatant denial to the most sophisticated and elegant rationalisation. After every atrocity one can expect to hear the same predictable apologies: it never happened; the victim lies; the victim exaggerates; the victim brought it upon herself; and in any case it is time to forget the past and move on. (1992: 8)

Despite the fact that there are such links between the psychological and the social nature of denial and manipulation of reality, which Herman herself points out (1992: 9), it is still common practice for those whose work sits more in the sociological camp to, ironically, deny the utility of the individual consciousness as studied by psychology. However, such arguments have been taken up by the sociologist Stan Cohen (2001) in his research on why people can be simultaneously aware of, and unaware of, atrocities, for example during war. Both of these writers will be discussed in more detail in later chapters.

Much of the work in this area is based on another of the key sociologists Max Weber, whose ideas on the dehumanising nature of bureaucracy and capitalism opened up debates about the nature of work and the stultifying tedium of day-to-day life in the modern world (1904, 1922). Weber's key contribution was to question the taken-for-granted acceptance of science as a rational enterprise. Science has answers to key questions, but what we do with those answers, the *meaning* we derive from them, is the key issue. In the early twentieth century science was able to show how to create products, from cars to radios, in the most efficient and profitable way possible. The industrial production line of Henry Ford's motorcar company in 1903 has become the blueprint for this phenomena and gave it a name, Fordism. However, F.W. Taylor is credited with an earlier system originating in America in the 1890s called Scientific Management, a term used interchangeably with Taylorism. A job was broken down into constituent parts, each one being performed by one person in contrast to the system of a person skilled in many or all of the techniques needed to produce the product. Over the twentieth century the skilled potter was replaced by the pottery factory, the clothes' maker by the sweatshop. Science answered the questions that capitalism asked of it, but the answers dehumanised society. As already noted, such ideas were modernist. The ambition was that through science, human progress could be assured. The problem was, at whose expense? Weber's contribution was to help us challenge the orthodoxy of scientific principles, not that science was flawed or that all ideas share equal importance; that would come later and characterised the view of postmodernity. What Weber sought to highlight instead was that bureaucracy, and here one might include the social sciences, was a method to control and constrain humans. Weber's ideas will be revisited in the last chapter where it will be noted that many of the advances in the psychology of crime have fulfilled Weber's warning that society was heading for rationality that was devoid of humanity. Suffice to say here that Weber's contribution has influenced many sociologists, especially those who question systems of risk management and control (Ferrell, Hayward and Young 2008). For some of these authors traditional psychological approaches are synonymous with this.

A similar movement away from scientific determinism was being made by those studying the individual. The pioneer of psychoanalysis Sigmund Freud has already been briefly discussed, but his ideas certainly belonged to the modernist world of creating rigid systems of classification. On the other side of this argument stand the lifespan psychoanalysts such as Erik Erikson (1964) who in the 1960s posited a lifetime of personality growth based upon a succession of seven challenges throughout one's life. Failure to successfully complete one challenge can be compensated by success at the next (see Table 1.3). Although in reality, if one does not successfully find intimacy, later challenges might be harder. Nevertheless, the flexibility of this personality theory is certainly a challenge to the static approach of the Freudian tradition. Certainly, Erikson's work is an elaboration of Freud's and reflected the new direction in social science in the 1960s to move away from the determinism of psychological, psychiatric and biological theories towards those that developed an integration of the psychological

Table 1.3   *Freud's psychosexual stages and Erikson's psychosocial stages compared*

Age	Freud's Psychosexual stages	Erikson's Psychosocial stages
Infancy	Oral stage	Basic Trust versus Basic Mistrust
Early childhood	Anal stage	Autonomy versus Shame and Doubt
Play age	Phallic stage	Initiative versus Guilt
Adolescence	'Latency'	Industry versus Inferiority
Young adulthood	Genital stage	Identity versus Identity Confusion
Adulthood		Intimacy versus Isolation
Middle adulthood		Generativity versus Stagnation
Old age		Integrity versus Despair

with the social (Taylor et al. 1973). Hence, Erikson's psychosocial stages reflected not just internal conflicts, but how such conflicts were linked to wider concerns in society. As will be noted in the final chapter, such ideas have contemporary relevance since there is renewed interest in what has become known as psychosocial criminology (Jefferson 2002, 2004; Gadd and Jefferson 2007). Although Erikson is not mentioned yet in this literature, his attempt to transcend the static rigidity of Freud's personality trait theory seems an untapped source of ideas.

Another approach that drew on theories being developed in social theory and sociology was Gestalt psychology. Developed as a response and revision of Freudian psychoanalysis, Fritz and Laura Perls were the figureheads for this approach (1947/1969). Gestalt psychology draws on many different elements and so is a synthesis of intellectual ideas from different traditions. Further evidence of the way that psychology draws on the ideas of others. The basic idea is that rather than focusing on just the verbalisations of the person in therapy, one should instead look to seeing the person as a whole. Their physical behaviour, how they move, sit, walk etc., as well as what they say. This has lead to the phrase, 'the whole is more than the sum of its parts'. It is a critique of the idea that the human can be studied in a purely rational way using the methods of the natural sciences. Consequently, Gestalt psychology is also a critique of **functionalism** and **structuralism**. Gestalt psychology introduced meaning into psychology, as humans perceived the world in ways that could not be explained by analysing the individual variables making up the phenomena. For example, the *phi phenomenon* describes the perception of two separate lights flashed in succession but perceived as one moving light by the subject. The subject is 'doing' something to the information and seeing something – movement – that is not there. This phenomenon is one common to anyone who has seen a film at the cinema, where single pictures are projected onto a screen sequentially at a speed that allows us to 'see' them as moving images.

Eysenck as atavistic throwback

However, as noted earlier, historical categories, such as modernism or postmodernism, are only ideal types and despite a move towards a questioning of positivism, one of the most influential theories in support of this approach also appeared at this time. Hans J. Eysenck's *Crime and Personality* (1964/1977) can be regarded as a direct descendant of the individual positivism of Lombroso. Eysenck argued that some people are biologically predetermined to be criminal due to their personality. This is determined by the physiology of their brains. Extroverted personality types had low cortical arousal, their brains 'ticked' over too slowly. To compensate such people sought out ways to energise their brains with excitement. Such excitement could be a bungee jump, or it could be through aggression or stealing. The introvert's brain in contrast works fast and so does not need to be stimulated by more adrenaline. Such people were less likely to be involved in crime.

The problem with Eysenck's theory, as with so much psychological positivism is that the categories are wholly invented by psychologists. What it means to be an introvert is determined by a questionnaire created by Eysenck and predicated on the assumption that such categories are stable traits. If you are an introvert at 10 years old, then you are one at 50. Similarly, social structure and the context in which action takes place is also ignored, such that the description of the neurotic psychopath might just as easily describe the head of a large corporation as it does a criminal. So we see overlap and complexity, rather than just a linear movement from one set of ideas to the next. Nevertheless, the period of an unquestioning and placid population in developed democracies was coming to an end. White, male hegemony was being questioned by feminists and the various racial equality groups and this was echoed by critical and radical academics.

The 1970s, the critical criminologists and the anti-psychiatry movement

Outside of academia, with the social world changing, there was a symbiotic relationship at work whereby intellectuals were responding to, and directing, the way that society developed. Traditional positivism was criticised as a method of social control used by the powerful elite. By the time the 1970s arrived the questioning of authority was well under way. The period of consensus, that all of western society thought similarly, began to crumble as more researchers from many disciplines began to present arguments directly questioning theories they believed were in the interests of government to control the population.

One of the most important of the critiques of traditional psychology and psychiatry was the work of the Scottish psychiatrist Ronald. D. Laing (Laing and Esterson 1964/1990). Laing argued that madness, specifically schizophrenia, was diagnosed by psychiatrists without them understanding what went on behind the obvious manifestation of seemingly disordered thinking and behaviour. Laing argued that the behaviour of those labelled as schizophrenic could be made intelligible if the behaviour was viewed in the context of the patients' everyday lives, specifically when with their families. Laing, with his colleague Aaron Esterson, observed the interactions between the person whose behaviour would have been diagnosed as schizophrenic and their family. The result was that the presentation of seemingly irrational behaviour could be seen in a wholly different way. It was argued that the diagnosed schizophrenic was expressing method in their madness. When they said they were being persecuted by their families, they were indeed being persecuted. Pearson argues that the anti-psychiatry argument of R.D. Laing is that the mad person is driven mad by crazy families *and* the madness is a rational response to mad situations, a breaking through of the restrictive chains of rational society and the restrictive envelope of the industrial demands on time and labour. This is in one sense tautological; madness is the symptom of a mad family and also the cure to the suffocating normality of existence in the conforming world (Pearson 1975). This whole movement can only be understood by looking at the context in which this argument is first expressed. Schizophrenia is as much a social phenomena as it is an individual pathology. This argument is taken to its most extreme form in the work of Laing, but we can see that the anti-psychiatry movement was also being supported by theoretical work in sociology and social theory. Authors like the French social theorist Michel Foucault (1971, 1977) questioned seemingly altruistic ideas like the individual positivist position that criminals should not be punished but treated. He suggested that they were in fact just new ways to gain control through surveillance. Through the idea of social welfare, people like doctors and social workers were able to gain access to the home and infiltrate families. The massively expanding disciplines like psychiatry, psychology and criminology were more concerned with control than help. Consequently, radical work in psychology, psychiatry, social theory and sociology began to question the deterministic accounts of individual and sociological positivism and pointed towards a new critical perspective. This is exemplified in the book *The New Criminology* (1973) by Taylor, Walton and Young that combined a Marxist perspective with symbolic interactionism to present a critical approach to the preceding theoretical perspectives such as the individual positivism of H.J. Eysenck, Becker's approach to labelling and the Mertonian tradition. The authors suggest that for 'fully social theory of crime' there needs to be a social psychology of crime. However, it has been argued that this has not been fully embraced and that there is now a more obvious split between psychology and sociology than there was previously (Webber 2007a). The historical continuity between the Mertonian tradition and *The New Criminology* will be discussed in more depth in Chapter 4.

Postmodern approaches to the theory of crime

Such attacks on positivism leads us to the ultimate expression of this critical approach to science, the advent of postmodern analysis. Postmodernity cannot be called a theory since the nature of postmodernity is to challenge the very construction of theory. It is an anti-theory. Many students new to the ideas of postmodernity find them difficult at first. This is, perhaps, because the ideas are counterintuitive and in contrast to conventional ways of seeing the world. For example, postmodernity challenges the idea that there is a story to life, a narrative that unfolds with a beginning, middle and end. Major influences in sociology were writers such as Jean-François Lyotard (1984) and Jean Baudrillard (1983). Psychology's position within the positivist paradigm sets it at odds with postmodern ideas. Postmodernists argue that theory is a human construction that is too ordered to adequately capture the chaos, confusion and contradictions of the human condition. Postmodern analysis does not sit easily on a historical timeline; in sociology and social theory the late 1970s and early 1980s are often cited as the period when the ideas became accepted. Postmodernity can be seen as a critic of the rationality of technological advancement. Whereas Weber argued that science and the rational methods that characterised it was a better system than common sense, postmodernity takes the problem with science further. As psychology moves more fully into the medical sphere, with psychologists having their research funded more frequently by medical research councils, so the critique of scientific rationality at the heart of postmodernity forms a central critique of psychology itself. The final chapter will explore these issues in more detail.

History as collective memory

The historian E.H. Carr wrote in *What is History?* that history is a dialogue between the past and the present (Carr 1987). One cannot understand our present situation without an awareness of the past. It is like a person who has lost their short-term memory. Everything has to be learned anew each day. So, in social policy an awareness of the past can alert us to the possible mistakes of previous methods of dealing with problems. However, there are numerous examples where this dialogue has ceased, and we forget the lessons of the past and remake policies devoid of a historical awareness of where they may go wrong (Herman 1992). Or we see a phenomena presented as if it is new and unique, and indeed uniquely troubling, when it is a phenomenon that previous generations have already confronted (Pearson 1983). Alternatively, a crime that is rare, such as serial murder, is given more media attention than it deserves and the method for preventing it given too much credence. The following chapter looks at the topic of serial murder, and discusses the way that the investigation techniques built up to tackle the crime often have very little to do with psychology and the risk of victimisation small.

Summary

- This chapter has traced the broad historical trends in the study of crime. It has pointed out that all psychological theories developed within specific historical moments and reflected the concerns of the time. Understanding this allows us to better judge contemporary research.
- Sociology and psychology were much more closely linked than in contemporary research. It is difficult to pinpoint when the separation occurred, but the questioning of positivism after the Second World War began a trend that saw sociological criminology become more dominant, especially the form that criticised the legitimacy of authority in the late 1960s and early 1970s.
- Nevertheless, even in one of the key books of this period, Taylor et al.'s (1973) *The New Criminology*, social psychology was presented as a key aspect for a 'fully social theory of crime'. However, this has yet to be fully explored.

STUDY QUESTIONS

1 Why is it important to be aware of the history of a subject?

2 Why might it be argued that terms like modernity, late modernity and postmodernity are social constructions?

3 Is a postmodern criminology possible?

4 Early criminological studies attempted to show how the offender was different from the non-offender. Conduct a content analysis of newspaper stories of crime. Can you still see evidence of this? If so, why do we still wish to see the offender as distinct from the non-offender?

5 Go back to Table 1.2 on page 9. Photocopy the page and add a column titled 'Major historical events' either to the right or left of the table. Using newspaper archives or books from your library add into this column major political or social events that you feel had a major impact on people at the time. What methods did you use to choose the events? Were these events equally felt locally, nationally and globally? How might these events affect our understanding of the causes of crime and solutions to them? In what ways were the concerns of the time reflected in the theories that were being developed and what does this suggest about how theory is created?

FURTHER READING AND USEFUL WEBSITES

Almost all introductory textbooks have a chapter on the history of criminology. Godfrey, Lawrence and Williams (2007), *History and Crime*, London: Sage, is a good place to start. Also, the chapter by Clive Emsley (2007) 'Historical Perspectives on Crime', in M. Maguire, R. Morgan and R. Reiner (eds), *The Oxford Handbook of Criminology* (4th edn). In the same volume Clive Hollin (2007), 'Criminal Psychology', provides a good overview of the links between sociological and psychological accounts of crime.

The following is a link to *The British Crime Survey: Measuring crime for 25 years*. This is a review of how this important survey has changed over its first 25 years:

http://www.homeoffice.gov.uk/rds/pdfs07/bcs25.pdf

Notes

1 The terms 'normal' and 'abnormal' are used throughout and placed in speech marks to illustrate the contested quality of these terms. They are still terms commonly used in Psychology, but which are problematised within some areas of sociology where the contention is that there is nothing fixed about what society sees as normal or abnormal, they are socially constructed categories.
2 This word refers to theories that are centred on the body.

2

Interpersonal Violence and Investigative Psychology

Chapter Contents

OVERVIEW

The following chapter is a discussion of the role of psychology in the investigation of violent crime. There is a particular focus on psychological attempts at profiling. The chapter will demonstrate the problems with many of the forms of profiling that have become well-known through cinema and television, such as that by the FBI in America. However, there will also be a discussion of David Canter's approach to Investigative Psychology which is based on a method for identifying correlations between crimes.

KEY TERMS

investigative psychology offender profiling serial murder

This chapter is an exploration of the contemporary fascination with serial murder and the role of investigatory psychology or offender profiling. This discussion will centre on both the FBI approach and the British psychologists such as David Canter and Paul Briton. The aim will be to demystify the myths that the media has helped create around this topic. The chapter will represent a critique of offender profiling and will draw on the work of David Canter's approach to investigative psychology to make the case that most representations of offender profiling are false and misleading. Contrary to the media depiction, murder is one of the most frequently cleared up crimes. This is because the victim and offender tend to be known to each other and so the investigation does not need to look too far for a suspect. However, a minority of murders are committed by someone who does not know the victim making the suspect less easily identified. It is here that offender profiling has traditionally been used.

Wanting to understand why some people do hideous things to other people is one of the overriding concerns of students taking courses in criminology. In many ways, we are asking what makes violent people different from ourselves. Why do *we* not do what *they* do? Explanations have ranged from the social to the individual, from social learning to inherited personality traits and mental disorder. Classifications have been created to distinguish one type of violent offender from another and to make sense of, often contentious, statistics that purport to show that crime is more often located in one group rather than another. Such classifications can be based on social class, age, race or gender and tend to lead to stereotypical depictions of who is and who is not a criminal. Many of the psychological studies on violence are essentially the creation of stereotypes used to categorise offenders into types.

Offender profiling and serial killers tend to be linked in the popular imagination. This is not surprising given the disproportionate amount of time that is devoted to the phenomenon by the media. Disproportionate because the offence is far less frequent than would be supposed if a survey of media representations of the offence were taken or an assessment of the impact of the offence in comparison to other forms of violence such as domestic violence or street violence. Furthermore, offender profilers have attained a mythical status out of all proportion to either their efficacy in solving crimes or their incidence in terms of how many of them there are. It is currently not a career option in the UK in the sense of there being a job titled 'offender profiler', indeed the term 'Behavioural Investigative Advisor' is replacing the term offender profiler (ACPO 2000 cited Alison et al. 2003a). Those who create profiles are more likely to be employed primarily as forensic psychologists or psychiatrists. However, Canter has argued that his version of geographical offender profiling could be used for higher volume crime like burglary, as will be discussed later in this chapter (Canter 2000). This chapter will discuss offender profiling and serial murder since typically profiles have been predominantly used for this offence. Sexual offences also tend to attract the call for profiles, but as this is the topic of another chapter this will only be briefly discussed here.

Personality disorders

Having already discussed the early theories of criminal behaviour such as phrenology and Lombroso's criminal anthropology, the following will be a brief review of some of the theories inspired by this form of individual positivism that tends to locate the causes of criminal behaviour within the individual and relegates social factors to the periphery. Associating mental illness with serial killers is one of the most common narrative devices seen in fiction. They are often described as psychotic, psychopathic or sociopathic. However, such terms are highly contentious. The terms psychosis and neurosis are now outmoded and largely avoided in diagnosis due to their overly general descriptions. Psychosis used to refer to the most serious forms of personality disorder where the individual had largely lost touch with reality. Hence schizophrenia would be a psychosis and post traumatic stress disorder (PTSD) or obsessive compulsive disorder (OCD) a neurosis. The problem is that within these two broad categories are a range of disorders that seemingly have very little in common with each other and have different **aetiologies**. For example PTSD and OCD clearly derive from different causes with PTSD being linked to an actual event and OCD caused by more esoteric and difficult to determine events. The point is that serial killers, on the whole, tend to be able to distinguish fantasy from reality and are not suffering from a serious neurological mental disorder. Nevertheless, some authors maintain that there is evidence that many serial killers are psychopathic (Holmes and Holmes 2002). An inability to empathise or sympathise with the suffering of other people and an inflated opinion of their own self-worth tends to characterise psychopathic individuals. Of course, as argued already, there are many people who have psychopathic characteristics but who have not engaged in serious criminal offending. So, the discovery that many serial killers are psychopathic does not by itself constitute a cause. Psychopathic personalities may just as easily rise to prominence in the movie industry or business (Blair et al. 2005). The aim of research into the mental health status of serial murderers (and other types of crime) is to identify, keep track of, and control potential offenders. Such research feeds into the risk society thesis where individuals become subsumed within one overall category and their individual differences become blurred (Hudson 2003).

Equally, there is a tendency, even a need, to pathologise the offender and treat them as different from everyone else in terms of their psychological or biological make-up. This raises two problems. The first is that the evidence for a clearly identifiable pathological problem in serial killers is ambiguous at best. The second problem is that, even if there were an internal fault of some kind, it does not help the police to catch the killer. Men who hate women rarely have 'women hater' tattooed on their forehead. This explains why work in the UK has moved towards a more pragmatic, practical form of research and away from the search for causes.

Furthermore, the media fascination with extreme violence tends to focus on the background characteristics of the offender. For the most part, this is a *post-hoc* observation, one that is made after the offender has been arrested or convicted and serves to explain what it is about the offender that distinguishes them from non-offenders. Typically, the discussion will centre on the types of interests that the offender enjoyed, highlighting those that are felt to be sensational. Interests in the military, the occult, heavy metal music, use of pornography and martial arts are typically mentioned as being enjoyed by the offender. Such activities have been defined as sensational interests and tend to refer to activities that elicit a physiologically arousing response (Brittain 1970). Clearly, such a definition is open to interpretation; an opera can be as violent as the goriest horror film. Such definitions are social constructs based upon, usually, right-wing or religious morals. Egan has argued that such interests may be shared by many non-offending people. He argues that '[t]he diversity of "normality" is rarely appreciated by those preoccupied with the pathological' (2004: 117). The amount of media devoted to such sensational interests, from the television through to the Internet, would over-predict the amount of violent crime committed if there was a causal effect. There are simply not enough offences to validate a causal link with sensational interests. Egan notes that little research has been conducted into the relationship between sensational interests and crime, particularly from within populations convicted of violent or sexual offending (Egan 2004). Egan and his colleagues present some interesting findings that highlight the role of background and the sociality of the offenders. Sensational interests are only related to crime when the person feels alienated from other people and they do not desire conventional achievement, presumably through such means as school, work and marriage or other such close relationships. It is not the quality of the sensational interests themselves that are related to offending, but the absence of relationships and ambitions. This is a finding that casts doubt on the veracity of offender profiles based on typologies that seek to identify the typical characteristics of an offender. In the final analysis, the sensational interests of many people are not sufficient predictors of crime and may potentially lead the police to suspects seen as outsiders. As will be seen later in this chapter, such an occurrence may explain the case of the psychologist Paul Britton and his advice regarding Colin Stagg who became a suspect in the murder of Rachel Nickell in London in 1992.

Contested definitions of serial murder

Typically, this depends upon the number of murders an individual commits. Holmes and Holmes (1998) argue that the number is three, in others four, whereas one definition is as low as two (Egger 1998). Fox and Levin do not find the distinction helpful or useful and use a far more wide-ranging definition that draws in many more female offenders (2005). Clearly, this is an important point since it determines who is regarded as a serial killer and who is not. By changing the definition to one where fewer murders constitute a case of serial murder you will increase the number of incidences of serial murder in any given country straight away. Each definition has a cooling off period between murders since this is what distinguishes this type of crime from mass murder (see Chapter 5). Obviously, there is an element of subjectivity in this. The question of how much time needs to have elapsed between murders is one that is open to interpretation. However, there is a further element in the definition that goes beyond the sheer numbers of people killed by an individual. The definition of serial killer also, implicitly, includes an evaluation of motive. The key requirement, for many authors, for a series of killings to be a case of serial murder is that they have no clear motive. Definitions including those of Holmes and Holmes (2002) and Ressler, Burgess and Douglas (1988) tend to equate serial killing with a motive that has no pecuniary or direct vengeful motivation and in the majority of cases there is a sexual component also. It is this that has lead to the perceived need to get into the mind of the serial murderer. Fox and Levin (2005), in contrast, include a range of motives that include revenge and crimes for profit. It is much easier to understand someone who kills for profit, or to seek revenge against people that have hurt or disparaged them. A gang member who shoots and kills four members of a rival gang would be a serial murderer in Fox and Levine's definition, but would not be in Holmes and Holmes' definition.

But, in the majority of definitions and the popular imagination the motivation of the serial murderer is opaque, requiring of an expert above and beyond the skills of a detective. A hit man or woman is rarely called a serial killer, or a burglar who kills three or more people during their burgling career is usually 'just' a murderer. In these cases, there is a motive, so the definition of a serial killer is someone who kills a number of people, over a period of time, for no obvious reason. Before moving on, one final problem with the definition of serial killing is that the crimes need to be linked through either modus operandi, forensic evidence or eyewitness testimony, all of which can be difficult (Woodhams, Hollin and Bull 2007).

The different styles of offender profiling

Offender profiling can be split between two distinct methodological approaches and they are summarised in Table 2.1.

Table 2.1   *The two methodological approaches to offender profiling*

	Top down	Bottom up
Type of approach	Comparison of crime scene with statistical research into other crimes	Getting into the mind of the offender by using empathy, using previous cases as evidence from which to make subjective comparisons
Main advocate	David Canter and Lawrence Allison	FBI, Paul Britton, Holmes and Holmes
Theoretical inclination	Quantitative, judgements based on correlations and analysis of locality of offending	Qualitative, but without reference to the social context of the interview, or a critical analysis of what is being said by the convicted offender
Method of research	Statistical comparisons of crime-scene behaviours	Interviews with captured offenders

Getting into the mind of the offender: the American approach to offender profiling

This method is based on interviewing convicted serial killers to see how they describe their offending and then to use that information to look at crime scenes to see what type of person might have committed the offences. An often heard phrase that exemplifies this method is 'getting into the mind' of the murderer. This style of offender profiling is associated with the FBI's Behavioural Science Unit in their headquarters of Quantico, Virginia, USA. In Britain, it was the psychologist Paul Britton who initially championed the idea (Britton 1997). The following is a discussion of this type of approach. Two of the most widely cited authors on this subject are Ronald and Stephen Holmes (1998, 2001a, 2001b, 2002). It is worth spending some time looking at some of this work since it summarises the kind of work associated with the FBI, and American investigative psychology more generally.

Holmes and Holmes assert that serial killers tend to be white males, between 25 and 34, intelligent or 'street smart', charming and charismatic and interested in police work (2002: 115). Holmes and Holmes outline a typology of different types of serial killer. The first distinction is the spatial patterning of the murder locations. This tends to be either spatially concentrated or dispersed, these are termed geographically transient and geographically stable. Such a pattern can provide investigators with information about the individual involved. Widely dispersed murders can indicate that the killer has access to a vehicle and travels to confuse law enforcement agencies. Equally it could indicate the killer drives for a living or has lived in various places. A geographically stable killer tends to live in one area for some time and kills close to home. As we will see later, this aspect of serial killing is key to the British psychologist David Canter's approach to what he terms investigative psychology. Within each of these two broad categories are more specific traits that have been collected into another typology.

The visionary serial killer

Visionary serial killers differ from other serial killers due to the fact that they seem to have lost touch with reality. Their violence is propelled by auditory hallucinations that direct the individual to kill broadly similar people, for example, women the killer believes to be involved in prostitution. It is not necessary for each victim to have been a prostitute, since the desire to kill may outstrip the availability of suitable targets, consequently the offender may settle for a women the killer believes is sexually promiscuous instead. The British serial killer Peter Sutcliffe, known as the Yorkshire Ripper, claimed to have heard voices telling him to kill prostitutes. Like many cases such as this, Sutcliffe's defence lawyers claimed a defence of insanity. In this case, the judge ruled against the defence arguing that he was sane when he killed his victims.

The mission serial killer

The mission serial killer is not psychotic, but like the vision serial killer tends to go after a certain category of people, for example, homosexuals, an ethnic group other than his or her own, women, etc. The mission serial killer is propelled not by voices but a perceived mission to eradicate the world or area of such people.

The hedonistic lust serial killer

The hedonistic serial killer's motive tends to be the eroticised nature of killing. The offender tends to spend some considerable time in planning and executing the murder, sometimes kidnapping and holding a victim for some time before killing them and then sometimes living with the victim for some time after death. Sexual pleasure is derived from the victim.

The power-control serial killer

According to the definition of this type of murderer by Holmes and Holmes there seems to be very little difference between the power-control and the hedonistic lust killer. Whereas the hedonistic lust killer derives sexual pleasure from the victim, the power-control killer derives sexual pleasure from the act of controlling and destroying life.

Of course, such typologies are ideal types and it is rare for a serial killer to completely conform to one of these types. Indeed, the essential problem with such typologies are that they tend to create an artificially static offender who seems not to change their behaviour. An example to illustrate the problem with this is the British serial killer Dr Harold Shipman who was convicted of killing 15 elderly patients initially without any clear motive. It could be argued that since there was no evidence of auditory hallucinations but that his victims were all elderly Shipman was fulfilling a mission, but equally it seemed that he gained a sense of power and control through the activity of killing. However, his killings were ultimately discovered because he had changed his behaviour when he tried to change a victim's last will and testament to favour himself. Although interviewing serial killers in prison may reveal some interesting data, it needs to be taken into account that the offender may be producing *post-hoc* justifications, reproducing their psychiatrist's assessment or repeating the defence lawyer's argument. Both such justifications may not correspond with the original motivation. Also, the FBI approach is unsystematic in the way it collects data. It is therefore possible to take any part of a respondent's interview and make it fit whatever category you want it to fit (Seltzer 1998). Furthermore, there is little awareness of the wider social structure so that there is an overly deterministic approach that cannot explain why it is that not everyone who shares the same background goes on to kill (Gadd and Jefferson 2007).

Fox and Levine provide another typology based on motivation rather than the amount of time between killings, or the cooling off period (2005). Their typology is able to encompass both serial and mass murder incidences, but it still suffers the same inflexibility. Under the headings, power, revenge, loyalty, profit and terror, Fox and Levine's typology has the advantage of being able to include killings for profit and even religious fundamentalism, thus overcoming the criticism of Holmes and Holmes' more moralistic approach that only includes crimes under the heading of serial murder where the motivation appears to be strange or esoteric. A further complication is that the FBI has categorised so-called lust offenders into two types, disorganised asocial and organised non-social (see Tables 2.2 and 2.3). Although this typology is primarily designed for when sex is a key feature of the offence, the terms have been used to include other offenders where sex is not an aspect of the offence. Indeed, it can be quite a confusing enterprise to disentangle the various typologies for offenders.

Table 2.2   *Organised versus disorganised offenders*

Organised non-social killer	Disorganised asocial killer
Planned offence	Spontaneous event
Targeted stranger	Victim unknown
Personalises victim	Depersonalises victim
Controlled conversation	Minimal conversation
Controlled crime	Chaotic crime scene
Submissive victim	Sudden violence
Restraints used	No restraints
Aggressive acts	Sex after death
Body moved	Body not moved
Weapon taken	Weapon left
Little evidence	Physical evidence

Source: Burgess et al. (1985b) cited Holmes and Holmes (2002: 81)

Table 2.3   *Perpetrator characteristics*

Organised	Disorganised
High intelligence	Below average intelligence
Socially adequate	Socially inadequate
Sexually competent	Unskilled occupation
Lives with father	Low birth-order status
High birth order	Harsh/inconsistent discipline
Controlled mood	Anxious mood during crime
Masculine image	Minimal use of alcohol during crime
Charming	Lives alone
Situational cause	Lives/works near crime scene
Geographically mobile	Minimal interest in media
Occupationally mobile	Significant behaviour change
Follows media	Nocturnal habits
Model prisoner	Poor personal hygiene
	Secret hiding places
	Usually does not date
	High-school drop-out

Source: Burgess et al. (1985a) cited in Alison, McLean and Almond (2007: 495–6).

Disorganised versus organised killers

Holmes and Holmes state that the *disorganised asocial offender* tends to be disorganised in all areas of their lives. However, in an example of the lack of research that has been undertaken to verify the veracity of offender profiles they state that there is no evidence for this. Despite this typology being based on nothing more than speculation, they go on to note that such people would be seen as loners and weird by those who know them, that they would have had educational problems and would find getting and retaining employment difficult. The crime scene would reflect this background with the offences being unplanned, the body and weapon left where the person was killed and the crime scene reflecting the spontaneous and sudden violence. Although they add that this is only theoretical (2002: 74).

The *organised non-social offender*, by contrast, is charming, employed, may live with a partner, they are socially and sexually competent and they tend to follow the media reporting of the case. The crime scene again, theoretically, reflects the personality of the offender, with the crime being planned, the victim targeted, the body may be moved to avoid detection or confuse law enforcement agencies, the weapon will be taken, the victim may be restrained and there is very little evidence left at the scene.

As noted, one of the major shortcomings of this research is the paucity of psychological evidence. For example, Holmes and Holmes talk about the work of Eysenck and note that despite criticism of his work, there is some evidence that the personality of the offender, especially as it developed during the early years of their lives, does have an impact on offending behaviour. It is noted that many offenders report in interviews an experience in their lives that lead them to a split in their personality allowing them to function socially, and have a 'dark side' that wishes to express a sense of power over others. They state that:

> This phenomenon is called 'Fractured Identity Syndrome'. Although this theory has not been empirically validated, it is based on Freud's and Goffman's principle that behaviour in adults is based on traumatic experiences in childhood that have left a lasting mark on individuals and their personalities. (Holmes and Holmes 2002: 51)

David Canter has placed questions of validity and untested assumptions such as this at the centre of his criticism of this approach. This Freudian notion that the early period of one's life shapes our personalities has, in any case, been challenged from within psychoanalysis, in particular the work of Erik Erikson (1964) and his belief that an individual is confronted by crises throughout their lifespan and that an inability to overcome a crisis at one time in our lives can be rectified at a later stage. Other critics of this form of trait theory, such as Maruna (2000), suggest that such an approach does not explain those who may desist from crime. This is especially the case with young offenders who tend to grow out of petty crime (Rutherford 2002), but equally it is the case for more serious offenders. Simply put, how can someone who exhibits a particular personality trait associated with crime stop committing crime? Similarly, why do people with a personality trait associated with crime never commit a criminal offence? The supposed stability of a personality, and the assumption that a particular personality is associated with criminal activity, such as Eysenck's extrovert, is deterministic and over-predicts crime amongst those who share certain characteristics. Moreover, some of the characteristics that are associated with, for example, serial murder, are never deconstructed. An asocial disorganised serial murderer is typically a white male, non-athletic, introverted, with an absent father. But, what is it about being white that propels an individual into a series of murders? Why are black males who share the same background less likely to be serial killers? Why males and not females? Clearly, one's personality is more than genetically determined, the content of that personality is made up from the cultural background of an individual and shared negative emotions are therefore expressed in different ways by different groups of people. Getting into the criminal mind, the ambition of many students of crime, is at best a waste of resources, at worst an impossibility.

Throughout Holmes and Holmes' book on profiling crime there are numerous references to the depiction of offender profiling in fiction, especially cinema. For example, they argue that 'the alert investigator must be able to get into the mind of the criminal, just as Will Graham did in *The Red Dragon* (sic)[1]', referring here to Thomas Harris' first Hannibal Lecter book (Holmes and Holmes 2002: 210). Elsewhere, the authors seem almost proud of the decidedly non-academic stance to offender profiling, for Holmes and Holmes, and for the American approach to offender profiling more generally, offender profiling is an art, not a science, that can be done by anyone (Ressler et al. 1988). A typical example of this is the following statement that also represents the main point of divergence between the American and British approach to offender profiling developed by David Canter and colleagues:

> It may be that we should return to an examination of the 'concentric zone theory' of years past to develop some theory of the relationship between criminal profiling and geography; but perhaps it is just as effective to consider our thoughts regarding our own mental maps and spatial behaviour. (Holmes and Holmes 2002: 212)

After suggesting that the Chicago School's ecological research into crime might be used, they then suggest that one's intuition might be as useful. By way of contrast, the following section discusses the British psychologist David Canter's approach.

The British approach to offender profiling: David Canter and Investigative Psychology

The British approach is based on a method that seeks to understand the actions of the criminal through the application of quantitative scientific methodologies. It is presented as a more objective approach than its American counterpart and is associated with the work of David Canter and his colleagues at Liverpool University. Canter calls this approach Investigative Psychology (Canter 2004). Canter is concerned to base this approach on the foundation of sound psychological principles. He argues that at the core of traditional American forms of offender profiling is the making of inferences based on little evidence. For, example, a crime scene that yields little direct evidence of who committed the crime is looked at to make an inference of the characteristics of the likely perpetrator. And yet, as the examples above show, the American approach is unverifiable and seems to associate itself more firmly with fiction than psychology.

Canter's approach to offender profiling is to apply psychological principles to the investigation of crime. His particular interest stems from his background as an environmental psychologist interested in the way that people make sense of their surroundings and become familiar with the movement around their environment. Through analysing the way that different offenders move between the crime site and their home, Canter argues it is possible to make some generalisations that are helpful to investigators. Since a profile is used for crimes where there is little evidence that would help link the victim to the offender, Canter argues that psychology may help in a far wider set of crimes than the current preoccupation with high profile serial crimes like murder and rape. However, the offence could just as easily be vandalism as a murder (Canter 1984). One issue that also needs to be understood is how a series of offences are linked in the absence of a forensic link such as DNA. Behavioural consistency across crime scenes can become an important factor in linking crimes. This is where the offender carries out similar acts at each separate crime scene. Canter's suggestion is that rather than looking for individual acts, behaviour should be categorised into themes. For example, gagging and tying someone up could be seen as two different acts, but they can be combined under the theme of control. An offender may choose one or the other due to the situational factors present at the time. For example, fear that someone will hear would lead to gagging, but where the location was more remote such caution may not be necessary. This is an important finding because two murders may not be classified as being the offence of one person because the two crime scenes do not appear the same.

From specifics to themes

There are a number of questions that need to be answered in a criminal investigation so as to find links between the crime scene evidence and the offender. The first question relates to the saliency of behaviours exhibited during the crime. Saliency here refers to behaviours that are specific to that offender. So the first question that needs to be asked is, 'what are the important behavioural features of the crime that may help identify the perpetrator?' The second area that an investigation must cover is the characteristics of an offence that makes it distinct from other offences. Canter puts this question as 'what are the most appropriate ways of indicating the differences between crimes and between offenders?' In order to move beyond the categorisation of offenders and offences and provide real and tangible assistance to the police the following question must be answered: 'what inferences can be made about the characteristics of the offender that may help identify him or her?' Finally, in order to determine if the crime is one of a series it is necessary to find links and answer the question, 'are there any other crimes that are likely to have been committed by the same offender?' (Canter 2000: 28). As Canter says, all 'four questions are derivations of questions crucial to other areas of psychology. They involve concepts associated with the significant differences between one person and another and the features of one individual's behaviour that remain constant over different situations' (2000: 28). In contrast, the FBI typologies as described above tend to talk about emotions and intangible motivations that are not necessarily useful for investigators. It is difficult to identify an offender who has auditory hallucinations telling them to fulfil a mission to kill non-believers just by knocking on their door and talking to them, but easier to identify someone who is highly religious and is likely to wear religious symbols or exhibit such symbols in their home because they act out religious symbolism at the crime scene and it has been found that such activity correlates with those who are demonstrably religious.

The most interesting element of Canter's approach is that criminal activity may well be an extreme reflection of non-criminal activity (Canter 1995). Crime scene behaviour that reflects elements of an offender's general lifestyle may be useful for investigators because it may be that people might notice such behaviour. Here, Canter makes links to a criminological theory called Routine Activities Theory (RAT) that posits the need of criminologists to focus on the crime event and the role of the victim in that event (Cohen and Felson 1979). By doing this, attention is shifted away from why some people commit crime whilst others do not and instead focus on crime prevention. For a crime to occur, there needs to be three factors coinciding in time and space. The first is a motivated offender, the second is a suitable target and finally the absence of capable guardians able to prevent the offence taking place. Importantly, offences are associated with the routine activities of everyday life. The rhythm of movements around the environment provides moments and opportunities for the commission of a crime. For example, many homes are empty between 9 am and 5 pm as people go to work resulting in the opportunity to burgle houses without the risk of someone being at home to prevent it. The argument that crime is linked to the routine activities of everyday life links into Canter's approach because Canter is less concerned with motivations than with the crime scene themes that might practically help investigations. For example, in homicides, it was found that previous offence history is related to what happens at the crime scene. Offenders who had previously had a custodial sentence are more likely to avoid leaving forensic evidence, and more likely to move or hide the body and steal non-identifiable property (Salfati and Canter 1999). Therefore, stolen property and a body that has been moved or hidden might suggest that a search of previously imprisoned offenders local to the area would be a good place to start the search. It could be suggested that this is another example of how some forms of psychology have moved away from causation and into risk assessment as suggested in the risk society literature (Beck 1992; Giddens 1990; Feeley and Simon 1992).

Canter's contribution to geographical profiling

There is also some good evidence that offenders tend to operate within a specific locality and use that area in ways that can be analysed to locate where they may live or work. This is termed the spatial consistency of the offences. Canter utilised his background in environmental psychology when he became involved in studying crime. The main finding in Canter's work is that offenders tend to commit crimes close to home or in familiar territory. This is true of many different types of offence. With regard to serial murder, this finding has been seen in different countries (Rossmo 2000; Snook et al. 2005).

Goodwill and Alison (2005) sought to understand the spatial patterning of three different types of offender: burglars, rapists and murderers. It was found that each type of offender was drawn to commit other offences of the same type near to the location of their first offence. There are other studies that have not showed this relationship or showed only a weak connection (Snook 2004). One conceptual problem is the number of crimes that an individual offender commits. In other words, how many offences need to be committed to constitute a series? Different studies have not been able to hold this variable consistent. Snook's study looked at the movement of residential burglars and how far they travelled to commit their offences. It was found that those with access to vehicles travelled further and stole goods of a higher value than those who walked.

They also tended to be older. One of the potential conclusions to this is that those who are older had a more developed cognitive mental map of their locality. The more sociological and practical reason is only alluded to; older people are more likely to have access to a car and a car allows for more goods to be placed in it. It may also be the case that there is more planning and the use of a car means that there is a need to move further afield than those without such an easily identifiable vehicle. In other words, those who travelled were more organised than the opportunist young offender.

However, the use of data from the police of recorded offences leaves this study open to question. How is it possible to know that the first offence recorded is the first committed? The discovery that the offender may offend near to their home is not new to criminology. The police routinely use criminal statistics to more efficiently deploy police officers. A group of criminologists who called themselves left realists carried out victim surveys and came to similar conclusions. Crime was mainly intra-class and intra-race. That is, crime was committed within the same socio-economic and ethnic group. Offender and victim were similar. Rather than psychological principles to do with location familiarity, these criminologists posited a more sociological account (Lea and Young 1993/1984). Relative deprivation was the major cause of crime, and for that to exist there needed to be some similarity. Relative deprivation is as much an emotion as an objective entity, in contrast to absolute poverty which can be more easily measured (Webber 2007a). Consequently, it could account for violence as a result of frustration and acquisitive crime for gain (this will be discussed in detail in Chapter 4). But, it represents another place where a similar finding from within psychology has an echo in sociological criminology and the reason for the finding reflects the focus of the discipline trying to explain the behaviour.

Racial profiling

One of the more controversial aspects of the application of psychology to crime and justice is the racial profiling of suspected terrorists. At places of heightened risk of terrorist attack, such as airports, police and customs officials have begun engaging in what is essentially a procedure for making stop and searches more efficient by targeting those groups of people more likely to be involved in terrorist activity. Stop and search has moved from the usual suspects (particular individuals known to be involved in crime) to the usual categories (groups, usually certain races, deemed to be potentially involved in crime) (Young 1999). The justification that it is more efficient to use limited resources on the most likely suspects, as opposed to stopping and searching a random sample of the population at an airport, is deemed by many involved in law enforcement a suitable justification for the potential infringement of an individual's civil liberties. What such a tactic has achieved is to shift the burden of suspicion onto entire groups of people, such as dark skinned men, and therefore suspicion onto a majority of innocent people. It is possible to see the problem with such tactics when one looks at the variety of people who have engaged in terrorist activity since the most vivid of the attacks in New York in 2001. From people born overseas to those born in the country they attack; from the disenfranchised and easily manipulated to professional doctors and teachers; and in the Middle East, women as well as men. This brings us back to the problem of categorisation, although useful in many contexts, it also has the potential to mask a variety of differences, and in so doing, create stereotypes that short-circuit the very real need to understand such behaviours at all levels of analysis, the individual, group, local, national and international.

Critique of profiles

The first and most damning criticism is that of Holmes and Holmes who say that a 'tremendous amount of interest surrounds the field of profiling. But we must remember that it is only one tool and by itself has never solved a murder case despite the statements made by some' (2002: 3). One of the problems of the idea of a profile is that it is a static and inflexible approach that may only have relevance for early stages in an investigation. As shown in Box 2.1 on page 49, a profile is similar to a snapshot of someone that may not reflect the way they look years, months or even weeks later. As police investigations develop, offenders can change their modus operandi in response to what the police do. This is particularly the case in high profile cases which may attract publicity. Similarly, there is evidence that when a serial killing is being investigated and reported in the media the residents in the area in which the murders are taking place show an increased fear level and take more protective measures, such as carrying pepper spray. In one study, fear of crime rose by 56 per cent due to the activity of a serial killer and the taking of protective measures rose by 46 per cent (Lee and DeHart 2007). Also, many studies are based on data from convicted offenders. Those who are caught may not correspond to those who are not caught. This is particularly true of the FBI approach.

A British study by Alison, Smith and Morgan (2003b) presented police officers with a 'bogus' offender profile designed to be deliberately ambiguous but based on a real murder and a description of the characteristics of an offender. The respondents were split into two groups and each were asked to rate the accuracy of the offender profile to the offender. One group was presented with a description of the convicted offender and the other group were presented with a description of a fabricated offender designed to have characteristics the opposite to that of the real offender. For example, the real offender was a 19 year old man and the fabricated offender was 38. This study demonstrated that police officers would treat an offender profile as an accurate description of an offender regardless of the characteristics of the offender.

In order to see if the same outcome would happen with a real offender profile the study used a real FBI offender profile and included other forensic professionals working in the criminal justice system, such as solicitors and psychologists. As before, the respondents were split into two groups with one presented with a description of the real offender and the other a fabricated offender. The majority of the police officers said that the profile would be a useful tool for an investigation and just over half of the forensic professionals thought it would be useful. Despite the different characteristics of the offenders the majority of the respondents felt that the profile was accurate. A useful analogy as to why profiles may be seen as accurate even when they contain ambiguous statements that could apply to many people are horoscopes. A horoscope is written as if for the reader alone yet that star sign is shared by approximately one-twelfth of the world's population. Ambiguous statements are assigned meaning such that the predictions are given personal relevance. For example, being told that your finances will be boosted could be finding a small amount of money in the street or getting a pay rise at work. Both are very different but both could be interpreted as fulfilling the prediction. Alison et al. argued that this was the result of a phenomenon that has been called the Barnum effect (Furnham and Schofield 1987). This is where ambiguous or false information is interpreted as accurate. In the example of a real offender profile below, it is clear that the statements could be interpreted in a number of ways. For example, what exactly does someone of average appearance look like? Could it not be argued that it is covering every eventuality to say that the offender may be unemployed, but his occupation will be blue collar or skilled? Whoever is caught, the author of such a profile could claim a high level of accuracy despite the ambiguity of such statements.

In a related study, Alison et al. (2003a) analysed 21 profiles used in major criminal investigations and found that 80 per cent of the claims made in these studies was unsubstantiated and 31 per cent were not falsifiable. In other words, the majority of the claims made could not be verified after the suspect had been caught because they referred to emotions, thoughts, feelings and other such factors that are subjective and personal to the offender. A falsifiable claim related to a point of fact that could be verified such as the age of the offender. Consequently Alison et al. found that nearly one-third of the claims were ambiguous statements. Ambiguous statements and statements that can be interpreted in two different ways, 'multiple outs', mean that the success of the statements are higher. An ambiguous statement in the profile in Box 2.1 would be: 'The murderer will not look out of context in the area'. This statement is clearly ambiguous since it can be interpreted in a variety of ways. Statements that would be multiple outs are the following: 'His occupation will be blue collar or skilled'. The profiler cannot be wrong once the offender has been apprehended since if they are a car mechanic then they are blue collar and could be described by some as skilled, whilst if an accountant is arrested then they are usually defined as skilled and the profiler is shown to be correct. In Box 2.1 the profilers give themselves even more potential for success with the following statement: 'He will not have a military history and may be unemployed'. Only the first statement is falsifiable since if the offender has been in the military then the profiler can be proved wrong, whereas the second statement when combined with the other statement about occupation means that every eventuality is covered from unemployed to skilled. Alison et al. argue that statements should be supported with evidence from research in order that they can be verified. Failure to do this can have serious consequences for the investigation.

In the murder investigation of Rachel Nickell on Wimbledon Common in London in 1992 a psychologist, Paul Britton, guided the police in an operation to extract a confession from a suspect, a local man called Colin Stagg. The operation involved a female police officer going undercover to befriend Stagg and attempt to extract a confession from him. Britton's involvement in the operation was highly criticised after the case against Stagg was thrown out of court and the Judge described the honey-trap operation as reprehensible. It took eight years from the original complaint in 1994 by Stagg's solicitor to the hearing by the British Psychological Society, which then collapsed after the delay was deemed too long. In consequence of such cases the Association of Chief Police Officers (ACPO) has called for more evaluation of profiles in order to attain greater accountability and effectiveness (Alison et al. 2003b). In December 2008, Robert Napper pleaded guilty to the manslaughter of Rachel Nickell on the grounds of diminished responsibility. A year after Nickell's murder, Napper murdered another women and her 4 year old daughter. In a study of investigations of murder and rape cases by Gudjonsson and Copson (1997) they found that a profiler helped to provide a second opinion rather than provided any major breakthrough. As Canter maintains, this can also mean that the police follow the wrong lead as happened in the Nickell murder. In this case, the wrong man was suspected whilst the real murderer killed again. As already noted, Holmes and Holmes assert that profiles on their own have never solved a murder. Copson (1995) further states that where a profile was used it was deemed useful in only 16 per cent of the cases, and lead to an identification of the offender in less than 3 per cent of the cases.

Box 2.1   Example of a genuine offender profile

Douglas, J., Ressler, R., Burgess, A. and Hartman, C. (1986) 'Criminal profiling from crime scene analysis', *Behavioral Sciences and the Law*, 4(4): 401–21.

The offender will be a white male between 25 and 35, or the same general age as the victim and of average appearance.
The murderer will not look out of context in the area.
He will be of average intelligence and will be a secondary school (High school) or University (College) drop-out.
He will not have a military history and may be unemployed.
His occupation will be blue collar or skilled.
Alcohol or drugs will not assume a major role.
The suspect will have difficulty maintaining any kind of personal relationships with women.
If he dates, he will date women younger than himself, as he would have to dominate and control in the relationships.
He will be sexually inexperienced, sexually inadequate and never married.
He will have a pornography collection.
The subject will have sadistic tendencies.
The sexual acts show controlled aggression, but rage or hatred of women was obviously present.
The murderer was not reacting to rejection from women as much as to morbid curiosity.
There will have been a reason for the killer to be at the crime.
He could be employed in the immediate area, be in the immediate area on business or reside in the immediate area.
Although the offender might have preferred his victim conscious, he had to render her unconscious because he did not want to get caught.
He did not want the woman screaming for help.
The murderer's infliction of sexual sadistic acts on an inanimate body suggests he was disorganised.
He probably will be a very confused person, possibly with previous mental problems.
If he had carried out such acts on a living victim, he would have a very different type of personality. The fact that he inflicted acts upon a dead or unconscious person indicated his inability to function with a live or conscious person.
The crime scene reflects that the killer felt justified in his actions and that he felt no remorse. He was not subtle. He left the victim in a provocative, humiliating position, exactly the way he wanted her to be found.

(In Alison et al. 2003b: 195)

What do the police do?

A further problem when trying to determine the characteristics of the individual responsible for any type of crime is that they may change their behaviour based on what the police are doing, if it is well publicised, but also in response to changes in the law. The police often hold information back regarding the details of a crime so that they can use it in an interview when the suspect is in custody. They also do this so that information that could prejudice the case is not in the public domain, making jury selection difficult. Nevertheless, it is not always possible to do this in high profile cases leading to possible changes in the offender's behaviour. Moreover, when laws are passed with harsher penalties then the chances of a rape turning into murder increase. If the penalty for rape is increased then the risk to the offender is increased so it may make more sense to kill the victim to avoid eyewitness testimony against the offender.

There is a common-sense notion that the police are crime fighters using their coercive authority to catch criminals. Some early studies supported this (Skolnick 1966). However, many studies have demonstrated that the majority of police work is about the maintenance of order rather than law enforcement (Reiner 2000). Similarly, we are presented with media fictions of police investigations that many people take to be representations of real police work. The image of the insightful detective solving crimes that baffle everyone involved is a common dramatic device. Most murders are solved, but not through the application of insightful intelligence, rather the murderer tends to be known to the victim and so is fairly easy to identify. Where that is not the case, the police rely on information from the public. Knocking on doors and gathering knowledge is the key investigatory tool used by the police (De Lint 2003). In this respect, the police act as amplifiers of the crime, talking to the media and making appeals on television in order to get more information from the public. It could be argued, then, that the finding that offenders tend to commit crimes close to where they live is one that the police already employ through their door-to-door enquiries. A more focused search is all that would be required to enact this finding in practice.

Nevertheless, the British police have recently set up what might be described as an equivalent organisation to the American FBI. The National Policing Improvement Agency (NPIA) is an organisation that is not part of any single police force, but instead acts like an umbrella organisation providing assistance and advice to police investigations. The aim is to centralise the tools for investigation and collation of crime data. Specifically designed for this purpose was the setting up of the Serious Crime Analysis Section (SCAS) in 1998. Its role was to spot emerging patterns in murders and serious sexual assaults so as to identify potential serial killers or rapists. Every force has an officer in the intelligence department assigned the role of passing all crime files to SCAS for the purposes of comparison with other similar crimes. Entered into a database developed by the Canadian Mounted Police called the Violent Crime Linkage Analysis System (ViCLAS), crime scene activity is coded and compared to data already entered to find potential matches both in terms of behaviour and forensic evidence such as DNA evidence. This is a career that is increasingly open to psychologists, termed assistant crime analysts; the role requires the coding of information not unlike that in many psychological experiments. This is then turned into a report for the Senior Investigating Officer (SIO) with salient points to help the investigation. It is worth pointing out that there are very few people employed in geographical profiling; as of 2008 there were only four people doing this job.

One of the main problems with the data upon which investigative psychologists must base their conclusions is that the police require that the research is in the service of their work. Not, in itself, an unfair position to take, but it remains unclear as to what impact this has on research that is critical of police practice. As the following demonstrates, the police can withhold permission to publish research findings.

- *Benefit to the Police Service*

  It is vital that NCPE Operations assesses the benefit of the research to the service in terms of its operational relevance, against the cost implications and the sensitivity of the data. The research must provide 'added value' for the police service as a whole. This, together with managing access to NCPE Operations data, will be discussed further in section three of this paper.

- *Publication*

  It must be made clear that access to data is for specific undertakings only. Any findings derived from it remain the property of NCPE Operations and can only be published, presented or otherwise placed in the public domain with NCPE Operations' explicit written permission.

(Internet Reference 1)

Moreover, there are very real legal and ethical issues with the use of police data. Not least the fact that confidentiality of both victims and offenders needs to be treated carefully, but also that any data that is not handled carefully may be rendered legally problematic for current investigations. Furthermore, there also needs to be awareness that a case can be reopened and challenged a long time after the original investigation through legal appeals. Finally, almost all profiles are based on data provided by the police to agencies like the FBI or the NPIA. Consequently, their accuracy is based on the initial accuracy of the police data collection. The computer program that links crimes together, essentially the tool that provides the initial suggestion that individual crimes may be part of a series, is dependent for its accuracy on a multitude of individual police officers collecting information. Information lost, distorted or ignored at any point in this chain will result in an end result that is less than accurate. Since most information comes from the public, and the public may not trust the police, a further distorting filter is placed in the chain. As Strangeland argues with regard to computer profiling models, the outcome of the program is only as good as the data that is put into it (Strangeland 2005). In one case of serial rape, for example, a system that is used to provide a geographic profile of the likely home base of the offender was wrong due to a series of errors. For example, the hypothesised home base was a choice between two distinct areas, a northern and southern sector. With a fifty-fifty choice, the wrong area was chosen. With regard to the offender's choice of transport, it was hypothesised that he would walk, when he used a car. The wrong choice of home base is perhaps the most significant, since there were only two choices and such errors could potentially mislead the investigation and waste time. Such profiling techniques as discussed in this chapter are clearly problematic, and police may need to trust in the basics of their job rather more than they trust offender profiles.

Serial killer as celebrity: popular representations of serial murder

Peter Sutcliff, Harold Shipman, David Berkowitz, Ted Bundy. The unifying outcome of each of these serial killers is that they became celebrities (Jenks 2003: 181). Each came from different backgrounds, were educated to varying levels and were parented consistently and inconsistently. The thrill of murder, the power it gave them and the potential fame at the killing spree's conclusion are the only unifying links between the killers. They cannot be linked by psychological variables such as introversion, extroversion, psychopathy, frustration, and so on.

One serial killer has even published a book. The Moors Murderer Ian Brady who, with Myra Hindley, kidnapped and killed four children between 1963 and 1964, wrote a book called *The Gates of Janus* (2001). The book reads very much like the kind of book that is prevalent in many bookshops in the 'true crimes' section. However, it is presented as a critique of the kinds of book that Holmes and Holmes, or Fox and Levine write. It attempts to undermine the whole apparatus of psychology by claiming that it is not possible to get inside the head of a criminal. Mainly because we are all to a certain extent criminal. Brady challenges those in power to take the same tests that are given to those in captivity to see if they would also score highly on tests of psychopathy, or if an EEG brain scan would reveal the same pattern as is sometimes ascribed to a killer or rapist. It makes for chilling reading since this is a man universally reviled who presents the case against the possibility of a science that could capture him. Essentially, those who are captured are lazy, losers or unlucky. It is not some psychological expert who tends to catch them. In many ways, then, Brady draws the same conclusion as some of the academics referred to in this book. He also makes for disturbing reading when he discusses the fascination that people have for killers like him. As can be seen in the following quotation, the public derive pleasure from reading about people like him. He also suggests that the public are complicit in the crimes committed by men such as him.

> The plain and perhaps regrettable fact is that it is part of the eternal human psyche and cycle for the normal individual to derive cathartic satisfaction and enjoyment from savouring the crimes of others, and from luxuriously dreaming of personally committing them. (Brady 2001: 41)

However, it says more about Brady that he thinks people are dreaming about doing the things that he did.

Conclusion

The serial killer industry is a massive money-maker. From the academics and the students they teach at one end to the filmmakers and novelists at the other, the fascination is real. Unfortunately, it is the sensational and gory aspect of the crime that becomes the media focus. The thousands of people unlawfully killed everyday due to faults in cars, workplace negligence and speeding or drunk drivers rarely get a mention. Yet, the rare cases of serial murder make the headlines.

Summary

- The psychological research into investigating such crimes has tended to mimic the sensationalist accounts of the entertainment media.
- The American FBI approach to profiling is based on interviewing incarcerated criminals. The result is profiles that some have argued lack scientific rigour and do not help the police.
- The work of David Canter and colleagues has put forward an approach they term Investigative Psychology. This term reflects the need for psychology to respond to the requirements of policing. The aim is to focus investigations by looking at themes and not attempt to get into the mind of the killer, as in the FBI approach.
- Until Canter and his colleagues, there was very little psychology employed at all in offender profiling.
- The job of profiling is not one that matches the media representations and there are not that many opportunities to work in the area. Currently, in the UK there are only five full-time Behavioural Investigation Advisers (BIA) and 30 part-time BIAs. These people tend to be academic researchers located in universities and are brought in to provide assistance when needed. Rather, what is needed is a change in perspective as to what the psychological and sociological realities of research in this area actually entails.

STUDY QUESTIONS

1 Is research into offender profiling worth the effort given the low success rate? How might it be improved?

2 Is it possible to get into the mind of a serial killer?

3 Is David Canter correct to say that trying to get into the mind of a serial killer does not help police catch them?

4 To what extent is Canter's investigative psychology an extension of the more common use of criminal statistics to more efficiently deploy the police?

5 Critically analyse the example of a real profile in Box 2.1 on page 49. What inconsistencies are there and how helpful would it be for the police in practice? Why might the police feel pressure to rely on such a tool?

FURTHER READING AND USEFUL WEBSITES

Peter Ainsworth's book *Offender Profiling and Crime Scene Analysis* (2001) is good for a more in-depth discussion of this topic.

The following is a good critique of the American style of profiling: L. Alison, M.D. Smith and K. Morgan (2003) 'Interpreting the accuracy of offender profiles', *Psychology, Crime and Law*, 9(2): 185–95.

For an example of the kind of research that the FBI produce then the following website has links to relevant publications:

http://www.fbi.gov/publications/leb/leb.htm

Also useful for looking at how the British police are using scientific methods, including psychology, is the following website for the National Policing Improvement Agency:

http://www.npia.police.uk/

Also, for information of UK government policy:

www.homeoffice.gov.uk

Note

1 The book is actually title *Red Dragon*, not *The Red Dragon*

3

Investigating
Sexual Violence

Chapter Contents

OVERVIEW

This chapter continues the theme of looking at the psychology of interpersonal violence, dealing with an issue that is wide-ranging in its scope. There will be a discussion of research on what causes people to commit sexual violence against adults and children. This will help to further unravel some of the misrepresentations of the problem and the overemphasis on the pathology of the offender. For example, in an ethnographic study by Bourgois (1995), *In Search of Respect*, the social learning of sexual violence is powerfully argued, a counter to the suggestion that there is an underlying individual pathology to the rapist.

KEY TERMS

child sexual abuse paedophile rape

Law and sexual offences

The psychological investigation of sexual violence takes many forms, but when it focuses on the victim it tends to research the validity of the accusation. This reflects the difficulty in getting convictions in rape cases due to commonly held, though mainly false, stereotypes. Not much has changed since the legal scholar Sir Matthew Hale noted in the seventeenth century that rape 'is an accusation easily to be made and hard to be defended by the party accused, tho never so innocent' (Hale cited in Rumney 2006: 128). There is a widespread assumption that many allegations of rape are false and the result of malice on behalf of the accuser. However, the evidence is ambiguous with some studies arguing that as many as 50 per cent of all allegations are false, whilst others are as low as 1 per cent (Rumney 2006). Moreover, a commonly cited statistic that only 2 per cent of allegations of rape are false is usually attributed to Brownmiller's *Against our Will* (1975). It is further stated that this figure is similar to the false reporting of other crimes. Certainly there is evidence of an occupational police culture that treats with suspicion allegations of rape (Reiner 2000). Even though the whole criminal justice system should be seen as contributors to the very low conviction rate, research by the UK government suggests a conviction rate of just under 6 per cent where 1 in 20 women report having been raped and of these it is estimated that between 75 and 95 per cent are not reported to the police (Her Majesty's Inspector of Constabulary 2007).

The work of Brownmiller (1975) raised awareness of how the law protected the interests of men and shifted the accountability onto women. It was not sufficient to prove that the women did not consent to sex, but instead the case rested on whether the defence could prove that the women *did* consent. Consequently, the background of the women, including sexual history and the type of clothing that was worn, became a key aspect of the legal defence (McGregor 2005). Women had to demonstrate 'utmost resistance' in order to show that they did not consent. This meant in practice that the women should have fought aggressively to protect her 'virtue' (McGregor 2005). Such a viewpoint does not take into account the threat of violence, or that violence does not have to be physical for it to be intimidating enough to elicit what could appear to be compliance. This imbalance in the criminal law serves to highlight the suspicion that women either lie about rape or consent to sex only to regret it afterwards and claim rape.

In response to this, the law on sexual offending has recently been strengthened in England and Wales by the Sexual Offences Act 2003. With the 2003 Act, for the first time, there is now a legal definition of consent that involves the active consent of one of the parties, free from factors that might mitigate against the freely given choice such as threats of violence, drugs, alcohol or being asleep. It is not sufficient for someone to assume that consent had been granted. Until this Act, a defendant only needed to show that they honestly believed that consent had been granted, however unreasonable that was in practice, they would have to be acquitted. Rather than the previous system where the victim was assumed to have consented, the new approach is based on the presumption that consent had not been given. This new law broadens out the range of people who may be charged with sexual assault. For example, a new offence of assault by penetration means that women who abuse children or adults can be charged, whereas previously this kind of offence would not be covered under sexual offences laws since the offence of rape is defined as the penetration by the penis of the vagina or anus. It may be surprising for many people to realise that the law had developed in such a way. The law developed in a similar way in the USA.

Widening the definition of rape

However, social attitudes to sexual violence are such that rape cases in particular have been very hard to prosecute due to a number of common assumptions about male and female sexuality. The most common assumption is that when a women says no, she really means yes. This notion of the reticent women who eventually succumbs is the basis for many stereotypes, most often seen in literature or films. But, more important than the depiction of this stereotype in literature is the way that such a belief is a common part of many people's understanding of sexual interactions. This is not just true of the general public, but also those who work in the criminal justice system and those who study it, such as psychologists. Consequently, we need to remember that theories of sexual violence tend to concentrate on only the most common forms of the offence. It has been argued that there are forms of sexual activity that rarely get treated as sexual offences by either the victims, the perpetrators or the criminal justice system. This is an area of sexual relations that tends to be a forgotten aspect of rape behaviour, or else it is not seen as rape at all. The criminologist Steven Box referred to these types of rape as 'seduction-turned-into-rape' and 'exploitation rape' (Box 1983: 128). The first refers to a situation in which an originally consensual meeting turns into rape when the offender does not stop their sexual advance at clear signals of unease, lack of consent or withdrawal of consent. The victim tends to blame themselves for misleading the offender and so few of these cases reach court. When they do reach court they tend to be defended on the basis that the accused misunderstood the signals. The second type of activity tends to be concerned with an offender of higher status, or who has an unequal power relation with the victim. This is a trade off between what the offender has to offer and what the victim may potentially lose. An example might be the casting-couch audition for actors, reluctantly having sex with someone for fear of losing the job. Such sexual relations are generally not considered to be rape and are difficult to prosecute. Consequently, there are gaps in knowledge because such behaviour is under-reported if it is defined by anyone as rape in the first place (Cowburn 2005). Koss and Oro (1982) began a survey in America in 1982 to determine the prevalence rate of women who report that they have been raped. It has been noted that the prevalence rate has remained relatively stable every year at around 15 per cent of the women surveyed (Rozee and Koss 2001). However, as noted below these figures should be treated with caution.

As can be seen, definitions of what constitutes a sexual offence can be contentious. How people define rape, or any other sexual offence, differs legally, culturally, by age, by gender and by ethnicity. One study in America found that Mexican-American women defined as rape demands by their husbands for sex when they did not want to, despite not saying anything to their husbands in protest (Ramos, Koss and Russo 1999). Kahn et al. (2003) conducted a study of 89 women who had experienced sexual assault. They found that 33 women defined as rape their sexual assault, whereas 56 did not. Those who did define it as rape were older, did not know the attacker well, had stronger negative reactions, the attacker used more force and they were more likely to have been assaulted as children. Women were less likely to define the assault as rape if they were impaired with alcohol or other drugs, or where the act involved oral or digital sex. As will be discussed later, date rape tends to be defined as rape less often than rape between strangers.

Consequently, prevalence rates for rape based upon victim surveys are as difficult to determine as police or court-recorded statistics since they tend to reflect these cultural variations in the definition of rape and the rapist. Similarly, our understanding of sexual offences, and indeed all crimes, tends to be based on officially recorded crime rates. This neglects an important factor, the **dark figure** of unreported crime. It is knowledge based on the official figures that feeds into popular representations of the criminal. In terms of sexual violence, this is where the overriding stereotype of the unknown stranger who attacks women and children developed (Kitzinger 1999) and so renders opaque the hidden, but more prevalent danger within the family (Cowburn and Dominelli 2001).

Statement validity analysis: testing for false rape allegations

Scientific research, either social or natural, reflects wider social and political attitudes. So, it is not a surprise that the same is true of psychological research into rape victimisation. However, it is also the case that such research is often unaware of the way it reflects such assumptions. One of the main issues in the above discussion of the way the criminal justice system deals with rape cases is that many allegations of rape are thought to be false and malicious. It could be argued that such an assumption underlies research into providing the police with a tool to determine the veracity of a women's account of rape. Research into the use of Statement Validity Analysis (SVA) by Parker and Brown (2000) is based on the assumption that there is a significant amount of false reporting of rape to the police. Parker, a Chief Inspector in the police, and Brown, a psychologist, report studies that demonstrate a range of false reporting from 2 per cent to as high as 41 per cent. They note that there are three types of false reporting, the first being an intentional deception that may be the result of revenge or guilt, the second being the result of erroneous memories or delusions caused by injury or illness and finally, false reporting of aspects of the behaviour, setting or offender. SVA derives from content analysis and is based on the Undeutsch hypothesis (Undeutsch 1982) which predicts that statements will be different if they derive from fantasy or reality. By performing content analysis on rape allegation statements Parker and Brown wanted to find out if this system, hitherto used mainly with child eyewitnesses, would work on adults who claimed they had been raped. The full procedure of SVA involves several stages aimed at determining the veracity of the statement and making predictions as to whether or not it is real or fabricated (Vrij 2008). The first stage is to evaluate documentary information about the case. This is usually derived from the police. The second stage is for the interviewer to elicit the statement by gaining trust and rapport from the alleger. This is followed by Content Based Content Analysis (CBCA) of the statement to compare this to the other evidence that has been gathered, this is followed with a check for similarities and discrepancies to determine the validity of the statement as it relates to other relevant pieces of evidence. Clearly, this represents a significant amount of work to get through before the alleged rape victim is trusted enough to proceed with the investigation. Such an exercise starts with the presumption of the alleger's capacity to lie, who in the majority of cases is a women. The alleger is guilty of lying until proven to be an innocent victim. It could be argued that if such a system was used widely, and if it were known that it was used, many people who would have falsely alleged rape would be wary of doing so. But, it might also have the effect of preventing many honest victims from coming forward to report a rape to avoid what might be felt to be a humiliating test of honesty. In England and Wales, this research is being applied in practice by Behavioural Investigative Advisers (BIA), the term preferred to Offender Profiler. The following extract from a report about the BIA contains the following:

> By combining a comprehensive understanding of the relevant research literature with their own behavioural and investigative knowledge and experience, a BIA may be able to assist in cases of sexual assault where there are believed to be issues with regards to the veracity of a victim's account. It is not for the BIA to provide a definitive judgement as to the truthfulness of an alleged victim but rather to offer some interpretation and advice in relation to what is said to have occurred (Crime Operational Support 2008: 7)

Of course, a system that uses the SVA on the alleged offender, if identified, would reverse this assumption of dishonesty and would as quickly identify anomalies in the case as the alternative of running the tests on the alleger would do. This study is a good example of psychology conducting research in a political void. The result is that it could further entrench stereotypes and police attitudes towards rape victims. Whilst if widely known that such techniques were to be used by the police then the likelihood of rape victims going to the police in the first place would fall even further than at present. Similarly, in one study it was found that it was possible to make a false statement look as if it was the truth and be judged as such by CBCA experts (Vrij, Kneller and Mann 2000). Clearly, such a system would have a short lifespan and would soon become redundant as a method of catching liars. The final issue that needs to be addressed is why SVA should specifically be used in the case of rape as opposed to any other form of crime, as Parker and Brown maintain (Rumney 2006). In summary, this research is a clear example of the need for psychology to become more fully aware of the political implications of its research.

The first part of this chapter looked at definitions of rape, both legal and informal, and then how one particular psychological tool has reflected social attitudes in the research. The following part of this chapter moves on from this to discuss the role of psychology in investigating what causes sexual violence. It will be argued that there is significant cross-over between feminist discourse and some psychological theories that rape is a normal, rather than a pathological activity. But, as will also be shown, the points of contrast between these two arguments are distinct.

Why men? sexual violence, masculinities and culture

One of the fundamental questions for criminology is why men appear to commit the majority of all crimes. Such a criminological truism, however, has been under-researched. What is uniquely criminogenic about men, as opposed to women, is rarely questioned and the literature on gender identity and crime is in its early stages (Silvestri and Crowther-Dowey 2008). With regard to sexual offending, it is usually an offence that is committed by men on women. The overriding stereotype of the rapist is usually of a surprise attack by a male stranger. The stranger tends to be seen as a psychopath or other pathologically damaged individual who needs to be locked up. Despite the illogical reasoning of punishing a sick person, this stereotype massively distorts the reality of sexual offending. One of the key early studies of rape was that of Amir whose study of convicted Philadelphia rapists challenged the stereotype of the pathological rapist jumping out on his victims (Amir 1967, 1971). However, in so doing Amir also seemed to be placing the blame onto women for what he termed 'victim-precipitated' rape. This refers to the retraction of consent to sex after initial agreement as well as the women not objecting in a strong enough manner. Amir argued that 19 per cent of the cases he studied could be categorised as victim-precipitated (Amir 1967). Although this study is methodologically flawed, since it is based upon police records which themselves could be biased by stereotypes of the type of women who might be raped, this research highlighted the ordinariness of rapists. This study also noted the role of alcohol in many rapes, although this issue had been rendered somewhat opaque until the recent media attention on drug-rape to be discussed below. However, Amir's study presented the argument that women are partly responsible for their behaviour around men. Amir suggested that a man who rapes a woman was less guilty if the woman acted in such a way as to provoke the man. The sexual reputation of the women also became a key factor to be taken into account. Such arguments lead to suggestions that there are deserving and undeserving victims, with only the former able to get help from the criminal justice system.

In response, there was a feminist critique of previous studies into rape and other forms of sexual offending (Brownmiller 1975; Jefferson 1997). However, rather than rendering men more complex, Brownmiller's work rendered all men the same. They were potential rapists, and by association all women were potential victims. This reaffirmed a form of homogeneous masculinity and femininity determined by socio-political and biologically predetermined factors (Box 1983). Rape, or the threat of it, was a weapon used by all men to retain their power over women. Rape was the weapon of a patriarchal system. Brownmiller's identification of a cultural and social element in rape was important, but it did not help answer why certain socio-economic groups tended to be over-represented in the statistics for rape. Psychological theories attempted to explain this finding, with one approach in particular causing much controversy – evolutionary psychology.

Evolutionary psychology and rape

Evolutionary psychology tends to claim that evolution is the ultimate form of explanation of the cause of rape and sexual abuse (Vega 2001). Essentially, natural selection has meant that humans, and other animals, have evolved to rape as a means of making sure the maximum number of men are able to mate and so ensure species survival (Thornhill and Palmer 2000). All other causes are secondary to this and so are subsumed by this explanation. Consequently, at the heart of Thornhill and Palmer's evolutionary psychology is the idea that sexual desire causes rape. But how does this explain the greater number of men from low socio-economic backgrounds charged with this offence? This has been explained by the suggestion that low status men rape women who would otherwise seek higher status males (Thornhill and Palmer 2000). Termed the 'mate deprivation hypothesis', the theory suggests reasons as to why lower-class males tend to commit more rapes than higher-class males. Women are presented as passive in their sexuality since men are essentially aggressive seekers of sex and women are presented as only attracted to high-status males. Discussion of the social context within which rape occurs, the self-reported motivations of the rapist or the victim's narration of the event, which, as we have seen, can often lead to varied definitions of the act, are all ignored, or they are suggested to be *post-hoc* rationalisations of innate adaptations to sexual urges (Gard and Bradley 2000).

Despite there being several evolutionary theories of rape, the evidence for their claims remains the same. Studies of different animals has shown that males force females into sexual copulation after initial resistance (Archer and Vaughn 2001). In Thornhill and Palmer's thesis, men will therefore rape when they are denied legitimate opportunities for sexual release. This theory is based on studying the sexual activity of the Scorpion fly so one should be more wary than usual with the extrapolation to human sexual behaviour (Segal 2001). But, as Burr has argued (2001), the main focus of Thornhill and Palmer is Susan Brownmiller's *Against our Will: Men, Women and Rape* (1975). This contains a similarly controversial statement that presents women as victims of men's power. It is noted that 'Man's structural capacity to rape and women's corresponding structural vulnerability are as basic to the physiology of both our sexes as the primal act of sex itself' (13–14). Whereas Thornhill and Palmer argue that physiological urges of inferior men are at the root of rape, for Brownmiller rape is integral to the weaponry of power used by men to control women through fear. Whereas for Thornhill and Palmer rape is about the urge for sex, Brownmiller's thesis is that rape is the use of violence for power.

This distinction is the key difference in this debate. Ignored are such typologies such as those noted below that seek to differentiate between a number of different motivations for rape. Similarly, the evolutionary account cannot explain child sexual abuse if it is committed against boys or girls yet to reach sexual maturity. Both Brownmiller and Thornton and Palmer overly simplify both men and women in the search for an overarching theory. Just as the physical shape of men and women is incredibly diverse, so also is the range of identities. The work of Bob Connell has highlighted that masculinity is not a single entity (1995) but split between hegemonic and subordinate masculinities. This has been extended to include issues like race, but the point is that masculinity is shaped by structural concerns.

Moving beyond traditional feminist concerns with the power differentials between men and women, more recent theory has focused on power differentials between men. Identity is shaped by these power struggles resulting in different forms of masculinity. This again raises the question as to why the official crime figures, and victimisation surveys, all seem to point to an over-representation of lower status, and therefore, less economically and socially powerful men being arrested and charged with rape. Box (1983) argued that the official figures and victimisation surveys all suffer from a bias in their focus. Official crime figures tend to highlight lower-status men in the rape statistics more often due to the types of crime they commit, namely that it tends to be more visible to the police. Similarly, lower-status men do not have as much access to the best defence lawyers. Box presents a critique of Brownmiller's all-inclusive male rapist, noting the different motivations for rape and how such differences are played out in rape behaviours. Box notes that the official prison population is likely to include an over-representative sample of rapists for whom anger and domination were the prime motivators for rape. It is less likely to include rapists who used seduction, or where they used their superior positions to cajole an unwilling victim to have sex. Box's point is that the legal definition of rape does not include the behaviours that occur daily and which men and women have been socialised to accept, but that could be regarded as rape (Box 1983). Through this argument Box maintains that the official figures for rape and our stereotypes of the rapist being a low-status man are a mystification of the reality of such offences. Similarly, stereotypes of the rapist vary culturally and tend to be based more on general stereotypes of sexuality. Many studies show that black men are more vigorously pursued by Criminal Justice agencies and more harshly punished than white men. Similarly, black female victims are deemed more culpable than white female victims (George and Martinez 2002). Consequently, rather than some innate, evolved instinct for procreation, or a simple quest to maintain power, rape is a complex crime that is not amenable to simple generalisations.

The rape myth

There is a commonly held myth that women who say no to sexual advances are either fooling themselves or are putting up an artificial resistance. This is the no means yes defence, or rape myth. Bohner et al. (2005) studied whether or not men who were more easily able to accept the myth have a greater proclivity, or inclination towards, sexual aggression. The research was survey based and so did not seek to study men who had been convicted of rape or who went on to rape. Based on a sample of male university students, it was found that men who accepted the myth were more likely to use it to justify sexual behaviour which would be classed as rape. Similarly, those who reported using sexually coercive strategies in the past were more likely to draw on their own use of the rape myth to justify sexual aggression. It is not possible to say whether or not such beliefs would lead to enacting of such attitudes. That such attitudes were so easily expressed by the research subjects in a clearly artificial setting should be concern enough. Such attitudes might be expressed even more vociferously in public.

Doherty and Anderson (2004), with the consent of the respondents, taped the conversations from men and women talking together about a vignette depicting a case of male rape. They found that a 'hierarchy of suffering' was created that posited a greater amount of suffering for heterosexual men, than for either gay men or heterosexual women. The act of consensual sex and rape was the same physical act and so was less traumatic for homosexual men and heterosexual women, and the ridicule of being a heterosexual male victim of rape added to their suffering. They argue that such a belief system negates the violence of all rapes, deflects accountability from the offender and so adds to the rape myth that women, and homosexual men, derive some pleasure from rape or are not emotionally or physically hurt by the offence. Davies and McCartney (2003) arrived at similar conclusions in their study specifically focusing on rape of a homosexual man. They found that heterosexual men were more likely to blame the victim than homosexual men. Although overall, most respondents tended to be pro-victim and were aware of the seriousness, it is the trend towards heterosexual men supporting rape myths that these studies demonstrate.

Differentiating sexual assault

As seen in Chapter 2, the majority of typologies of serial crimes were initially developed where the crime had a sexual element to it. Sexual behaviour during an offence is, perhaps, the most intimate expression of an offender's activity at the crime scene and, it is assumed, reflects the most obvious manifestation of the offender's personality. Sexual activity at the scene of a murder manifests in the way the victim's body was left and so the job of the police and the psychologist is to make inferences about the offender's motivation. As noted in the last chapter, this is a difficult process. When the victim is alive, a more detailed evaluation may be possible if the victim is able to recall the events. Consequently, the profiling of sexual violence where the victim is left alive, or where some victims in a series are left alive, produces more useful evidence from which to develop investigatory profiles and practices.

A number of different researchers have put forward typologies for differentiating between the actions of rapists. Groth (1979) identified three types of rapist based on the motives they had for the offence, these being anger, power and sadistic needs. Hale (1997) identified eight different motivations for rape by summarising existing studies. These were: revenge direct and indirect, anger, satisfy sexual urge, excitement, challenge – especially group rape, domination, evolutionary opportunity theory and to fulfil a fantasy. These typologies, however, share similar problems to those discussed in the previous chapter whereby inferences are made about an offender's internal psychological motivations that serve little use for investigators. The police are not mind readers and so cannot observe the unobservable.

In contrast to this is Canter's approach of looking for crime scene behaviours that can be statistically correlated and catalogued into themes. This was discussed in more detail in the last chapter, but it is worth repeating here since the original study that lead to Canter's work on geographical profiling began with a study of rape. Canter and Heritage (1990) put forward several themes that classified the behaviours of different rapists. This is based on the proposal that crime scene behaviour reflected interpersonal relationships the offender had in their everyday lives. This is based on two hypotheses, the first is that there is *consistency* of behaviour across separate offences, and *variability* between the actions of one offender and other offenders. In other words, two offenders will not act in the same way. The notion of consistency between one crime and another should not be taken to imply that the offender will perform the same actions in each separate offence, rather that each separate offence committed will share a similar theme. The themes that have been identified by Canter and his colleagues with regard to stranger rape, both singular cases and serial cases are:

- *hostility* which involves forcing the victim into sexual acts;
- *involvement* which concerns the offender attempting to create some interpersonal attachment through kissing and complimenting the victim;
- *control* which involves using a weapon, binding the victim or using blindfolds. (Canter, Reddy and Alison 2000)

As can be seen from the last theme, each of these crime scene actions are different. An investigator looking at three different crime scenes might suspect three different offenders. One who uses a weapon, one who ties the victim up and another who blindfolds the victim. However, Canter and Heritage (1990) point out that each act is consistent with the theme of control and so could be the actions of an offender who wishes to control the victim. The actions may similarly change depending upon the context in which the crime takes place. For example, an offender who finds his victim in a quiet area may not need to use a weapon and may instead bind the victim to gain their compliance. Over a series of offences a witness description of the offender may be circulated by the police and so the use of a blindfold may be used. In each case, the theme is to *control* the victim despite the seemingly different crime scene behaviours. A further theme of *theft* was added to this to account for the taking of belongings from the victim as a primary goal (Canter et al. 2003).

Alison and Stein (2001) positioned themselves differently from Canter and Heritage by drawing on research into interpersonal interactions in order to present an approach to the way the victim verbally narrates the offence to the police. Alison and Stein argue that accounts of rape reflect everyday processes of interaction, but they tend to take on a more abusive and manipulative approach. They develop three themes to account for the different ways that victims narrate the sexual assault to the police; these are *hostility*, *dominance*, and *compliance-gaining*. Consequently, this approach is based on the victim's account of the event. They argue that these themes are based on a wider and more established theoretical base than those of Canter and Heritage. Furthermore, the advantage of this approach is that most studies of sexual offenders present theories based on the offender's actions which are then presumed to be a reflection of their underlying narrative. Alison and Stein's approach takes the point of view of the victim. Perhaps the best method would be to combine the two approaches. One of the problematic legal issues that is often raised about acquaintance rape allegations is whether or not the victim consented to sex. By combining the two research methods above it would illuminate the ways that men and women narrate both compliant and non-compliant sexual interaction. This is perhaps best illustrated in one of the most contentious developments in sexual assault, drug rape.

Drug rape

There is very little research around the topic of rape involving drugs to incapacitate the victim. Indeed, there is very little evidence that specific drugs such as Rohypnol are implicated in many rapes. Alcohol was the drug most commonly used to incapacitate the victim (Association of Chief Police Officers [ACPO] 2006; Horvath and Brown 2007). However, the real extent of drug-facilitated rape is likely to be higher than the statistics suggest since victims are often unaware they have been targeted. But, it is useful to note that the media fascination with this crime tends to suggest it is a new and unique activity. The moral panic that this can cause when there is a suggestion of a new and unique crime has been well documented by others (Cohen 1972/2002; Jewkes 2004). Slipping someone a 'Mickey Finn', essentially putting a drug in a drink, has long been a staple of literature and cinema since the term, whose origins are unknown, came into existence in the 1920s.

According to Horvath and Brown (2005) it is necessary to provide two different definitions of the crime, one that is suitable for researchers and a more restricted definition that serves a legal function. The legal definition includes rapes where the victim has voluntarily taken drugs, including alcohol, after which the offender has raped the victim. Another definition is intended to allow psychological researchers to determine if drug rape is at the extreme end of normal sexual activity or is instead committed by individuals with pathological impairments. This distinction has the advantage of suggesting that those who commit drug rape are in need of treatment rather than punishment. This definition explicitly states that the offender deliberately introduced a substance knowing that it would incapacitate the victim in order to facilitate sex without the victim's consent. As can be seen, this definition takes crime to be a manifestation of a pathological illness. Research for the Home Office in the UK by Sturman similarly differentiates between different types of rapist. Sturman (2000) maintains that there are three distinct types of offender. The first is the rapist who plans an attack ahead of time; the second is the rapist who offends within a relationship; and finally the opportunistic rapist who takes advantage of a situation, or assists in the deliberate incapacitation of the victim with drugs or alcohol. In the first and last types the offender needs to be in possession of the drugs if that is the intended method of inebriation. The contentious legal question for the last type of offender relates to whether or not the victim consented or was able to consent to sex. Santilla, Junkkila and Sandnabba (2005) refer to this type of offender in their typology as the deceptive involvement style. The offender has a confident manner to persuade the victim to join them voluntarily. Such an approach has been difficult to prosecute in Britain. Sturman (2000) noted the demographic breakdown of victims and offenders involved in drug rape. Out of 123 victims of both heterosexual and homosexual assaults the majority were female, with 14 (11 per cent) of the victims being male, 42 per cent were in their 30s (see also Abarbanal 2001).

In summary, research on the sexual assault of adults suggests that there are a variety of reasons for its committal. The most problematic aspect of this offence is not that there is insufficient clarity on the causes, but that when it is committed the criminal justice system is distrustful of the accuser. This distrust has been taken on by psychologists who have begun the process of formulating a strategy for detecting the deception of women with the SVA method. The following section looks at the sexual abuse of children.

Child sexual abuse

A potent media folk devil is the predatory child abuser or paedophile. The Internet opened up a new forum for the dissemination of child pornography and consequently lead to a global policing operation, called Operation Orb in the UK, tasked with searching out those who shared such images of abused children. Yet, whilst the media focused its attention on such activity, a less publicised, but arguably more widespread and so more problematic phenomena goes unnoticed by many people: familial child abuse committed by a child's relatives (Cowburn and Dominelli 2001). Less obvious in its manifestation since it is committed by people known to the victim, and so initially at least, trusted by them, child abuse within the family does not have the same news values as the child who is snatched from the street and held against their will. Yet, familial abuse is usually a longer-term imprisonment with no home to return to when it ceases or the perpetrator discovered. Indeed, one typical response is to take the child away from home and into foster care. To put it simply, most serious crime does not happen on the streets, but in the home. And whilst the public protest against the re-homing of paedophiles in their community, the majority of children are not being abused by strangers, but by their own family. A further side to this is the number of abusers who are themselves young. This has been estimated at between 25 and 33 per cent of all sexual offenders, and they are predominantly male (Grubin 1998; Green and Masson 2002).

History of recovered memories

As the criminologist Geoff Pearson has shown (1994) society suffers from 'historical amnesia' whereby we forget our own recent past and believe that the problems of the contemporary period are unique, or far worse than anything that came before. A similar argument is put forward by Herman (1992), one of the leading proponents of the recovered memory syndrome, that there is 'intermittent amnesia' in the study of child sexual abuse. It is often stated that only relatively recently has child sexual abuse come to be seen as a serious social problem in the English speaking world (Pratt 2005). Yet, perhaps this should be regarded as a resurgence of interest in the issue since many concerns were expressed at the end of the nineteenth century, and early in the twentieth century by people such as Sigmund Freud, who argued that hysteria was a consequence of early premature sexual experience (Freud 1896/1962). On noting that the number of women who could be diagnosed as hysterical was so high, Freud turned away from the study of hysteria because it suggested that so many women had been sexually assaulted as children that it was endemic (Herman 1992). Such an idea was unthinkable. Consequently the theory of premature sexual relations, child sexual abuse, was inverted. Hysterics invented such a past, they were fantasists. This situation remained for the next century. The sexual abuse of children, the inability to tell anyone at the time and the subsequent burying of the pain in subconscious memories fell out of favour with investigators.

The extent of child sexual abuse is beset by similar methodological problems to the estimation of the prevalence of adult rape. But, in addition to factors that inhibit the reporting of adult rape are such issues as the age of the child and their lack of understanding of their own victimisation, the familial setting of the majority of such offences and a lack of knowledge in the procedures for reporting such incidents. The methodology for getting to the 'dark figure' of unreported child sexual abuse tends to be victim surveys conducted with adults. Such a methodology requires someone to recall their victimisation many years after the offence. Consequently, such an approach can be prone to problems due to faulty memory (London et al. 2008). Such a problem can be seen in the 'discovery' in 1992 of recovered memory syndrome and the linked discovery of false memory syndrome, to be discussed below, whereby an adult is able to recall that they were abused as a child, usually during psychoanalysis or hypnosis (Herman 1992). This was often enough to warrant a criminal investigation, and in some cases enough to get a conviction in the absence of any other physical evidence (Pratt 2005). Nevertheless, some studies have attempted to provide an estimation of the prevalence of child sexual abuse and have arrived at very high incidences (Gallagher 2000). In the USA, research suggests that as many as 62 per cent of women were abused as children (Showalter 1997) and in the UK 60 per cent of women and 25 per cent of men were abused as children (Bauman 1997 cited in Pratt 2005). Given the problems with generating such statistics, such figures should be treated with caution. But, equally we should be cautious of returning to the neglect of child abuse that meant its existence became hidden.

Understanding recovered and false memories

The issue of recovered memories lead to a series of allegations in the US, UK, Australia and New Zealand of systematic satanic sexual abuse. Such claims were based on shaky evidence, but for a while such claims were taken seriously. Driven by a series of 'experts', from doctors to psychiatrists, social workers and psychologists, children were taken into care and interviewed about the range of abuses they supposedly suffered. Providing the children with anatomically correct dolls to facilitate communication of behaviours that the children did not have the language to articulate, social workers were able to elicit testimony that was deemed sufficient to proceed to trial. Fusing crime, psychology and religion, such allegations became increasingly bizarre and **due process** ignored because of a belief, supported by Summit (1983), that children's responses to child sexual abuse can look unconvincing and manifest in a delayed response. The unconvincing nature of such allegations should not be taken as evidence that the offence has been fabricated. In contrast, a child will undergo a series of developmental stages that may appear in contradiction to the usual stages that would garner credibility. These stages are:

- *Secrecy,* keeping the abuse a secret;
- *Helplessness,* feeling that no one will be able to help;
- *Entrapment and Accommodation,* the feeling of entrapment engenders an accommodating attitude towards the offender where fear of reprisals or little hope of help results in acceptance;
- *Delayed, conflicted and unconvincing disclosure,* such feelings lead to an indirect and haphazard disclosure of the offences, which may lead to the final stage...
- *Retraction,* where the disclosure is retracted.

Each of these stages is usually taken as evidence by adults that the allegations are untrustworthy. However, there is no empirical evidence presented by Summit to support these stages. Since Summit's original paper, various researchers have attempted to discover the validity of these stages with the result being ambiguous. For example, Sorenson and Snow (1991) presented empirical evidence from studying 117 cases of child sexual abuse that provided support for Summit. By contrast, Sjöberg and Lindblad (2002) argued that it was probably not possible for professionals to discover sexual abuse by relying on what a child said since they may not disclose sexual abuse for a variety of reasons. Bradley and Wood (1996) could also find no evidence for Sorenson and Snow's empirical support of Summit. It is therefore unclear if there is any pattern to the way that children talk about their victimisation. London et al. (2008) in a review of the literature suggest that there is more evidence against Summit's suggestion that children recant their allegations. Perhaps a better method of researching this issue is to look at the wider social networks open to individual children and the willingness of childcare professionals to both listen to such allegations and to investigate them properly. Without an empathetic listener, it is unlikely that a child will say anything at all, let alone about something so traumatic.

This debate about the validity of a child's recovered memory of abuse, and indeed an adult's recovered recollection or belated revelation of being sexually abused as a child, has lead to psychological research that attempts to measure the validity of a statement. This can be linked to a discussion above regarding Statement Validity Analysis for adult rape victims. The investigation of child sexual abuse involves both physical investigation, but also narrative investigation through interviews. In a review of the literature Davies (2001) notes that there is a distinction between an allegation that is completely and deliberately fabricated, a statement that is the result of suggestion whereby the alleger is not aware of the falsity of the allegation and an allegation that is based on a real event. Although there may be some difference between the maliciously false allegation and the unconsciously manipulated false allegation, this is not yet of sufficient distinction for CBCA to draw conclusions. But, overall, the message is the same as that for SVA in adult rape investigations. Such techniques can short-circuit police investigations, engendering reliance on psychological analysis at the expense of sound police investigative techniques.

Effects of child sexual abuse

One of the possible effects of child sexual assault is post traumatic stress disorder (PTSD) (Browne and Finkelhor 1986). But, it is often claimed that there is a cycle of abuse that goes beyond the traumatic damage to the individual. One of the most common ideas is that those who were abused as children are highly likely to be abusers themselves. Such is the power of the theory that it has become an almost common-sense truism. Nevertheless, there is some evidence that females who were victims of sexual abuse as children have a higher chance of being involved in a variety of criminal activity (Siegal and Williams 2003; Swanson et al. 2003). The idea has been heavily criticised and it has become marginalised from mainstream psychology and other social services dealing with families (Hooper and Koprowska 2004). One of the essential problems is that it suggests a deterministic, intergenerational causation for child sexual abuse. Such a concept victimises survivors of sexual abuse a second time and places blame within the family. Wider structural issues such as inadequate care for survivors of abuse, poor access to education for adult survivors, help and support to deal with abusive relationships and stigmatisation through the cycle of abuse label becoming a hindrance to adequate social care. All of this requires a non-pathologising system of support (Hooper and Koprowska 2004).

Summary

- This chapter has discussed some of the research on sexual offending. There has been a focus on the investigation of sexual assault and victimisation.
- Techniques such as SVA are becoming a psychological tool frequently used to determine the veracity of an alleged victim. The ethical, social and political problems with this have been identified and the way that such methods act as a shortcut for a thorough police investigation noted. Such seemingly objective psychological techniques are wittingly or unwittingly reproducing stereotypes about women and sexuality.

- David Canter has suggested that research should focus on the investigation of offences rather than on the causes. Finding out what makes an offender tick is less useful than finding out where they might live. Psychology is increasingly being directed towards this end.
- Research into false memories of child sexual abuse remains controversial, but the evidence for a cycle of abuse is limited, as is support for Summit's contention that children who report that they have been abused go through several stages that might suggest lying, but should be taken as the truth.

STUDY QUESTIONS

1 Critically discuss the arguments for and against the use of SVA to test the veracity of a victim's allegation.

2 It has been argued that the use of SVA on female rape victims reproduces the 'no means yes' stereotype. How can psychology overcome this?

3 With reference to SVA, what accounts for the way that some psychological research seems to be unaware of the political aspects of the study?

4 Can human behaviour be explained by evolutionary theory?

5 There is little evidence in its favour of Summit's contention that when a child tells the truth about sexual abuse it seems as if they are lying. However, this proposition had a major effect on the lives of many children and their families. Why is there pressure on policy makers and the legal profession to rely on such unsubstantiated claims? What can be done to avoid such problems?

FURTHER READING AND USEFUL WEBSITES

For a general introduction to this area that includes a historical discussion see:

McGregor, J. (2005) *Is it Rape? On Acquaintance Rape and Taking Women's Consent Seriously.* Aldershot, Hampshire: Ashgate.

Pratt, J. (2005) 'Child sexual abuse: purity and danger in the age of anxiety', *Crime, Law and Social Change*, 43: 263–87.

Thomas, T. (2005) *Sex Crime: Sex Offending and Society*, 2nd edn, Cullompton, Devon: Willan.

The following website contains a link to a guide for the Sexual Offences Act 2003:

http://www.homeoffice.gov.uk/documents/adults-safe-fr-sex-harm-leaflet

4

Crime in Groups: Explaining Subcultures, Groups and Gangs

Chapter Contents

OVERVIEW

This chapter moves the focus from looking at crime as committed by individuals to crime committed in groups. It could be argued that this area is the one that sociological criminology is better able to explain. It is certainly the case that sociological criminology has some very well-known theories, such as subcultural theory. However, there are also social psychological theories that have been developed. This chapter, then, represents a theoretical synthesis between sociological and psychological explanations of group criminal behaviour.

KEY TERMS

ingroup and outgroup relative deprivation self-categorisation theory social identity theory subculture

Tracing the psychological study of crime and disorder in groups

Before we begin to look at some psychological research into group formation and behaviour, it is useful to look at the work of George Herbert Mead, a social psychologist who is 'accepted' by sociologists. In an introduction to his writing on social psychology, the sociologist Anselm Strauss points out some of the reasons why his work is accepted (Strauss 1964). Strauss notes that many sociologists saw social psychology as inseparable from sociology. As noted in the first chapter, such sentiments were expressed as early as the first *American Journal of Sociology* in 1894. However, only some of Mead's ideas were incorporated into sociology. Strauss points out that Mead's ideas on socialisation and a very social concept of 'self' were used by sociologists in criticism of biological and individual psychology. Mead's social psychology could also be used to counter Freudian notions of the self as being a general typology of personality types forged and constructed through close interaction in the family. Mead put forward a more fluid interpretation of how humans interact. Human communication differs from other animal's communication through an ability to construct shared meanings. This insight formed the foundation for the elaboration of some of Mead's ideas in the approach known as symbolic interaction. The main idea that was taken by sociologists is the way that social control becomes internalised as self-control. Mead's concept of the 'generalised other' was elaborated into reference group theory, where group behaviour and shared emotion can be analysed as a function of how that group perceived itself relative to other groups, the 'other'. It is possible to see in this the foundations for ideas on subcultural group formation. In particular, how gang culture develops in opposition to outgroups. From the outset, then, social psychology has been an influence on ideas that inspired many of the germinal debates in criminology, such as the anomie tradition of Robert Merton and its influence on subcultural theory (1938). The chapter discusses these ideas and shows how an integration of psychological and sociological ideas can create a powerful and robust tool for understanding crime at the level of the group.

The social psychology of the group

Early writers on the group or mob, such as Gustave Le Bon, regarded such entities in reductionist terms whereby the individual became subsumed by the group and individual choices somehow transformed into a 'group mind' (Le Bon 1908/1896). Reflecting back on the French Revolution just over 100 years previously and with concerns over newly formed trade unions agitating for better conditions for the working class, there was a sense among some that there could be impending revolution. Throughout the world from Russia, the Ottoman Empire and China, fear of the mob was rife. The writings of Karl Marx and the effect they had throughout the world added to this sense of instability. Le Bon's work was also influenced by the work of Lombroso, discussed in Chapter 1, and so the crowd was seen as **atavistic**, a primitive state of affairs where the individual conscience disappeared to be replaced with animal instinct. The crowd was, therefore, deeply pathological where the rationality of the individual is surrendered to the collective mindlessness of the crowd. Nevertheless, it was an influential book and a version of its basic ideas were taken up by Robert Park and E.A. Ross and became part of the Chicago School (Nye 1995).

The idea of losing self-control in the crowd is a precursor of more contemporary research into deindividuation. Work by Festinger, Pepitone and Newcomb (1952), Zimbardo (1970) and Diener (1979) noted that in groups, under certain conditions, people could feel a sense of 'losing themselves' where their personal identity becomes anonymous. The Stanford Prison experiments present a similar case where the 'prison guards' became increasingly authoritarian and controlling of the 'prisoners' (Haney, Banks and Zimbardo 1973). In contrast, Floyd Allport (1920) saw the group not as a place where individuality was lost, but rather where individuality was accentuated. The individual in the group saw their normal human instincts, such as aggression and territoriality, become liberated from an upbringing that taught that such instincts should be held in check. These early approaches made way for an understanding of the group that was more flexible, yet still reduced the complexity to singular causes. One of the first was Muzafer Sherif's work on group interaction which presented competition as the cause of hostility.

Sherif and the Robber's Cave experiment

Muzafer Sherif and his colleagues conducted several experiments at the Robber's Cave summer camp for boys in America (Sherif et al. 1961). The boys were all picked for their 'normal' characteristics. There were several stages in this experiment with the first being an occasion where the boys could freely associate with each other. The boys formed distinct friendship groups as would be expected at such a venue. Several days later the researchers split the one group into two others. This was done by surreptitiously breaking up established friendships without the boys being aware of this manipulation. Each group worked on various tasks without the other group. New friendships emerged and the boys created their own group identities calling themselves the Red Devils and the Bulldogs respectively. In the next phase, the two groups were told they had to compete for points that would go towards a treat for the winning group such as a cinema trip. This lead to the creation of ingroup codes and the groups actively distinguishing themselves from the other group. Obvious competitiveness emerged and the boys took to calling their rivals denigrating names. The final stage occurred when the boys had to work together to solve a problem that affected the entire camp such as trying to fix the water supply. The old rivalries were slowly overcome as the boys sought to work together for the common goal.

Cooperation and the dissipation of old rivalries were further achieved when a third group from another summer camp was introduced. It was as if a common enemy created a greater sense of togetherness. Sherif has argued that prejudice and hostility is caused by competition over resources and that such hostility can be overcome through mutual cooperation for a common goal. Several problems have been raised about this study. There is a suggestion that without competition for resources prejudice and group solidarity would not exist or would not be necessary. So, for example, if there were enough jobs to go around and everyone who had the ability could have the job they wanted then hostility towards immigrants would cease since there would be no perceived competition over jobs. Such a theory oversimplifies complex social and historical dynamics where discourse about other groups can often occur even where no competition existed. Also, the methodology is questionable because the subjects were all boys from a similar social demographic background. The findings may not be generalised to other, more mixed groups. Finally, the influence of the researchers who acted as summer camp helpers is not considered. However, the study did show that prejudice was a flexible and changeable entity in contrast to earlier theories that suggested that prejudice was due to a personality type. For example, in Adorno et al.'s (1950/1982) theory of the authoritarian personality, it is suggested that there was something natural about prejudice. In contrast, Sherif's approach suggested that there was a social element. However, Sherif's work noted that there would be conflict only when there was a competition for resources. This suggests that racism, for example, is due to a conflict over resources. Where no conflict exists then no racism can exist. However, in the real world, not manipulated by psychologists, competition for resources is a more complex phenomenon and an issue that sociologists have been trying to understand for as long as the discipline has been in existence. The most well-known is subcultural theory.

Subcultures in America

Merton's theory of social structure and anomie

The concept of subcultures is one that is important to criminology and will form a major part of this chapter since it can be looked at from both sociological and psychological positions. Within this discussion of subcultures, note should be made of the almost casual way that ideas that developed principally within psychology are used and developed within what are essentially sociological theories. I will note the points of contrast between them, but also point out where collaboration between these theories would create more robust theorising. I will also discuss the way that one author, W.G. Runciman, was ignored within sociological criminology but became a central concern of social psychology. The idea of relative deprivation is central to one criminological school of thought called left realism. Runciman wrote a book on relative deprivation in 1966, yet his book is not central to left realism despite Runciman's work sharing a theoretical lineage with more well-known theorists such as Albert Cohen and Richard Cloward (Webber 2007a).

Subcultural theories developed initially in America and then in Britain. Although centred mainly on youth, it is an important set of ideas that allows us to see the way that crime in groups has been explained, as well as to show the way that the application of psychological ideas can help the sociological approach. The American version is indebted to Robert K. Merton's social structure and **anomie** thesis (Merton 1938). Two of the leading proponents of American subcultural theory, Albert Cohen and Richard Cloward were both research students under Merton's tuition (Merton 1995). In short, Merton proposed that the American Dream of success through wealth was common to all, but the means of achieving such a goal, such as education, was not universally accessible to all. Consequently, this lead to an anomic situation. There was a strain between what was expected from life and what could be achieved, hence the theory is sometimes referred to as strain theory. Because of this, American culture was inherently structured towards crime (Merton 1938). Nevertheless, although economic goals were central to the theory, the social structure and anomie approach was not exclusively about economic goals (Merton 1957: 181). Notwithstanding this caveat however, Merton argued that people could either accept, reject or abandon the goal of success through wealth and accept, reject or abandon the legitimate means of gaining the goal. He proposed five 'modes of adaptation' that people could take in response to this social system made up of different responses to the means and the goal based on their position in the social structure. These were conformity, innovation, ritualism, retreatism and rebellion (see Table 4.1).

Table 4.1   *Merton's modes of adaptation*

Modes of adaptation	American Dream of wealth and success	Legitimate means to achieve the goal (e.g. education, job, marriage)
Conformism	Accepts	Accepts
Innovation	Accepts	Rejects
Ritualism	Accepts, but knows the goal cannot be achieved	Accepts
Retreatism	Rejects	Rejects
Rebellion	Rejects and replaces goal with an alternative	Rejects and replaces means with an alternative

All modes of adaptation except conformity were regarded as deviant responses. Therefore, innovation described typically working-class responses to the social structure of American society. The goal was accepted but because the legitimate means to achieve it were blocked then alternative, deviant means needed to be found. Ritualism is a typically lower-middle-class response where the ambitions of reaching the pinnacle of success are abandoned, but the means are adhered to in almost mechanical and zealous manner (Merton 1957). Retreatism involves the rejection of both the means and the goal and results in a withdrawal from the world. Such a response is seen as explaining why some drug addicts, alcoholics and the homeless opt out of traditional routes to success. Finally, the rebellious response is one of rejection of both means and goals in favour of a new set of social values. Merton's theory began with a premise that the crime statistics were accurate reflections of the social world, showing as they did crime concentrated in the working class. Moreover, they assume a homogeneous cultural consensus to the American dream of wealth. Also, different classes were seen to exhibit quite specific responses to the social structure. Such modes of adaptation were limited in their applicability to the types of crime and deviance typically carried out by young people, namely vandalism, petty theft and violence.

Albert Cohen and delinquent boys

Albert Cohen's discussion of distinct youth subcultures elaborated the work of Merton by extending the social structure and anomie tradition to explain the non-acquisitive vandalism and violence that is the most common form of crime committed by young people (Cohen 1955; Merton 1995). Cohen argued that working-class youth subcultures internalised middle-class values, but finding the legitimate routes to these goals blocked sought to reject these values through the Freudian process of reaction-formation, that is excessively denigrating that which was once cherished. We see in this a further example of the use of psychological or psychoanalytic ideas within a sociological account. This results in non-instrumental actions such as vandalism and interpersonal violence due to status frustration and an active rejection of middle-class norms and values (Cohen 1955). Central to this argument is an acceptance by working-class young people of the values of middle-class culture, which in Cohen's approach is occupational status. In this definition of status frustration, Cohen borrows narrowly from Merton's American Dream concept of the goal of wealth. As already noted above, Merton did not confine his theory to economic variables. However, Cohen notes that within classes there are distinctions of attitude and conduct, and accordingly he makes use of the distinction between 'college boys' and 'corner boys' in W.F. Whyte's *Street Corner Society* (Whyte 1993/1943). Although both these 'ideal-types' are the product of working-class families, college boys take on middle-class values which help facilitate upward mobility, whereas corner boys have the benefits of solidarity in close-knit groups but a culture that makes upward mobility less likely. The problem with this is the assumed consensus to middle-class values of upward mobility, a criticism that also pertains to Merton.

Cloward and Ohlin's delinquency and opportunity

A similar elaboration of Merton's earlier work by Richard Cloward resulted in the extension of the concept of blocked access to the legitimate opportunity structures, such as schools, work and family. Cloward argued that there was also differential access to *illegitimate* opportunity structures and with Lloyd Ohlin provided a typology to account for the different modes of adaptation that resulted from such differential access (Cloward and Ohlin 1960). Subcultures were therefore split into three distinct 'types'. The first being the violent gang, to be found in socially disorganised working-class areas, akin to the zone of transition in Burgess, Shaw and McKay's sociological research in Chicago (Bottoms 1994; Shaw and McKay 1942). The second adaptation was the criminal subculture, where access to legitimate opportunities is denied, but access to illegitimate opportunities is plentiful. This results in the transmission of criminal acquisitive values and skills. Finally, the retreatist subculture exists where access to both legitimate *and* illegitimate opportunities are denied, leading to subcultures that are fatalistic and characterised by drug and alcohol abuse. Both the work of Cohen and Cloward and Ohlin elaborated that which was only tacit and implied, but not fully brought to the foreground, in Merton's earlier work (Merton 1995).

Nevertheless, as Matza argued, all of these approaches assume a commitment to deviancy (Matza 1995/1964). Matza regarded such approaches as positivistic because they delineated the criminal from the non-criminal. He contended that young people drift in and out of deviancy rather than being committed to it (ibid.). Moreover, the values associated with deviant groups are not so different from those associated with 'conventional' values, such as the quest for excitement and status, what Sykes and Matza termed 'subterranean values' (1957). Therefore, the main criticism of the American subcultural theories are that they overdetermine crime among certain young people, mainly the poor, and ascribe an all-encompassing cultural homogeneity, in other words, given the right circumstances they will all be compelled to deviance.

Applying American subcultural theory to the UK

Reviewing British criminology between 1960 and 1987, David Downes argued that academics in Britain acted as if it were an 'off-shore laboratory' testing American theories (Downes 1988: 176). Nevertheless, over time British subcultural theory developed a tradition somewhat different from its American counterpart, in that the identification of distinct gangs did not apply to the British situation.[1] However, there was, instead, a focus on cultural forms and their links to leisure activities. Then later research, taking a more politically radical and Marxist approach, became interested in moral panics and the problematisation surrounding the activities of certain young people.

Two important examples of British research drawing on American studies is Terence Morris and his attempt to replicate the findings of the Chicago School's ecological theory of social disorganisation (Morris 1957; Shaw and McKay 1942; Bottoms 1994) and David Downes' study to see if American subcultural theories were applicable to postwar Britain in his study of Stepney and Poplar in 1960 (Downes 1966). Downes' study differentiates working-class young people[2] into college boys and corner boys in a manner similar to W.F. Whyte's American study, focusing mainly on the latter (Whyte 1993/1943). The research also represents a critique of the Mertonian anomie tradition as it was presented in Cohen and Cloward and Ohlin's subcultural theories. The critique of these earlier American studies centres firstly on the argument that the focus of Cohen and Cloward and Ohlin on gang delinquency is too narrow. Downes takes issue with the definition of subculture in the American studies and argues that there is little evidence of structured gangs in Britain, although pointing out that there has been little research into the phenomena. He notes that there is an implicit conflation of subculture with a structured gang formation in Cohen and that this conflation is rendered explicit in Cloward and Ohlin, such that the subculture *is* the gang and vice versa (Downes 1966: 21). Consequently, Downes argues that a delinquent subculture can exist even when there is no structured delinquent gang. This leads to the second main point that subcultural theory can explain adolescent corner groups where delinquency is the sole purpose of the group, as in the American approach, *and* where delinquency is secondary to the group's activities as it is in Downes' study. In this assertion Downes is close to Matza (1995/1964) in the sense that young people drift in *and* out of delinquency and that, as such, their non-delinquent phases are still important. It is this latter point about non-delinquent phases that foreshadows work on youth culture in the 1970s to be discussed below. Downes argues that the young people in his study were not afflicted by class-based status-frustration which manifests in a reaction-formation, as in the work of Cohen. Neither were they alienated from 'conventional norms' and so withdrew support for their legitimacy, which is the analysis advanced by Cloward and Ohlin (Downes 1966: 236). This is because, in the main, the young people did not express a 'problem of adjustment' to working life. Consequently, Downes' key concept, 'dissociation', is used as a replacement for status-frustration in Cohen's study and alienation in Cloward and Ohlin's research (ibid.: 237). Dissociation refers to the elevation of non-work over work. Paid work becomes something that you do to make money and not the manifestation of one's status in life. Rather than status frustration caused by lack of opportunities and the attendant frustration or rebellion, there is, instead, inertia. The dullness of a job, the lack of prospects for the future hardly register because work is not a highly salient category of comparison between individuals or within one's own status universe (Cohen 1955: 85). It simply does not matter for many working-class young people. Access, or lack of access, to leisure is the key to the lives of young people. Lack of leisure opportunities causes frustration. Nevertheless, it needs to be pointed out that the methods employed by Downes were limited to those who would talk to him. Downes notes, for example, that an attempt to conduct unstructured interviews failed because only four out of ten of a pilot group responded positively to a request to be interviewed. Consequently, Downes had to carry out fieldwork in a 'caff'[3] in Poplar and a more fleeting series of encounters with young people in youth clubs in Stepney, both in East London. Downes' conclusions, as he points out, may have been different had he studied young people in schools that contained the most deprived children (Downes 1966: 253).

The Birmingham Centre for Contemporary Cultural Studies: the British subcultural tradition

Downes' research forms a theoretical conduit between American and British subcultural theory. Downes' theory of dissociation was taken forward in other British studies where culture and leisure became the main focus of research. The main impetus of this approach stemmed from the abundance of research from academics working in the Birmingham Centre for Contemporary Cultural Studies and those attending the National Deviancy Conferences in the late 1960s and 1970s influenced by Marxist and conflict theories. The Birmingham School took the 'non-work' side of subcultural activity a stage further. Criticising the assumption within the American tradition that there was a cultural consensus against which one could judge the behaviour of deviant groups, British subcultural theory employed a more critical, class-based approach to society. Subcultures were seen as a resistance to authority and took the form of an often playful expression of this resistance in clothes, style and music. The emphasis was on play rather than work. Work for the mod was a means to the weekend, a necessary intrusion to fund their leisure time (Hebdidge 1976a: 93).

By focusing on the leisure activities of young people British criminology marked a further move away from the American tradition of Mertonian strains in the social structure towards an analysis of cultural symbols and the meaning they had for those who used them. This argument was part of a larger movement in the social sciences that sought to criticise traditional or modernist theory and so was a general shift away from positivism and theories seeking to pathologise behaviour deemed deviant (Downes 1988). Such arguments were not just concerned with subcultures or crime (see e.g. the anti-psychiatry movement associated with Laing and Esterson 1964/1990, but also Foucault 1977 and Pearson 1975 on punishment and social work respectively). Consequently, this period represents the separation of sociology and psychology. In the main centre for subcultural studies in Britain, the Birmingham School of Contemporary Cultural Studies, there was an eclectic use of theories from different traditions, such as the use of Levi-Strauss' discussion of the transformation of one object of meaning into another or *bricolage*, as well as a cautious appraisal of Becker's labelling perspective (Clarke 1976: 177; Hall and Jefferson 1976; Levi-Strauss 1966, 1973; Becker 1963). Phil Cohen's 1972 study of subcultures in a working-class community became the catalyst for an enormously productive period of research into youth cultures, style and fashion (see, for example, the edited collection Hall and Jefferson 1976; Cohen 1972). With regard to criminological theory more particularly, the response was to blame crime on poverty and inequalities in the system, and to neglect low-level street crime or shift the focus to those who produce the label, hence crime becomes a social construct.

The high point of this approach in British criminology was *The New Criminology* in 1973 (Taylor et al. 1973), which was itself an extension of the new deviancy approach associated with the American sociologists Howard Becker and David Matza, and a general appreciation of the labelling approach. In *The New Criminology* social, biological and psychological positivism were attacked, theories that found favour with the conservative right and which were central to psychology. They argued that crime was a social construct, created through the labelling of marginal groups as deviant when judged against a supposed cultural consensus. However, such an approach was not finding support in the public at large, and was increasingly a position at odds with the statistics.

Subculture as class resistance

Moreover, the overtly Marxist approach overplayed the political determinants of youthful interaction, and in a similar way to the American subcultural theorists, there is an overemphasis on conflict between the working class and middle class. This bipolar classification is overly simplistic and disguises very real differences inside specific subcultures. For example, there are very real differences within what might be defined as the working class such as differences of race or sex. Moreover, it has been argued that this approach focused too much on the 'spectacular' youth subcultures prevalent at the time, such as the punks, mods, hippies, skinheads and rastafarians (Pearson 1994). Stan Cohen presents a powerful critique of the Birmingham Centre for Contemporary Cultural Studies in the second edition of *Folk Devils and Moral Panics* (Cohen 1980). Cohen argues that groups such as the mods, punks or skinheads were held up as examples of working-class resistance. However:

> Studies which start in a particular biographical location – school, neighbourhood, work – come up with a much looser relationship between class and style. They show, for example, the sheer ordinariness and passivity of much working-class adolescent accommodation and its similarities to, rather than dramatic breaks with, the respectable parent culture. (Cohen 1980: xix–xx)

Studies of youth by Parker (1974), Willis (1977) and Gill (1977) all point to the ordinariness, even boredom, associated with youth activity. Gill's study of the Luke Street kids (Gill 1977) found that there was little work available, and that which could be found was repetitive and dull. The result was dissociation from work as a source of satisfaction and the elevation of idleness to the forefront of their lives, punctuated by phases of often frenetic illegal activity. In Willis' study of the reproduction of social structure through the education system he found that the 'lads' unwittingly helped to determine their own later position in the workplace. Willis shows how for these working-class lads, manual labour becomes an almost inevitable outcome of their progress through education (Willis 1977). A similar sense of inevitability is present in Parker's study where the stealing of 'cats-eyes', slang for car radios, is undertaken as a means of affording the 'good times' from within the context of a social environment without excitement (Parker 1974). In each of these studies young people are represented not as politically aware resisters of an unfair dominant system, as expressed through the appropriation of cultural symbols, but in many respects as passively accepting their position in life. In the early 1980s, however, politics had shifted to the right and with it the arguments about crime. This was also a period of massive social upheaval across the world as one socialist country after another underwent often rapid disintegration and tentative rebirth as a form of capitalism (Hobsbawm 1994). Margaret Thatcher's government in Britain had replaced poverty and inequality as a cause of crime with freewill and immorality resulting in often intrusive and increasingly militarised policing tactics. In response to both this shift towards new right policy and the criticism of earlier Marxist and radical criminology, left realism developed.

Locating left realism

The paucity of a law and order policy in the British Labour party, at least one that appealed to the common sense of the electorate, capitulated this area of social policy to the new right political parties of Margaret Thatcher in Britain, and Richard Nixon in America. This is illustrated most dramatically by the election victory of Margaret Thatcher in 1979, ostensibly elected on a tough law and order manifesto. The two sides of the political spectrum were, therefore, split between moral and psychological individualism on the right and a variety of Marxism on the left where working-class crime, as noted above, became a romanticised expression of rebellion (Hall et al. 1978; Young 1994). The British Labour party's lack of a voter-friendly criminal justice policy during the 1980s lead to a *volte face* by a criminologist associated with *The New Criminology*'s Marxist-inspired argument that it was the powerful elite that defined what is to be criminalised (Taylor et al. 1973). In an attempt to provide a coherent law and order policy for the Labour Party, Jock Young had moved his position from treating crime as a social construct, and hence not real, to accepting that crime was a reality for many people, and that crime made other social problems worse and so was especially serious for the poor (Lea and Young 1993/1984). This position was termed left realism.

The left realists moved away from Marxist analyses and towards a version of relative deprivation based on Robert Merton's social structure and anomie that included elements of American subcultural theory (Lea 1992; Young 1997). They argued that absolute poverty could not account for crime rates during times of affluence since as people became richer crime rates also increased. Relative deprivation therefore replaced absolute deprivation. The left realists still focused on the inner-city poor, epitomised by their methodological tool of the local crime survey which tended to focus on areas of high unemployment such as Islington and Hammersmith in the 1980s (Jones, MacLean and Young 1986; Painter et al. 1989). But, it was argued that poverty and unemployment leads to marginalised communities, divorced from the forces of politics and control, such as the police. In other words, they replaced a simple determinism that saw poverty leading to crime with a more convoluted determinism. Political marginalisation leads to a Mertonian anomic situation of blocked opportunities engendering a feeling of relative deprivation that leads to crime. So, despite arguing that relative deprivation could affect anyone, rich or poor, they still focused on predominantly poor areas. But, the left realists did not just talk about relative deprivation as a cause of crime, but rather relative *economic* deprivation. Thus, the perception of economic inequalities relative to others leads to resentment that leads, somehow magically, to criminal behaviour. Therefore, the importance of relative deprivation theory to the study of crime stems from the role it plays in superseding overly-deterministic theories that sought to trace the causes of crime to problems which have their roots in poverty. However, the left realists did not base this approach on the work of W.G. Runciman whose book *Relative Deprivation and Social Justice* (1966) provided one of the fullest accounts of the theory and despite a focus on the inner-city riots of the 1980s, there is no mention of T.R. Gurr, whose 1970 book utilised relative deprivation to make sense of the motivations for collective violence. The next section will elaborate on these themes and seek to reposition the work of W.G. Runciman at the centre of debates concerning relative deprivation.

Relative deprivation: a fair-weather concept?

Runciman, like Albert Cohen and Richard Cloward, was a former student of Merton and shares a concern with the problem of poverty (Merton 1995; Runciman 1989). However, Runciman adds to his approach a more subjective interpretation of social class. Where Merton takes someone's class position from their income, Runciman bases his approach on the self-defined class position that someone gives themselves. Crucially, this may not be the same as the objective definition given by demographic statistics such as income or job title and is based on social comparisons. Hence, a feeling of deprivation is relative because it can exist even with a healthy bank balance if your neighbour is better off than you. Relative deprivation has been discussed within numerous different disciplines from sociology to criminology, political science and psychology. Consequently, it represents an idea that illustrates very well the way that sociological and psychological theories develop in isolation from each other. Moreover, it has been in and out of fashion at different times and within different disciplines. But, to begin with, a brief definition of relative deprivation needs to be provided on which the rest of the chapter will expand. Various researchers have offered definitions (Young 1992: 33; Lea 1992), with the term being first used by Stouffer et al. in a book called *The American Soldier* (1949). Runciman has provided a paraphrased summary of the key idea:

> If A, who does not have something but wants it, compares himself to B, who does have it, then A is 'relatively deprived' with reference to B. Similarly, if A's expectations are higher than B's, or if he was better off than B in the past, he may when similarly placed to B feel relatively deprived by comparison with him. (Runciman 1966: 10)

In essence, the distinction is between expectation and aspiration. If we *expect* something to happen then we are likely to feel discontented if it does not materialise, if we *aspire* to something then we may feel less discontent if it does not materialise. It could be argued that an aspiration is a subjective perception of future potential, whereas an expectation is more fully based on an assessment of objective probabilities. By asking young people what they would like to do when they are older we key into aspiration; asking them if they think they will achieve this aspiration keys into expectation. Relative deprivation can occur when expectation is blocked.

Relative deprivation as the outcome of comparisons

Runciman's work is based on a survey that focused on self-defined class position. Comparisons could be made between the self-elected class position and that which would be imposed when reference was made to economic indicators and occupations. Such a methodology allows the actor to subjectively place themselves within a stratified hierarchy, arguably a more accurate reflection of how people perceive themselves. Such self-labelling is a more interactionist interpretation of society whereby groups actively construct their roles and status with reference to ingroup/outgroup relationships or reference groups (Hogg and Abrams 1988; Abrams and Hogg 1990). Moreover, such a method allows for a more fluid interpretation of how people place themselves within society. The theory is also useful because it overcomes the bipolar structure/agency debate that tends to either emphasise structural causes of crime such as the economic system or causes derived from the agent's choice to commit an offence. Relative deprivation includes both structural factors, such as objective indicators of a group's income, and the subjective element of how people perceive their position.

Therefore, Runciman is concerned with identifying the circumstances that lead to feelings of resentment. Runciman highlights three main sources of relative deprivation, class position, power and education. Unlike Merton's opportunity theory (1938), Runciman is not only interested in the negative problems associated with the blocking of goals (which for Merton can lead to crime), but in the ambiguities that can arise when there are institutional blocks, but an ambivalent attitude or no feelings of resentment. He is also interested in the opposite phenomena, feelings of resentment when there are no objective reasons. For example, it is argued that the middle class felt more relative deprivation with respect to inequalities of class between the end of the Second World War and the survey conducted by Runciman in 1962. This means that middle-class non-manual workers felt that there was a narrowing of the class divide, even though this was not in accord with 'reality' (Runciman 1966: 94). Thus, whereas Merton tends to focus on those denied access to legitimate opportunity structures, in particular the poorest sections of the population, Runciman looks at all classes and argues that relative deprivation can be found in those with money as well as those without. Runciman argues that:

> Relative deprivation should always be understood to mean a *sense* of deprivation; a person who is 'relatively deprived' need not be 'objectively' deprived in the more usual sense that he (sic) is demonstrably lacking something. (1966: 10–11; emphasis in original)

This provides a broader framework and, in so doing, could be characterised as a synthesis between Durkheim's emphasis on the effects of anomie on the better off (1897/1951), and Merton's emphasis on the poor. Runciman himself points out that his book should be regarded as an eclectic mix of history, political philosophy, social psychology and sociology (Runciman 1966). Indeed, as Runciman argues, the related terms 'relative deprivation' and 'reference group' are both borrowed from social psychology (ibid.: 6), but they are used to forward an argument which Runciman regards as political theory and social history. It is for this reason that his work is important in the context of this book. Runciman integrates psychological and sociological theories.

The existence of relative deprivation is mediated by the choice of reference groups that a person or group makes. The term 'reference group' was first used, according to Runciman (ibid.: 11), by Herbert Hyman (1942). Runciman notes that reference groups can work in one of two ways: we can either direct our attention towards those that are doing better than we are and feel aggrieved, or we can look down to those worse-off than ourselves and feel satisfied with our position. There are many factors that determine the choices we make and our choices of who to compare ourselves to can change depending upon the social context. This complex set of possible comparisons seems to preclude any attempt at predicting social action. For example, which groups will we compare ourselves to, and when? This is one of the problems highlighted in a social psychological set of ideas called social identity theory and the related self-categorisation theory (Hogg and Abrams 1988).

How do we choose reference groups? Social Identity theory and Self Categorisation theory

As noted earlier, the work on groups by Muzafer Sherif suggested that the main cause of conflict was competition over resources. However, the social psychologist, Henri Tajfel, put forward the suggestion, based on his group experiments, that intergroup conflict could occur without competition. Identification with a group was sufficient to create conflict if comparison with another group took place. This was because a social group had the need to positively distinguish itself from what became known as the outgroup. People needed to create or maintain a positive social identity. This hypothesis was tested in experiments based on a 'minimal group paradigm' (Tajfel and Turner 1979). This involved placing people into groups based on chance. So a person would clearly see, for example, that the toss of a coin was all that determined which group they were in. Through a variety of experiments, however, it was possible to get the groups to negatively discriminate against the other group. John Turner, a former research student of Tajfel, produced a more general theory based on Social Identity theory called Self Categorisation theory, the two terms are sometimes used interchangeably (Turner 1988). However, as Turner says, both are based on the same hypothesis 'that individuals define themselves in terms of their social group memberships and that self-defined self-perception produces psychologically distinctive affects in social behaviour' (Turner 1988: XI). Consequently, who we are, our identity, is made up of elements based upon our belongingness to different groups.

For example, 'I am English' denotes membership of a specific group of people who derive from part of a small island to the west of mainland Europe. This is quite a specific category and the members are linked by location, language and history. 'I am a man' is a more general category that denotes membership of approximately half of the entire world's population. Apart from sex, this category shares less in common. 'I am a supporter of Arsenal football club' is even more specific. And 'I am a member of a local gang' more specific still. The interesting point about social identity theory is that each of these groups provides us with a sense of who we are – our social identity. We can make membership more or less salient, or uppermost in our minds, by changing the social context. Take for example a dinner table at which sits a child, her father and her grandmother. Her father may tell the child to eat slowly and not play with her food. He, in turn, may be told not to put his elbows on the table by his mother, the child's grandmother. Each of these people have multiple group memberships, but in this scene the father's social identity would have switched from a scolding father to a scolded son. Social identity theory describes a hierarchy of categories which overlap and can contain others. The utility of this theory is that it is able to show how changing social contexts result in changing social identifications. In many ways, there are similarities here with the criminologist, David Matza's concept of 'drift' (1995/1964). Traditional criminology and psychology posited an identity that was stable and unchanging. We have already looked at Eysenck's theory in Chapter 1 where stable personality traits are said to be related to crime (1964/1977). In sociological criminology, the subcultural research such as that discussed above by Albert Cohen (1955) or Cloward and Ohlin (1960) present a similarly static account where gang membership is seen as deviant and the individual is seen as immersed in this deviance such that their social identity *is* deviant and nothing more. The social identity perspective is a psychological theory that can overcome this static account of crime as unchanging and allow for drift in and out of a particular identity.

One of the key studies was conducted by Tajfel and Wilkes (1963) which asked subjects to judge the length of a series of eight lines that were each slightly different in size and arranged in size order. The four smallest were labelled 'A', and the longest 'B'. The lines were arranged sequentially in ascending order. It was found that when judging the length of the 'A' group and the 'B' group, subjects exaggerated the differences between the lengths of the two groups. They also overestimated the similarity of the length of the lines within the groups. Subjects, therefore, created groups that were artificially more distinct from each other. For example, the longest of the lines labelled 'A' was closer in size, and therefore more alike, to the shortest line labelled 'B' than the shortest 'A' line. Yet, the subjects saw these abstract lines as sharing more in common simply because of the labels attached to them. This led to the suggestion that we categorise a group of people as more similar to each other and more different from an outgroup based upon whatever characteristic becomes most salient. So, football supporters may suggest that the team they support is inherently better than their rival's team due to the better skill of their players. However, if the team started to lose, in order to maintain a positive social identity they might focus on the loyalty of the fans in the face of defeat when compared to their rival supporters.

One problem with such an account is that the theory suggests a universal set of cognitive functions regardless of nationality, history or upbringing. Stereotyping is regarded as a natural response to intergroup comparisons. So if a predominantly white neighbourhood was located adjacent to a predominantly black neighbourhood this theory would posit that racism would result due to the universal cognitive processes possessed by all groups. However, anthropological research has shown that such assumptions do not pertain for all people or all cultures. Consequently it has been argued that much of the research into the psychology of groups has been from within a positivistic paradigm based on small group experimentation (McGrath, Arrow and Berdahl 2000). The results of this experimentation are thought to be applicable to all people. Sami Timimi in a critical review of Attention Deficit Hyperactivity Disorder (ADHD) argues that there is a distinct western approach to the creation of problems by psychologists and psychiatrists (2005). Furthermore, Lena Robinson has argued that western psychology is inadequate in its approach to black young people. This is because the majority of all psychological research is based upon white Europeans, who are mostly middle class (Robinson 2004). However, it is possible to show how social identity theory can be synthesised with sociological approaches, as it has already been done with Runciman's relative deprivation thesis. The following part of this chapter, therefore, returns to this.

Synthesising social identity and relative deprivation theory

The following discussion looks at the evolution of relative deprivation theory after Runciman and its re-emergence in the discipline of social psychology, in particular the social identity approach (Hogg and Abrams 1999). The concept of relative deprivation has enjoyed mixed fortunes since Runciman's book appeared. In a historical review of the changing fortunes of relative deprivation in the social sciences, Brush has noted that sociology became less interested in the theory at the same time as psychology began to make use of the theory (Brush 1996). In 1970 T.R. Gurr's study of collective violence, *Why do men rebel?*, was based on a theory of relative deprivation and was initially well received (Brush 1996). Gurr, a political scientist, provided a psychological critique of previous theories of collective violence. Earlier theories proposed a number of different explanations for the instigation of collective violence ranging from the individual who acted emotionally because they were socially isolated to social contagion theory, whereby through a process of symbolic interaction, people were drawn into collective action by motivated instigators. All such theories presumed collective protest to be irrational and against the common good (ibid.). Gurr proposed that collective violence could best be explained as resulting from the discontent suffered by members of society; discontent refers to a discrepancy between what they have and what they believe they should have. In other words relative deprivation provides the motive for violence. Gurr incorporated the psychological proposition that this leads to frustration, which then leads to aggression, or the frustration-aggression hypothesis (Dollard et al. 1939). After a number of empirical studies that sought to empirically test Gurr's hypothesis (most notably Muller 1972, cited in Brush 1996) the theory fell out of favour with political scientists and sociologists. This was because such studies found that relative deprivation was not as important as other variables. However, the theory underwent a revival during the 1980s within social psychology at the same time that it fell out of favour with sociologists (ibid.). As Brush states: 'One reason for this may be that relative deprivation theory is viewed as a "reduction" of sociology to psychology, which thus tends to annoy sociologists and please psychologists' (1996: 535). However, one important caveat needs to be added to this, and that is the re-emergence of relative deprivation within the criminological school of left realism. But, as already noted, the left realists focused their theory on the work of Merton, not Runciman, which was a missed opportunity given Jock Young's earlier call for a social psychology of crime (Taylor et al. 1973).

When relative deprivation is discussed in social psychology, the concern is mainly with Runciman's differentiation between egoistic and fraternalistic relative deprivation. The former refers to individualistic feelings of deprivation, whilst the latter refers to feelings of deprivation on behalf of a group, be that a social class, locality or nation. Despite much of the focus of the social psychological approaches to group behaviour being small-scale quantitative experiments, it has been employed in the understanding of large-scale social protest, as the ethnographic work of Stephen Reicher has revealed in his studies of the St Paul's riots in Bristol and student demonstrations in London (Reicher 1987, 1996). Perhaps the most important contribution that these social psychological theories can offer is their discussion of the way in which categorisation processes are recursive. This is to say that when an individual categorises something else, be that a group, an individual or an object, we do so with reference to ourselves, that is we reproduce an aspect of our own self-identity (Turner et al. 1987). The social psychological approach suggests that groups have a psychological reality akin to structural entities which organise behaviour. Having said this, it should not be assumed that these approaches are new or unique. Sutherland and Cressey argued that 'differential association' rather than social disorganisation shaped criminal interaction. In other words, crime is a social process relying on interactions with other people (Sutherland and Cressey 1974). Therefore, in order to understand crime we have to understand the networks and social context in which people operate (see Hobbs 1997 for a review of the literature; Canter and Alison 2000).

But, still the question arises: which reference groups do we choose, and when? Self-categorisation theory uses the term 'saliency' to refer to the category that is uppermost in the mind at any given time. For example, it is often hard to see oneself as part of a group unless there is an outgroup with which to compare ourselves. To illustrate this, the criminologist Tony Jefferson has argued that crowd demonstrations would not escalate into riots if the police remained passive, and did not resort to aggressive, paramilitary tactics (Jefferson 1987). If we were to introduce self-categorisation theory into this proposition, the police would become salient as a group the more they acted in unison, for example tactical baton charges and riot shield manoeuvres, which are characteristic of paramilitarism. Such tactics would create a greater differentiation to occur between the crowd and the police, leading to the crowd as a group becoming salient. In other words, when ingroup and outgroup differentiation is greatest so is the salience of each group. This has been expressed as follows:

> [A]ccording to self-categorisation theory, social self perceptions can be perceived as a continuum ranging from perception of self as an individual to perception of self as an ingroup member. A person's self-categorisation at any given moment depends on the salience of personal or group identity in the social situation. Salience refers to the conditions under which one or the other type of identity become cognitively emphasised to act as the immediate influence on perception and behaviour. (Kawakami and Dion 1993: 526)

How salient a group is can depend on a multitude of different variables. Politics and the media are for ever creating outgroups, both positive and negative. Moral panics and the creation of 'folk devils' are good illustrations of the latter. Thus, categorising groups into stereotypic entities is context dependent (Oakes, Haslam and Turner 1994). Similarly, comparisons can be made at differing levels of abstraction, or identity. This means that two people could share the same job, both be married with the same number of children, have the same level of income, but because one of them is older this is the level of identity on which the comparison might be made. Therefore, reference group theory is a dynamic approach that transcends purely 'functionalist' ideas that tend to emphasise 'social' groups, such as the family, occupations and religious affiliations. For example, it has been argued that: 'frames of reference vary by age, sex, ethnic group, occupational, class, and prestige-group comparisons' (Downes 1966: 7). This does not mean, however, that relative deprivation is too broad a concept to have any theoretical use because it is delimited in terms of the possible reference groups a person or group will choose. Of course, this may vary over time, and the impact of globalisation illustrated by the increase of information technologies potentially increases the scope of reference groups and consequently increases aspirations (Giddens 1990; Young 1999). This perhaps accounts for evidence that suggests that crime rates rise during upturns in the economy allowing more people to purchase products they could not afford previously. The advertising and purchase of new products increases the likelihood that relative deprivation will be more acutely felt and the greater quantity of goods results in the rise of theft (Maguire 1997).

Towards a synthesis of social psychology and criminology?

The idea of relative deprivation has, therefore, been discussed by both sociological and psychological theorists and the discussion here serves to demonstrate the utility of combining ideas from different approaches. Where traditional psychology tends to be positivistic, social identity theory and self-categorisation theory *can* overcome this. The work of Stephen Reicher and his more qualitative research demonstrates this. Also interesting is the way that sociological ideas like those of Runciman can be neglected in the discipline within which they developed but resurrected in another. The utility of thinking in terms of reference groups also allows us to move beyond the simplistic understanding of subcultures and gangs being static entities and their members seen as uniformly deviant. More contemporary research has questioned the social-class based subcultural theories in both the USA and UK and posited a more postmodern approach that shares some issues in common with Matza's concept of drift (Blackman 2005;

Muggleton 2000). Muggleton, for example, has argued that youth cultural groups are much less cohesive than the Birmingham subcultural theorists assumed. Social class was not the unifying identity since class has become much less important to young people. In contrast, Shildrick and MacDonald (2005) have argued that Muggleton's approach neglects the very real effect that class has on people. This is especially the case with young people where class affects what forms of leisure they take part in. Social psychology has not been used as much as might be expected to understand gangs or subcultures. There is significant scope for a concerted research strategy that synthesises the social psychology of intergroup relations with the sociological approaches. This area is, arguably, the most obvious one for such a synthesis to occur due to the focus on social interactions as opposed to the individual focus of the majority of psychological accounts. Sociological accounts have also been better able to explain crime of a less serious nature. Crimes like murder tend to have more explanations emanating from psychology than sociology. However, some forms of death are caused by fundamentally social causes. This will be explored further in the next chapter.

Summary

- This chapter explored the way that social psychology can be integrated with sociological arguments to provide a more robust and flexible account of small group-level crime.
- Subcultural theory originated in the work of sociologist Robert K. Merton, and was elaborated by his students Albert Cohen and Richard Cloward to account for non-acquisitive youth crime.
- David Downes applied the American ideas to Britain, and argued that they did not fit the pattern of youth crime. Downes focused instead on differential access to culture and leisure. Crime could result if access was blocked.
- The Birmingham School took this further, added a Marxist analysis, and argued that spectacular youth subcultures were a form of resistance to authority.
- Such arguments can be criticised as being too deterministic. David Matza argued that young people drift in and out of deviant groups.
- The left realists utilised the Mertonian form of subcultural theory, and added the argument that crime was caused by relative deprivation. However, this was not directly based on the work of W.G. Runciman.
- Runciman's work is an integration of ideas deriving from sociology, political science and psychology.
- Where this research was peripheral for sociological criminology, it became a major theme in some forms of social psychology. Runciman's work allows for a more flexible approach to youth gangs and other forms of group-level criminal activities because it overcomes the deterministic element of both Mertonian and the Birmingham versions of subcultural theory.

STUDY QUESTIONS

1 Is social psychology really sociology?

2 What subcultures exist today? Are they still as distinct as they were in the past, such as the punks, skinheads or hippies?

3 List the reference groups with which you compare yourself. What effect do these comparisons have on your self-identity?

4 What reference groups cause you to feel relatively deprived? Describe the feeling.

5 Is the left realist argument that relative deprivation causes crime too deterministic?

FURTHER READING

There are many excellent books on this subject, perhaps the best introduction is J. Muncie (2009) *Youth and Crime*. London: Sage.

Others include:

Blackman, S. (2005) 'Youth subcultural theory: a critical engagement with the concept, its origins and politics, from the Chicago School to Postmodernism', *Journal of Youth Studies*, 8(1): 1–20.

Canter, D. and Alison, L. (1999) 'The social psychology of crime: groups, teams and networks', in D. Canter and L.J. Alison (eds), *The Social Psychology of Crime, Groups, Teams and Networks*. Aldershot, Hampshire: Ashgate.

Muggleton, D. (2000) *Inside Subcultures: The Postmodern Meaning of Style*. Oxford: Berg.

Shildrick, T. and MacDonald, R. (2005) 'In defence of subculture: people, leisure and social divisions', *Journal of Youth Studies*, 9(2): 125–40.

Webber, C. (2007a) 'Revaluating relative deprivation theory', *Theoretical Criminology*, 11(1): 97–120.

Notes

1 Whether or not this was due to the British researchers looking in the wrong places is another debate, but one that needs to be borne in mind.
2 In common with many other studies, Downes' study mainly includes boys.
3 The colloquial phonetic pronunciation of Café.

5

Mass Murder, Political Murder and War Crimes

Chapter Contents

OVERVIEW

Continuing to explore the wider scale of crime, this chapter seeks to extend the topic of mass murder as it is usually discussed in the psychological literature and begins to elaborate the applicability of criminological psychology at a global scale. Mass murder is often conceived as different from serial murder, with a typology as to what makes it unique. This chapter seeks to extend this debate by including discussion of mass murders as they are committed both by individuals (or rarely dyads as at Columbine or the Washington snipers), and on a global scale where the book will highlight the paucity of research on issues such as genocide, terrorism and war crimes.

KEY TERMS

genocide homicide-suicide mass murder war crimes

What is mass murder and how does it differ from serial murder?

Dietz (1986) has defined mass murder as the wilful injuring of five or more people, of whom three or more are killed by a single offender in a single incident. Mass murder results in the suicide of the offender in around 50 per cent of all cases. For Fox and Levin (2002) mass murder is the killing of four or more people by one or a few assailants within a single event, lasting from a few minutes to several hours. Fox and Levin argue that their definition is better able to distinguish between mass murder and killing more generally. This is in contrast to definitions by Dietz, Holmes and Holmes (2001a) and Ressler, Burgess and Douglas (1988) who define it as two or three killings. For example, two or three people may be killed during a bank robbery. This would not constitute a mass murder in the sense that Fox and Levin would like to promote. In an attempt to distinguish between instances of serial and multiple murder, Fox and Levine present a summary of the types of activity and the causes for it (see Table 5.1). A note of caution should be borne in mind when looking at Table 5.1 in that the causes presented are extremely vague. Social theorists have grappled over terms like power and revenge in an attempt to define them, but no such struggle has been undertaken by these authors. Generally, mass murder is distinguished from serial murder due to the former's lack of a cooling off period between instances of murder. Clearly, with no agreed definition of what is and what is not an example of mass murder, it is difficult to pinpoint exactly what we are studying. This has implications for trying to understand causation as shifting definitions do not help us to be precise about the phenomena. What constitutes mass murder is more commonly defined by the media, especially with regard to school shootings. Such murders tend to result in the perpetrator committing suicide, termed homicide-suicide. However, there are various forms that homicide-suicide takes, with school shootings being the rarest, but most frequently publicised. Before moving on to looking at mass murder a discussion of the various forms of homicide-suicide will take place in order to demonstrate the many forms that it can take.

Table 5.1 *Generic examples of motivations for multiple murder*

Motivations for multiple murder	Serial murder	Mass murder
Power	Inspired by sadistic fantasies, a man tortures and kills a series of strangers to satisfy his need for control and dominance.	A pseudo-commando, dressed in battle fatigues and armed with a semi-automatic weapon, turns a shopping mall into a 'war zone'.
Revenge	Grossly mistreated as a child, a man avenges his past by slaying women who remind him of his mother.	After being fired from his job, a gunman returns to the work site and opens fire on his former boss and co-workers.
Loyalty	A team of killers turns murder into a ritual for proving their dedication to one another.	A depressed husband/father kills his family and himself to spare them from a miserable existence and bring them a better life.
Profit	A women poisons to death a series of husbands in order to collect on their life insurance policies.	A band of armed robbers executes the employees of a store to eliminate all witnesses to their crime.
Terror	A profoundly paranoid man commits a series of bombings to warn the world of impending doom.	A group of anti-government extremists blows up a train to send a political message.

Source: Fox and Levin (2005: 20).

Homicide-suicide

Homicide-suicide usually involves one perpetrator and one or a few victims. Consequently, only at the more extreme form of this behaviour can it be classed as mass murder. However, it is worth discussing the range of forms that this type of killing takes and end on the one that is most familiar, and yet rarest. In a review of the literature on homicide-suicide, Hillbrand (2001) has echoed previous research when stating that there is little research into homicide-suicide due to the very low incidence, which might explain why much of the literature is from American research. What is known is that those who commit homicide-suicide share similar characteristics around the world. The majority are men (95 per cent in the USA), the victims are mostly women (85 per cent in USA), and most of these are relatives or shared a close relationship with the perpetrator. Ninety per cent of all cases in the USA involve one killer and one victim. Many perpetrators have been treated for depression, as many as 75 per cent in the UK. The majority of these perpetrators do not have a history of prior violence, but many have attempted suicide and so the genesis of the problem shares more in common with the general characteristics of suicide than they share with homicide.

Marzuk, Tardiff and Hirsch (1992, cited in Hillbrand 2001) in an American study presented a typology of the various forms taken by homicide-suicide based on the relationship between the offender and the victim. Not discussed here is the topic of politically motivated homicide-suicide which will be discussed in the next chapter.

- *Filicide-suicide*: A father or mother kills their child followed by their own suicide. Being murdered by a parent is the most frequent form of child homicide belying the more usual media stereotypes and panics regarding stranger danger.
- *Familicide-suicide*: Spouse, children and other relatives and family members, including pets are killed followed by suicide. The perpetrator is usually an older male, depressed and a substance misuser.
- *Jealous spousal/consortial-suicide*: This form accounts for half of all American homicide-suicides. Mostly involving males, this involves the murder of a sexual partner by a jealous spouse or partner, and may include the murder of another implicated party.
- *Declining health spousal/consortial-suicide*: A spouse or partner kills their partner due to their declining health. It could be argued that this type could be split into two forms, the first where the killing was agreed by both parties so that it becomes euthanasia-suicide, and the second type where there is no agreement and the victim is killed due to frustration on behalf of the care giver.
- *Extrafamilial homicide-suicides*: This occurs infrequently. One person, more rarely two people, attack and kill a number of people for a real or perceived grievance. This type is the least common, but most frequently publicised, and can be further broken down as will be discussed below with reference to mass murder in schools. However,

before getting to that, another type of homicide has been identified by Wolfgang (1959, cited in Hillbrand 2001).

- *Suicide by victim-precipitated homicide*: Sometimes called *suicide by cop*, this phenomenon occurs where an individual deliberately threatens a police officer leading them to kill the individual in self-defence.

The rarest form of mass murder is the one that attracts most media attention. It is to this that we now turn.

Mass murder in schools

Harding, Fox and Mehta (2002) argue that death in school is a rare occurrence. Schools are still the safest place for young people. In the last three decades of the twentieth century rampage mass murder has occurred in America between 30 and 50 times, depending upon how an event is defined. According to Hagan, Hirschfield and Shedd (2002) media coverage of lethal gun violence in schools tends to focus on the rare mass murders committed by one person over a short time period and leading to a number of deaths. The more common form of gun crime is a single attacker and a single victim, usually with a clear social context that provides some meaning for the incident, such as gang members targeting rivals. Hagan et al. also point out that what we know about such incidents is usually heavily distorted by the media.

In support of the risk-society thesis outlined in Chapter 1, one of the key aims of psychological research into this form of mass murder is to identify possible perpetrators before they commit the offence. Mulvey and Cauffman (2001) point out that this form of prediction is extremely difficult. This is because the event is so rare. Consequently, the risk of falsely identifying individuals is very high – a so-called false positive result. Such an activity stigmatises many young people who are, perhaps, least able to deal with such surveillance and may make matters worse. One way to overcome this is to widen the definition of school violence that this strategy is designed to predict. This may be to include bullying or fighting. However, Mulvey and Cauffman cite research by Bosworth, Espelage and Simon (1999) showing that 80 per cent of young people have engaged in bullying behaviour thus diluting the specificity of the prediction. Also, school violence tends to take place within a process of quite specific interactions, a failed relationship, or a perceived humiliation by a teacher or peers. Consequently, such predictions would have to take into account an infinite series of interactions with those who had been identified as potential perpetrators to predict the outcome. Add to this the rapid process of developmental change that young people go through and the prediction of violence

Table 5.2   *Types of violence in school*

Source of action in relation to agent	Locus of effect in relation to agent	Mode
External	External	Adaptive
Internal	External	Expressive
Internal	Internal	Integrative
External	Internal	Conservative

Source: Fritzon and Brun (2005: 57).

becomes even more difficult. It is better to focus on school-wide strategies of support where young people feel trusted rather than suspected and an understanding that it is often the environment outside school that is a better predictor of violence than what takes place in the school. Such an holistic approach, more common to sociological criminology is often at odds with the understandable desire for specific prediction tools.

For example, Fritzon and Brun (2005) put forward an approach that seeks to identify the motivation for why individuals commit school-associated homicide based on the meaning that the offender assigns the victim. The authors present a model that describes four different motivations for school-based violence. This is based on a model developed by Shye (1985) whereby the crime is seen to be a way for an offender to alter a part of their internal or external world. This involves a source of anxiety, anger or frustration and a target for the perceived alleviation of these emotions. Both source and target can be either external or internal. This results, according to Fritzon and Brun, in four hypotheses describing different types of violent school behaviour and how the offender interacts with those around them (see Table 5.2):

- *Adaptive mode*: The target is external to the individual. The types of actions that result are instrumental and directed at external sources. The activity is a means to an end, such as monetary gain, and might describe the activity of a gang engaging in opportunistic crimes where the victim has no specific significance.
- *Expressive mode*: The victim is not significant in this mode but becomes the target of the actor's emotional state. It is argued that violent incidents of this mode are a form of communication rather than revenge. Violence can therefore occur without much provocation by the victim, and tends to take place over a longer timeframe. The source of the anxiety comes from a source other than the victim, who is a proxy for that conflict.
- *Integrative mode*: This mode is directed inwardly and takes the form of actions designed to demonstrate the actor's distress and, at its most severe, takes the form of suicide. Actions tend to take place in private areas.
- *Conservative mode*: The conflict is caused by an external source and the actor feels the need to change their internal psychological frustration or anger. The target will

be a specific individual or group upon whom the actor can take revenge for some actual or perceived injustice and may take the form of a violent outburst in order to satisfy the actor's internal emotional state. This might take the form of a rampage killing spree, and in the USA this tends to be with a gun.

The most common mode was the adaptive mode characterised by gangs targeting specific individuals to rob or against whom they wanted to express their status. This supports the point made earlier that the media overemphasise the spectacular at the expense of the more common. The integrative mode was a close second in frequency and tended to be a homicide or series of homicides followed by suicide (Palermo 1994). This research is based on categorising behaviours into distinct themes after the event and based on reports from eyewitnesses, newspaper reports and others involved in creating accounts of the events. As the authors point out, such conclusions that are drawn from this data are not suitable for predicting future crime, although the study could indicate clinical interventions with those deemed at risk. But, this risks stigmatising those who may never go on to commit a crime.

Palermo (1997) presents a psychoanalytic account of the cause of mass murder which argues, somewhat vaguely, that the cause is related to the Superman complex – Nietzsche's concept of a superior being able to control a weak and easily lead humanity. Such killers are narcissistic and when that sense of superiority is threatened then this leads to an attempt to restore that sense of self-control. Applying Freudian concepts Palermo argues that a breakdown in social norms leads to the release of Id impulses in vulnerable people. Although not referenced, such an idea echoes those of the French sociologist Emile Durkheim and his concept of **anomie**, or normlessness, discussed in Chapter 1. The title of the article 'The Berserk Syndrome' relates to the idea that we often see such killers being described as going 'berserk'. Berserk is the name of a mythical Norse warrior and came to represent a particularly violent group of Norwegian warriors. Palermo does not take this idea any further and so it is not clear what conceptual use such a typology would have for research.

Mass murder and the quest for celebrity

Palermo argues that the quest for celebrity may be one cause of serial killing, but he argues that the impulsive nature of mass murder makes this cause less likely (1997). However, in the Virginia Tech mass murder in the USA on 16 April 2007, Seung-Hui Cho murdered 32 and wounded 25 people before committing suicide. The killer had sent a package to the news channel NBC on which was recorded 27 videos in which Cho expressed his hatred for various groups along with an 1800 word document detailing similar animosities and likening himself to Jesus Christ. Such a murder spree was clearly planned, even if many of the targets of the killer were randomly shot. The video contained images of Cho seemingly copying poses from the Korean Film *Old Boy*, and one sociologist, Loren Coleman, suggested that the murders were a copycat of the Columbine massacre in 1999 (see also Coleman 2004). A similar series of school shootings have occurred in Europe, with recent plots being foiled after police viewed Internet chatrooms detailing the plans (Internet Reference 4). The issue of copycat violence is a contentious one in criminology, with many academics wary of attributing violence to copycat explanations because it suggests a **deterministic aetiology** and over-predicts the likelihood of violence. Since media representations of violence, both real and fictional, are so pervasive, the extent of copycat violence should be higher. From Bandura's BoBo doll experiments to more recent research looking at the introduction of television to previously unconnected areas, the evidence is varied (Jewkes 2004; Boyle 2005).

A more thorough review of the American literature on young people who have committed mass murder by Meloy et al. (2001) identified a number of factors common to a range of mass murders by young people committed in America. The author's criteria of what constituted an adolescent mass murder included 'the intentional killing of at least three victims (other than the perpetrator) in a single incident by an individual 19 years old or younger' (Meloy et al. 2001: 720). Note that such a definition would not capture within its remit the Virginia Tech shooting where the perpetrator was 23 years old. Twenty-seven incidents of mass murder were found between 1958 and 1999, with 14 of these occurring in only the last four years of the range, 1995–99. The authors attribute this to a copycat effect. It was found that all subjects were male, between the ages of 11 and 19, with an average age of 17. Seventy-nine per cent or 27 were white, 3 were Hispanic (8.8 per cent), 2 were African-American (5.9 per cent) one was Native American and one was Asian-American. This distribution is similar to the ethnic population distribution in America, but not to the firearm homicide rate where white adolescents using guns are outweighed by a factor of 10 by African-Americans. This reiterates the point earlier that the majority of school murders involves one victim and one perpetrator.

The majority of those involved in mass murder were described as loners (70 per cent). In 17 per cent of the cases the perpetrator had bullied others, however in 43 per cent of cases the perpetrator was themselves the victim of bullying. Nevertheless, bullying is experienced by many young people so its effect is difficult to separate from the everyday experiences of school life. Thirty-seven per cent of the perpetrators came from families where their parents had separated or divorced. Here also, it is not possible to state that this had any causative effect since many children grow up in a single parent family. It was noted in this study that in two-thirds of these cases there was reported to be a 'trigger' that preceded the violence. This took the form of rejection or failure from a real or unrequited girlfriend or some other rejection or failure within the school setting, such as by a teacher. Second to this form of trigger was a sense of injustice caused to the perpetrator by other people. Guns were the most frequently used weapons with two-thirds of them being obtained from the perpetrator's own parents or purchased by the offender. Most of these events were planned. Almost a quarter (23 per cent) had a documented psychiatric condition, although the authors suspect the number to be higher due to privacy laws with regard to minors meaning that the data was not available to them. Almost half were reported to be interested in war or weapons and a similar number were regarded as fantasizers (sic) by the authors if they were reported to be interested in fantasy games, books or hobbies.

One of the essential problems with such statistics is that without a comparative context it is difficult to know how common such fantasizers (sic) are amongst those who do not go on to commit mass murder. With the wider use of games consoles it might be argued that such a finding becomes somewhat redundant. Therefore, research needs to separate out the cultural factors from the clinical factors, and set the whole study within a wider context. Perhaps the most important difference between those who go on from these factors to actually commit a mass murder is that 44 per cent discussed killing people with at least one other person before the event and 58 per cent made threatening statements regarding what they wanted to do beforehand. Yet, caution about how such findings should be interpreted must be taken. Many people express a desire to kill their boss, tell an aggravating peer that the next time they see them 'they're dead' and so on. Meloy et al. (2001) note themselves that mass murder is such a low frequency activity that prediction is 'virtually impossible'.

Nevertheless, Leary, Kowalski, Smith and Philips (2003) argue that rejection by peers, such as bullying, might be a strong predictor of school shootings since there is an established body of research that suggests that real or imagined rejection leads to aggression. Reports into the Columbine shootings suggested the killers had been publicly taunted. Such overt teasing adds a further sense of humiliation into the mix. Rejection can occur in a number of ways, such as teasing, ostracism and romantic rejection. Despite these being common occurrences in childhood Leary et al. point out that few go on to commit mass murder. They used a case study method to look at all cases of school shootings that matched their criteria. The shooting had to occur during the day, result in at least one student being injured or killed and did not include shootings where the only death or injury was to a non-student. This last omission from the criterion of inclusion is perhaps somewhat strange given that it suggests the only people who can precipitate extreme violence through rejection are other students. It suggests that teachers rejecting students, belittling them or otherwise humiliating them in front of their class mates would not be a powerful factor. Nevertheless, they identified 15 cases that matched the criteria between 1995 (when they argue school shootings became widely publicised) and 2001. As noted earlier, suicide after a mass murder is rare and in only one of these cases did the perpetrators commit suicide – Eric Harris and Dylan Klebold at Columbine High School, Littleton, Colorado in 1999. In 12 of the 15 cases the perpetrator had been teased and bullied and there is evidence they were on the periphery of their school peers' social life. Romantic break up also preceded many of the shootings. In many cases, a victim was part of the ostracising, rejecting and bullying group. In only two cases were these factors not present. Other factors associated with school shootings also appeared: fascination with death, an interest in weapons and mental health problems. Ten of the fifteen had a history of mental health problems such as depression, six cases involved perpetrators interested in guns and weapons, four were interested in 'Goth' music and expressed an interest in Satanic ritual. Despite concurring with Mulvey and Cauffman's (2001) point that it is probably not possible, or ethical, to attempt to predict who will become a school shooter, they present a profile regardless. For Leary et al. the profile of a typical school shooter is:

> a male student who has been ostracized by the majority group at his school for some time, and has been chronically taunted, teased, harassed, and often publicly humiliated. Moreover, he probably demonstrates one or more of the three risk factors identified in the present study – an unusual interest in guns and explosives; a fascination with death, Satan, and other 'dark' themes; or psychological problems that are characterized by depression and/or a personality disorder that involves antisocial behavior, poor impulse control, or sadistic tendencies. (2003: 213)

Ultimately, the question turns to culture and social factors. Many other countries have easy access to guns and one would assume that rejection is a common experience of childhood. So why does America suffer disproportionately from school gun crime?

Perhaps the most that can be achieved is to follow the suggestion by Mulvey and Cauffman (2001) that a greater focus on the social context is the most important policy to pursue, rather than try to target individuals. However, as the report into the Virginia Tech murders pointed out (Internet Reference 4), in that case, at least, there were several clear signs that the perpetrator was seriously disturbed, but that not enough was done to tackle the problem due to misunderstandings between various agencies as to what information could be shared about the deeply disturbed killer. Similar issues may pertain in the UK with the Data Protection Act (1998) preventing organisations from sharing personal data with each other without permission. Consequently, whenever psychological research suggests that certain procedures should be followed, wider social, ethical and legal factors that might hinder this need to be borne in mind as well.

War and mass murder

The following section explores an area of human behaviour that has not been focused on by criminology. State sponsored mass murder, such as during a war, and the mass murder committed by terrorists are areas that have not been looked at in much depth by criminologists despite the subject matter seeming to fit within their domain (Yacoubian 2000; Friedrichs 2000; Edward Day and Vandiver 2000). As Fox and Levin argue (2002) this area is better contained within the theory and methods of political science. This is what tends to happen when the media call an expert to discuss an event such as the World Trade Center and Pentagon attacks in 2001. Political scientists or historians tend to be the expert of choice for the evening news programmes.

The reasons for the neglect of genocide and other forms of political mass murder can be explained, according to Yacoubian, by four factors. Firstly, the way research is funded leads to a tendency to study crime at a national level rather than the more expensive international level necessary to understand genocide in countries other than your own. Secondly, linked to this is a culture of localism with researchers forming relationships with local practitioners and the aim to create domestic social policy. Thirdly, criminological research methods are not always appropriate for the study of genocide. Although Yacoubian is partly correct in this, criminology is a field and can draw on many methods from other disciplines. The research costs would seem to be the more important barrier to research overseas. The final reason for the neglect to study this area is that there is no history of studying this subject in the recent history of the subject. Consequently, few criminologists regard the subject to be relevant to them. The following is a review of this area and the contribution that criminological psychology can make to it.

War, genocide and psychology

Genocide was defined in the Convention on the Prevention and Punishment of the Crime of Genocide which became International Law in 1951. This Convention was a direct consequence of the mass murders during the Second World War. Article II states that:

> In the present Convention, genocide means any of the following acts committed with intent to destroy, in whole or in part, a national, ethnical, racial or religious group, as such:
>
> (a) Killing members of the group;
> (b) Causing serious bodily or mental harm to members of the group;

(c) Deliberately inflicting on the group conditions of life calculated to bring about its physical destruction in whole or in part;

(d) Imposing measures intended to prevent births within the group;

(e) Forcibly transferring children of the group to another group.

There are, of course, other groupings who may fall outside of this definition, such as groups defined by their social class, as in the murder of street children in Brazil; or their sex, as in the murder of female babies in China; or, as in the case of Nazi Germany, their presumed intelligence or their sexuality.

Stanley Milgram and obedience to authority

Despite many studies being conducted during and immediately after the Second World War, discussion of the massive shifts in global culture engendered by the war are hardly mentioned. This is a strange omission given the fundamental effect the war had. However, the war did have an effect on psychology, in particular work such as Stanley Milgram, whose research on obedience to authority can be seen as a response to events during the war (Milgram 1963). The Second World War alerted psychologists to the role that ordinary people had in the genocide of thousands of innocent people. Milgram's work is one attempt to answer the question of why normal people do extraordinary violence to other innocent people.

Milgram invited people to participate in an experiment into memory at Yale University. The volunteers were introduced to a man they were told would be the subject of the experiment who was then strapped into a chair. The volunteer was told they would be giving the man, a confederate of the experimenters, increasingly powerful electric shocks. This was demonstrated by giving the volunteer a small shock. The man strapped in the chair was trained in how to respond and no shocks were given to him. The more voltage administered the more reaction he would give, at 300 volts he would kick the wall, after that level he ceased to say anything. The volunteers could not see him. On giving a wrong answer to a set of memory questions the volunteer pressed a switch on a panel which had various buttons labelled with increasingly dramatic descriptions. These ranged from 'Slight Shock' to 'Danger: Severe Shock', and ranged from 15 to 450 volts. No punishment would be given for failing to obey. How obedient the volunteers were depended on how much voltage they would administer. Many volunteers questioned the experiment the further they went and they were given increasingly encouraging phrases to persuade them to continue. Milgram found that 65 per cent went all the way through the range of shocks giving 450 volts. No one stopped prior to 300 volts, the point at which the confederate kicked the wall. This finding suggested that obedience to authority was easy to achieve and that people who would not normally wish to inflict pain on someone could be compelled to do so. In this case the authority was a researcher from Yale University, but it is not too difficult to extend this to actions during war. The remoteness of the volunteer from the man to whom they thought they were giving electric shocks might explain some of this obedience. The fact they could not see him and the shocks were being administered by pressing a button created a sense of anonymity. Termed a buffer, Milgram showed that the levels of obedience dropped to 40 per cent if the volunteer was in the same room as the confederate.

What is also important is that as part of this experiment Milgram needed to discover what people would predict would happen in the experiment. Milgram asked 14 students (admittedly a small number) to predict how many people would go through to administer the highest shock from a hypothetical group of 100 Americans from diverse backgrounds. The response was that very few would do so. Although this is not a representative sample the low prediction is in stark contrast to the outcome of the experiment. Milgram argued that obedience is an ingrained behaviour and an 'impulse overriding training in ethics, sympathy and moral conduct' (Milgram 1963: 371). Of course, it is possible to argue that the volunteers were aware of the artificiality of the scenario and that the social context during a war is very different. Nevertheless, despite the dubious ethics of this experiment, it is still a reminder that obedience to authority is an easily manipulated human behaviour.

A more wide-ranging account of genocide was put forward by Staub (1989, 1996, 1999). Staub applies a range of established psychological concepts to an analysis of why groups engage in genocide. Staub sees the catalyst for genocide where there are persistent difficult life conditions. In an echo of Durkheim's concept of anomie and the Chicago School's major cause of crime (social disorganisation), Staub argues that this could be economic depression, or the aftermath of war where social breakdown is evident. This has to be combined with other cultural factors such as strong acceptance of hierarchical authority, antagonism towards an outgroup, such as the Jews in Nazi Germany, and a prior history of resorting to violence to deal with conflict. This results in scapegoating a designated group against whom the frustrations can be targeted. This is a theory of gradual escalation from small harms to the ultimate act of genocide. However, this is not an inevitable outcome and along the continuum the escalation can be abated or quickened either by those within the aggressive group or by bystanders, such as other countries. What this cannot explain, however, are genocides committed by nations against an indigenous population, such as in America and Australia. The aggressors in each case were not living through particularly hard times relative to other cultures. Similarly, many countries have suffered hard times and not engaged in genocide. One of the major problems with Staub's account is the lack of reference to sociological theories that would add weight to the argument. As noted, much of Staub's account is similar to the idea of anomie in Durkheim and the Chicago School's concept of social disorganisation, but these are not noted. Similarly, there is no mention of relative deprivation or social identity theory despite the argument that frustration and blocked goals were a key element in the creation of genocide. As noted in the final chapter, these ideas have been used to explore the way that we compare ourselves with others and how we relate to our country and create a sense of belonging. A fuller analysis of genocide would need to take on these points.

War, crime and states of denial

What explanations have been put forward for why ordinary people do extraordinary violence? Or indeed, why ordinary people do not do anything to stop such violence? One book that sought to answer this was *States of Denial* by Stan Cohen (2001). Cohen was interested in the notion that ordinary members of the German public were living in a state of denial over the Nazi atrocities, a state of knowing and not knowing at the same time. This idea can be seen as an extension to Cohen's earlier research into moral panics. It was argued by Cohen and other criminologists that big corporations and the state itself hide the impact of their crimes by diverting the public attention towards less serious crime committed by the powerless (Hall et al. 1978; Cohen 1972/ 2002). However, this Marxist analysis does not take into account the myriad people who work within the state and big corporations who are themselves relatively powerless at an individual level. For example, employees of oil companies that pollute the environment are probably more aware of the mismanagement and shortcuts taken than any number of external observers like Greenpeace. What Cohen is talking about in *States of Denial* is a powerful psychological principle of not wanting to put oneself in the line of fire. Very real in Nazi Germany, metaphorical in a large corporation but transferred into fears for the loss of one's job. Milgram's research on obedience to authority, and Zimbardo's prison experiment can all be drawn upon as psychological evidence for this phenomena. Such research moves the debate about involvement away from purely Marxist political ideas of subterfuge and misdirection, which in any case presents the majority of the world as dupes unaware of their exploitation even as they live it every day. In its place is a different kind of explanation that is still able to include political exploitation for financial gain, but adds to this an element of agency on behalf of those who were dupes under traditional Marxist accounts. Cohen's book combines structural accounts of war, such as politics and history, with agency approaches, such as individual responsibility.

Cohen makes use of the work of Sykes and Matza's Techniques of Neutralisation to account for the ways that people involved in genocide deny the severity of their involvement (1957). Although Sykes and Matza developed this theory to account for juvenile delinquency, Cohen argues that it is relevant in this context also. To the original five techniques used by juvenile delinquents in Sykes and Matza's account, Cohen adds two more: *denial of knowledge* and *moral indifference*. The following summarises this argument.

Denial of knowledge

Those who deny knowledge of an atrocity to avoid being found guilty make claims like, 'I was not there, so could not have known', or more simply, 'it wasn't me'. Cohen notes that for the majority in Germany it was plausible that many did not know about the full extent of the Final Solution to eradicate all Jewish people. For others, especially those more directly involved, although not to the extent of actually being there at the moment of death, Cohen asks if it is possible that something is known and not known at the same time. In the sense that the genocide was being denied at the time it was being committed there is certainly a sense where this is possible.

Denial of responsibility

This form of denial is the most common form. In many forms of denial of responsibility the denier uses attempts to redirect responsibility onto other people. The individual's freewill has been taken over or manipulated by someone else. Cohen argues that there are four versions of this form of denial. The first is *obedience to authority*, which we have covered in detail earlier in this chapter, but I will discuss how Cohen applies it directly to genocide. The three other forms are *conformity*, *necessity* and *splitting*.

1 Obedience

Denying one's responsibility by claiming that you were only following orders and that you were obeying people higher in a chain of command links directly to Milgram's research on obedience. Cohen's work on the topic of mass murder is one of the few recent examples where a sociologist employs research from psychology to enable a fuller understanding of the issues. In discussing Milgram, Cohen points out the complexity of the experiments Milgram conducted. As already noted, Milgram manipulated the conditions and found varying degrees of obedience. For example, people were less likely to follow orders if they were in the same room as the confederate being given fake electric shocks than if they were separated by a wall. With regard to mass murder, Cohen refers to Kelman and Hamilton's application of the concept *crimes of obedience* (Kelman and Hamilton 1989). Kelman and Hamilton apply this concept to the 1968 My Lai Massacre in Vietnam during which American soldiers killed between 350 and 500 women, children and elderly people after being ordered to wipe out the enemy.[1] The enemy had already left the village.

Crimes of obedience occur in organisations with a hierarchical chain of command. This could be the police, the army or terrorist groups. The event is either criminal or immoral, but tends to be neutralised by the justification of following orders. Consequently, the event is committed by lower ranking individuals. Kelman and Hamilton argue that there are three conditions that need to be met for such events to occur. The first is *authorisation* to commit the act by those higher in the command structure. The morality of the perpetrators is not changed at a general level, only for this particular case. That is, the event is context dependent and when the individual returns to being a civilian they are not likely to do the same again. There does not need to be an ideological or moral justification because someone else has that responsibility. The second is *dehumanisation* of the targets. They are an outgroup lacking in the same human characteristics as oneself, literally a target and not a person. The final condition is *routinisation* where the initial reluctance to kill has been overcome by the first kill. Once the first risky activity has been completed subsequent acts are easier. In the case of murder, the soldier needs to overcome their moral reticence. Once the first person has been killed it becomes harder to stop since that would raise questions over the morality of the first kill.

Cohen argues that Milgram's obedience to authority seems to be devoid of ideological factors. In other words, no justification is made regarding the political necessity of killing people, orders were unthinkingly followed. However, Cohen notes, in contrast to Milgram's more biological evolutionist account, that obedience is not natural. Rather than obedience being a natural response evolved in the human species for the purpose of survival, obedience is a socialised behaviour. It is learned, not instinctive.

2 Conformity

At its most basic level, when this justification is used by delinquents it makes sense and it is something many people will recognise as an excuse they have used. 'Everyone else was doing it, so don't blame me'. When used by soldiers to account for why they raped and killed someone the justification is more troubling. However, as Cohen notes, there is another version of this denial of responsibility that is more chilling still. The argument that if you were there you would do the same is the most disturbing of all. As Cohen says this 'claim is frighteningly plausible' (Cohen 2001: 91).

3 Necessity and self-defence

At the basic level such denial of responsibility is plausible and may be justified. To shoot someone in self-defence because there was a clear threat to one's own life tends to be more easily accepted than the other justifications discussed so far. However, there is another form of this denial which became familiar during the second Gulf War. It was claimed by America and the UK that the president of Iraq had weapons of mass destruction, commonly referred to as WMD. Iraq was required to destroy these weapons and allow inspectors from the UN to check this was being done. This request was turned down and so followed a lengthy diplomatic standoff resulting in an ultimatum. The weapons need to be destroyed or the so-called coalition of the willing would invade Iraq and destroy them itself. The justification for the invasion of Iraq was that Saddam Hussein could use these weapons to destroy our own military and neighbouring countries such as Israel. They could be deployed in as little as 45 minutes. Therefore, the justification for the second Gulf War was necessity and self-defence.

4 Splitting

One of the problems of much early psychological and sociological theories is that they over-determined criminality. By this is meant that the cause of crime was seen as a powerful factor in making people commit crime. It overcame freewill and pushed or pulled them into deviant activities. In psychological accounts, it also meant that such approaches posited a criminal type, a personality predisposed to criminality and therefore relatively stable. As we saw in the last chapter, our identity changes depending upon the situation. In social identity theory, for example, our self-identity changes depending upon how we regard the outgroup. An example of these multiple self-identities can be seen when people engage in atrocities during one part of their life and are then able to switch back to an identity that seems at odds with the earlier one. It has been argued that Nazi doctors were able to split their identities into two distinct selves so that they could dissociate the activity of killing people with lethal injections or performing experiments on death camp inmates from their home life. The idea is that at one moment they are doing morally repugnant crimes, whilst at the next they are tucking up their children in bed. Cohen is not convinced by such theories since it does not take into account the wealth of evidence that there was an ideological reason given for doing these things based on the idea of Jewish impurity.

Denial of injury

The way that young people deny the effect of their crimes on other people is less easily used by those involved in atrocities such as might happen during a war.

'It didn't really hurt' is not a denial that is resorted to easily, although there are occasions where the victims are so ideologically dehumanised as to make such denials plausible. Nazi Germany successfully forged a propaganda war that sought to present the Jewish population as subhuman.

Denial of the victim

In the same way that ideological constructions of otherness leads to denial of injury, so also it leads to denying that there is a victim. This is often the result of excessive and overt patriotism. Essentially, this is akin to social identity theory where the ingroup needs to be made salient and obvious by referring to an outgroup. The ingroup ceases to have an obvious characteristic without a contrasting outgroup. Often, patriotism is created by reference to an enemy. The construction or reawakening of an enemy tends to diminish the sense that the enemy can also be a victim. All of which leads to the denial of victim status and the feeling that 'they get what they deserve'.

Condemnation of the condemners

In contemporary politics this form of denial is very clearly articulated. Osama Bin Laden justifies terrorist attacks by claiming that western democracies are corrupt; Saddam Hussein questioned the legitimacy of the court that sentenced him to death; and the kidnappers and murderers of the British volunteer in Iraq, Kenneth Bigley, released pictures of him in an orange jumpsuit – this was a clear message that the condemners of this murder were hypocrites who held hundreds of people hostage at Guantanamo Bay and made them wear similar orange jumpsuits. Questioning the legitimacy of those who condemn them is a common form of denial.

Appeal to higher loyalties

Hitler's speeches spoke about the 'German people', their bravery and hard work that saw them through the depression of the loss and reconstruction following the First World War. As the economic position of Germany improved, so Hitler created a sense of potential loss of these hard-fought-for gains. Linked to this, Hitler presented a nostalgic picture of the larger German Empire that was broken up after the First World War and the creation of the smaller Weimar Republic. Such an approach positioned Hitler as the champion of the German people, his actions were taken for a German population humiliated after the war. Essentially, Hitler was denying personal responsibility by claiming that Germany needed someone to lead them back to a position they had prior to the First World War, this is the idea of appealing to higher loyalties. We see this kind of justification in wars and terrorism, as well as the group fights of gangs.

Moral indifference

Moral indifference refers to living outside of a moral universe to which those outside of the atrocity belong. Similar to one of Robert K. Merton's modes of adaptation discussed in the last chapter, rebellion, the moral goal that may have been there in the past is replaced with another. An act like the Holocaust does not need to be neutralised since there is nothing to neutralise. Not that it did not happen, but what happened occurred within a universe where it was not wrong. The ideology of Nazi Germany had created a moral universe where it was right that the Jewish inhabitants of Germany should be eradicated. This will be further explored below.

The indifference hypothesis

The indifference hypothesis is another explanation as to why a great many people from one nation engaged in the machinery of genocide. It is not sufficient to explain the psychology of those who shut the doors on the gas chambers or who shot the prisoners standing over the mass grave they dug themselves. What is necessary is a broader understanding of the people who were not directly involved in the moment of death, but who could be said to be complicit through silence and inaction. Moreover, there is a sense in some accounts that the motivation for the genocide was simply a political-legal matter of following orders. This is what Hannah Arendt (1964) called the banality of evil whilst following the trial of a former member of the Nazi Party, Otto Adolf Eichman. Arendt describes the testimony of Eichman when he was involved in the Final Solution to the 'Jewish Problem'.[2] Eichman claims that he was not guilty for his actions because they were not criminal under the laws of Germany at that time. Consequently, Arendt puts across the idea that the motivation was not a deep-seated hatred against Jews, or other outsiders deemed at odds with Nazi ideology. However, Glass has pointed out that the genocide of the Jewish population during the Second World War needed more than indifference from the population to have occurred on the scale that it did. Instead it was 'more than acquiescence, but a willed desire, throughout the population, for the elimination and extermination of persons of the Jewish race' (Glass 1997: 130).

Glass goes on to argue that the German public, in particular the children, were indoctrinated with the idea that Jewish people were an unhygienic intruder. Creating an 'other' based on concepts of disease and illness became widespread to the extent that many in Germany came to accept as fact these ideas. Instead, this ideology lead to a massive sense of 'cooperation and enthusiasm for the elimination' (Glass 1997: 132). This propaganda was widespread in both academic fields such as medicine and psychology with concepts like racial intelligence and racial inferiority, and in popular culture through posters, newspapers and literature. Glass suggests it lead to a phobia of Jewish people because they were thought to spread disease, and that mixing the races would lead to a poisoning of the supposedly superior German race. As noted, this was not confined to the equivalent of the mass media tabloids, but was established scientific orthodoxy. Glass uses his own term *Kultur*-group to refer to the shared set of beliefs that were accepted by a majority of the German population at this time.

It should also be noted that such beliefs were widespread throughout the world. It was also not confined to fascistic far-right politics. Based on social Darwinism and the work of Darwin's own cousin Francis Galton, the Eugenics movement was widespread and held in some regard by many leading politicians from both the left and right of the political spectrum. In Britain, when he was Home Secretary in charge of law and order policies, the future wartime Prime Minister Winston Churchill expressed an interest in Eugenics but was told that it would not be a good election strategy. Churchill was also a sponsoring vice president of the Eugenics society. Other advocates of eugenics were the socialist writers George Bernard Shaw and H.G. Wells, Beatrice and Sydney Webb founders of the socialist Fabian movement, as well as Harold Laski who went on to be the head of the British Labour Party and who had Jewish ancestry (MacKenzie 1976).

The psychology of war is more advanced than that of sociological criminology's discussion of the topic (Jamieson 1998). This is a very strange situation when a discipline that tends to be regarded as one that focuses on the individual is more advanced than sociological criminology when studying such a social, even global, phenomenon. However, as the final chapter of this book will note, we should be cautious of the role played by psychologists in times of war or heightened states of anxiety such as after '9/11'. The creation of research into Intelligence Quotient (IQ) during the First World War, the further enhancement of medical and psychological techniques for differentiating people with abnormalities during the Second World War in Nazi Germany and the interrogation rooms in Guantanamo Bay should serve as a warning that the power of psychology can be misused. Hegarty has powerfully argued that the history of IQ research is also the 'recognition of psychology's indebtedness to past military collaborations for its current position of legitimacy' (2007: 83).

Summary

- This chapter has explored some of the research into a topic that tends to be neglected by sociological criminology, that of mass murder.
- There are several types of mass murder, with the least common being the one that tends to be most frequently publicised in the media – mass murder committed by young people.
- Mass murder during war suggests that many people who may not be directly involved may be complicit in the offence. Others who previously showed no signs of violence may become involved in mass murder.
- Research by Stanley Milgram attempted to explain why ordinary people get involved in extraordinary acts of violence. He suggested that there was an inbuilt, evolved tendency towards obeying authority.
- Stan Cohen used Sykes and Matza's techniques of neutralisation to show how individuals and nations can deny suffering.

STUDY QUESTIONS

1 Discuss what might be done if research suggested that it was possible to predict a school shooting? How reliable would the prediction have to be to make intervention ethically sound?

2 Critically discuss Cohen's question about involvement, either actively or through inaction, in genocide. If you were there, would you do the same thing?

3 Do some research into the second Gulf War and try to find other techniques of neutralisation used by politicians and the Military. How did these change during the course of the war, especially after no WMD were found?

4 Go to the following website that will take you to the British Psychological Society Code of Ethics:

http://www.bps.org.uk/the-society/code-of-conduct/ethical-principles-for-conducting-research-with-human-participants.cfm

Then go to http://www.holah.karoo.net/milgramstudy.htm which will take you to a brief summary of Milgram's study on obedience. To what extent does Milgram's study conform to the ethical codes? Is the potential harm of this study justified by the outcome?

FURTHER READING

There is a small, but growing literature on mass murder in schools and the criminology of war. A good place to start is the following;

Day, L.E. and Vandiver, M. (2000) 'Criminology and genocide studies: notes on what might have been and what still could be', *Crime, Law and Social Change*, 43: 43–59.

Friedrichs, D.O. (2000) 'The crime of the century?: The case for the Holocaust', *Crime, Law and Social Change*, 34: 21–41.

Fritzon, K. and Brun, A. (2005) 'Beyond Columbine: a faceted model of school-associated homicide', *Psychology, Crime and Law*, 11(1): 53–71.

Notes

1 The army did not take a definitive body count leading to the disparity in figures.
2 The First Solution was expulsion from homes and the Second Solution was concentration in camps and towns closed off to outsiders such as the Warsaw ghetto. The Final Solution was genocide.

6

Terrorism: From Pathology to Normality

Chapter Contents

OVERVIEW

This chapter aims to look at the psychological accounts that have been put forward to account for why some people resort to terrorism. Some psychological accounts suggest that terrorism is a form of pathology, echoing early criminological and psychological ideas on the pathology of the criminal. More sophisticated research suggests a more complex causative process. The chapter begins by setting out the historical backdrop to the current focus on the Middle East, arguing that only through this context can a fully social understanding be forged.

KEY TERMS

state crime terrorism 'War on Terror'

This chapter looks at another aspect of mass murder – terrorism. The 'War on Terror', lead by the American administration of George W. Bush after the terrorist attacks of 11 September 2001, has set the political agenda for the beginning of the twenty-first century. After the world-wide consensus of condemnation, the political initiative was squandered after the invasion of Afghanistan failed to capture Osama Bin Laden and the American-led invasion of Iraq widened the conflict in the Middle East to a country that had nothing to do with terrorist attacks on America. Making the peace is the hardest aspect of war, yet it tends to be treated as the least important. The planning for the war in Iraq seemed to take no account of the aftermath, scattering Saddam Hussein's allies and so leaving Iraq with a political vacuum fought for by a variety of factions, not least of whom were the self-styled 'Al Qaeda in Iraq'. But, an understanding of history might have cautioned against such folly. During the World War of 1914–18 one of the many battlefields was the Middle East.

At the time it was a very different geopolitical entity with different country names, Iraq was Mesopotamia for example, and with different political allegiances. Much of the Middle East was part of the Turkish Ottoman Empire during the war. Because Turkey supported Germany, the country became an enemy of the Entente Powers (Russia, France, Britain and later Italy and the United States) and the Middle East, particularly Arabia, became a battle ground. Promises by the Entente Powers that after the war the countries would return to Arab rule formed the backdrop for future problems. The breaking of these promises and the splitting up of the Middle East into spheres of influence separately administered by the Entente Powers lead to resentment that reverberates today. Rather than tracing the terrorist attacks on America to internal psychological traits, the best way to prevent terrorism is to read a history book and try to solve the long-standing animosity that created artificial countries drawn on a map in London and headed by political leaders put in place by their western administrators.

Indeed, we can trace many of the tactics used against the West today from this period, and before. In Iraq, the use of Improvised Explosive Devices, known commonly as IEDs, to blow up military vehicles are no different than the guerrilla tactics of the Arabs, using expertise and training by the British, most famously T.E. Lawrence, or Lawrence of Arabia, during the 1914–18 war. Then, Lawrence and the Arab tribes enacted a revolt against the Turkish rulers and used explosives laid near the railway line to move personnel and equipment. The explosives were set off as a train passed and the Arabs moved off to another site undetected due to their small numbers and ease of movement across the desert on camels and horses. The Turkish army by contrast needed the railway for its equipment. Exactly the same technique is being used against coalition forces in Iraq by those who see them as invaders. A case of history repeating itself. There are, of course, many terrorist techniques. This alone should caution against some of the more deterministic psychological approaches that seek to find one cause for terrorism in the individual. Setting an IED near the roadside to blow up an armoured truck is a very different technique from someone walking into a queue of men waiting to join the police and exploding a bomb attached to their chest. The outcome of each violent episode is clearly very different for the perpetrators and the emotions involved equally diverse enough to suggest a different causative process. This chapter will explore the psychological explanations for terrorism.

The battle over the definition of terrorism

We must remember that who we define as the enemy is a matter of which side you are on. This is one of the fundamental problems in the definition of terrorism. It has come to mean almost any form of violence (Victoroff 2005). Essentially, terrorism is violence that is not validated by those who govern. Victoroff reviewed the literature on terrorism in a variety of psychological and sociological academic databases ranging from 1887 to 2003 and found 109 academic definitions for terrorism. However, he notes that there are two main points that are common to many of these accounts: '(1) that terrorism involves aggression against non-combatants and (2) that the terrorist action in itself is not expected by its perpetrator to accomplish a political goal but instead to influence a target audience and change that audience's behaviour in a way that will serve the interests of the terrorist' (Victoroff 2005: 4; see also Badey 1998; Lacquer 1999).

The problem with this definition is that it posits an outcome from the violence: to change the way an audience behaves. But, some violence is carried out to maintain ingroup solidarity, to be one of the group. Or, the act may have a minor goal of vengeance or further recruitment. How the audience's behaviour changes may have no consequence except in that they died (Freedman 2007). Similarly, an audience's behaviour can only change if the terrorist group takes responsibility. As Post argues in the late 1980s and early 1990s, for nearly 40 per cent of terrorist acts no responsibility was taken. For example, when committed by Islamic fundamentalists, no recognition was sought – they were killing for God – and so the only entity that needed to know was God (Post 2005). If we define terrorism with relation to the dominant word in the term, namely terror, then we could argue for an inclusive approach that seeks to understand those cases where the main point is to cause political change by using terror against civilians. Such a definition moves away from the moral problem of determining whether or not a group has a 'just' cause and does include those elements of 'legitimate' military activity where civilians are targeted alongside military or other strategic targets. For example, the so-called 'shock and awe' tactics during the second Gulf War designed to intimidate military and civilian alike. This is an example of the complexity of the real world and the need to draw from many other sources outside of one's own specialism.

Psychology, religion and terrorism

Religious fundamentalism is often associated with Islam. However, the Christian Republicanism of George Bush Jr's American Presidency has also been compared to fundamentalism. Richard Dawkins even called them the American Taliban (Dawkins 2006). Nevertheless, most commentators regard religious fundamentalism as a disruptive and potentially dangerous ideology:

> From a psychological perspective, the significant feature of 'taking religion seriously' is that it implies not just consistency in one's belief(s), but also in *behaviour*. A quality of the fundamentalist believer is, therefore, the expression of the particular fundamentalist priorities in behaviour of some form. (Taylor and Horgan 2001: 37; emphasis in original)

Many people regard Islamic fundamentalism as a negative retreat to a more conservative and illiberal form of social and moral organisation. Taylor and Horgan note, however, that this may not be the correct way to characterise this ideology. Rather, it should be seen as a renewal of a former system that has been eroded. It is a progress *to* Islam, not a retreat *from* secularism. Moreover, many commentators struggle to understand the psychological and behavioural factors associated with the rise of Islamic fundamentalism. This seeming complexity is in contrast to the explanation by the fundamentalists themselves, that it is the word of Allah.

Behaviourism, rule-following and terrorism

One psychological approach that has been applied to religion is behaviourism. This explanation is one that posits a set of rules that needs to be followed if the outcome is to be achieved or avoided. Called behavioural contingencies, a rule sets out what a person can expect if they behave in a certain way. The outcome can be positive or negative. Non-fundamentalists follow a complex set of rules, whose outcome or contingency is not so easily attained. The religious fundamentalist, in contrast, follows a relatively simple set of rules. The contingencies are straightforward. This is especially the case with regard to Islam. The rules known as *Shari'ah* govern all aspects of behaviour. The following of these rules constitutes being a Muslim. They are, therefore, a very powerful set of rules, with a very negative contingency for failing to follow them. Similarly for the fundamentalist Islamist the Islamic world order is under attack by plotters intent on overthrowing Islam. This logic is the only way a believer can explain why their devotion to the practices of the religion have gone unrewarded. If you follow the rules and the outcome is bad then rather than question the belief system a conspiracy theory is developed instead.

These rule-based behavioural psychologies are not just an explanation for religious membership, but can also explain other behaviour such as being involved in politics. However, the problem with the rule-following idea is that it does not explain motivation to follow the rules. Many people smoke despite the rule that smoking is detrimental to health. Moreover, why is one rule followed whilst another, perhaps equally compelling rule, is ignored. This is a highly deterministic account that does not do justice to real world situations. Other psychological principles are also ignored. Although some mention of authority is made, Milgram's research on obedience is ignored. Similarly ignored is peer pressure and social influence such as that in social identity theory. Subcultural theory can be employed to explain the attraction to belonging to a group. Also, the extent to which we follow religious rules is also linked to upbringing. Firstly, in the choice of religion, secondly in the extent to which the rules are accepted; the degree of fundamentalism. Of course, many people are brought up in families that are religious and do not follow that religion, or who become religious later despite a secular upbringing. More fundamental issues pertinent to humans could also explain religiosity. Religions purport to answer questions about one of the unique features of being human. Humans are unique due to our knowing about our own mortality. Knowledge that we will die raises deep psychological anxiety in many people. The comforting story that there is life after death is a powerful one.

Terrorism as a syndrome or tool

Psychological accounts tend to take one of two general approaches, although combinations can be found: a top-down approach that seeks to find cause in social factors such a politics, history and economics; and a bottom-up approach that looks at why certain individuals or groups turn to terrorism (Victoroff 2005). Another way to look at the psychology of terrorism has been put forward by Kruglanski and Fishman (2006). These academics split the various approaches to terrorism into two distinct types – the 'Syndrome' and 'Tool' perspectives. The former tends to be more psychological and the latter more sociological, where the emphasis is on the intention of a terrorist act. The following concentrates on the approaches that see terrorism as a syndrome.

Syndrome: the terrorist personality

The 'Syndrome' perspective draws together a variety of psychological theories, all of which see terrorism as akin to a pathology. Essentially, these approaches are variations on individual **positivism**. The first area to fall under this category is the idea that there is a distinct terrorist personality that distinguishes them from non-terrorists. The most commonly cited personality trait is psychopathy. In reviews of this literature, both Andrew Silke (1998, 2003) and John Horgan (2003a, 2003b), both well-known for their work in this field, argue that despite the extensive number of studies none of them have been able to demonstrate a difference in the terrorist personality. In addition, there are many different types of terrorist and terrorist techniques (Victoroff 2005).

One of the main problems in the study of terrorist personality traits is that few terrorists wish to fill out a personality questionnaire. However, there has been one study that sought to do just this. The Red Army Faction, formerly the Baader-Meinhof Gang, a prominent post-Second World War German terrorist organisation were studied in some detail by researchers (McCauley 2002). Using a control group that closely matched each gang member, a series of records were examined (such as school and university records) and friends and family were interviewed. The researchers concluded that there were no differences in personality between the gang and the control subjects. Moreover, many were well-educated and originally had tried peaceful means to reach their goal of getting American nuclear weapons out of Europe. It was also noted that many members of the gang had willingly died for the cause. A certain amount of collective responsibility and sympathy for the cause is needed to give up your life for the furtherance of a belief. As McCauley notes, this is not in accord with any research into a psychopathic personality.

Indeed, the collective organisation and cooperation needed to carry out the 11 September 2001 attacks on America is diametrically opposed to the usual descriptions of psychopathic personalities found in the current Diagnostic and Statistical Manual (DSM IV-TR) for mental disorders. However, research into psychopathic personalities has also criticised the often stereotypical idea that all psychopaths are necessarily engaged in criminal activity or under psychiatric supervision. What this means is that psychopathy may be a personality trait that could be exhibited by someone who works in business, politics or the arts. In other words, psychopathic personalities may be present in every profession in much the same way that any of the other personality traits might be. In research by Forth and Hare (1989), they discovered that people with psychopathic personalities exhibited a greater ability to focus on a goal and ignore other stimuli that might inhibit their quest to reach that goal. There is also evidence of a thrill-seeking aspect to the psychopathic personality. This set of factors may describe someone in business seeking a goal of greater wealth by ignoring the impact of their quest on family, friends and their business rivals, or the world economy. It might also describe the leader of a terrorist group charismatic enough to convince others of the moral superiority of a suicide attack. However, this might only account for the leaders of a group. Theories of terrorist psychopathy, and more general pathological causes, fail to realise the many and varied humans that are involved in terrorist actions such as those on 11 September 2001. Just as early subcultural theory posited a unified gang who all shared a similar outlook and so negated individual difference, so the same is true of these theories of terrorist pathology. The point is not that research into the lack of a psychopathic cause of terrorism is wrong, but that the search for any singular cause is liable to miss those who do not share that cause.

One study that also showed the problem with the static determinism of personality theories was one by Echebarria-Echabe and Fernández-Guede (2006). This study looked at the attitudes of Spanish respondents to Arab and Jewish people before and after the Madrid bomb attacks on 11 March 2004. The study showed that attitudes changed after the bomb attacks. Some of this change was hypothesised and confirmed such as a move towards a more anti-Arab and anti-Jew prejudice, greater authoritarianism, an increase in Conservative values and a reduction in measures of Liberal values. The anti-Semitism demonstrates a general mistrust of outsiders since there was no evidence of any Jewish involvement in the Madrid attacks. Authoritarianism is traditionally seen in the work of Theodore Adorno and colleagues (1950/1982) as a stable personality trait across the lifespan. However, this study demonstrated that such attitudes can change and should perhaps be seen as ideological resources that are employed to cope with collective and personal anxiety. A further finding from this study is that despite a shift to a more conservative attitude this was not reflected in voting behaviour. The Madrid bombs took place four days before a general election but the Conservative Spanish government were voted out of office. Aware that the majority of the population were critical of the government's deployment of troops in Iraq and the effect the bombs would have on their re-election, the government suggested that the bombings were caused by the Basque separatist movement, ETA. Yet many commentators were suggesting that the cause was Islamic fundamentalists and many in Spain had accepted this. Clearly, just because a person's attitude shifts towards one political position does not mean that they will act out that attitude in an election, a form of national cognitive dissonance (Festinger 1957). Other factors thought to be associated with terrorism, or support for terrorism are an increased interest in one's own death, called Mortality Salience, and right-wing authoritarianism. However, these personality traits were also predictive of support for anti-terrorist military interventions. Consequently, what this suggests is that such traits only predict the use of force to deal with problems and that the political context determines against whom that force should be directed.

Other possible contributory factors that fall within the category of 'Syndrome' explanations are collectivism, sensation-seeking, cognitive styles and group dynamic.

- *Collectivist attitudes* towards political change, as opposed to individualist attitudes, have been linked to a greater motivation towards using force against outsiders (Post, Sprinzak and Denny 2003). This is similar to Runciman's concept of fraternal and egoistic relative deprivation, discussed in Chapter 4.
- The idea that terrorists might be *sensation seekers* is limited since it does not explain why terrorism is chosen rather than an extreme sport, for example. This idea is similar to that suggested by the cultural criminologist Mark Hamm that terrorists seek celebrity and find the act of terrorism seductive (2004).

- *Cognitive styles*, or the way people think, may be linked to motivation towards terrorism since there tends to be the creation of conspiracies in many terrorist groups. The attribution of malicious intent towards the dominant majority may be seen as a cognitive error. Similarly, thinking in terms of binary oppositions, such as good and evil, and assigning negative attributes to outgroups is common in all terrorist agendas. The reduction of complexity, however, is a common and necessary human practice and is undertaken by everyone every day. For example, a stereotype is a form of cognitive shorthand that speeds up thinking and allows decisions to be made more rapidly (Oakes et al. 1994). Consequently, it cannot be said to be a necessary condition of terrorism since it is common to all people.
- Research into the *group dynamics* of terrorist groups has not shown any consistent correlation. Different groups are organised differently. Taking Al Qaeda as an example, it is difficult to call this a distinct group. It is more akin to a political ideology followed by various groups. Many such groups may never have met the main figure Osama Bin Laden. Other groups are structured around a leader or are organised along military lines, the latter indicative of the IRA.

The problem with the search for causes such as these are that they over-predict the behaviour they seek to explain. Whatever cause is posited, many more people live under those conditions than go on to act out the behaviour such factors are thought to cause. The idea that there is a terrorist personality distinct from a non-terrorist personality is not borne out by the evidence. In many ways, this should not be surprising to those who read the previous chapter where the work of Stanley Cohen and Hannah Arendt was discussed. Many people can be pulled into conflict. The speed with which the former country of Yugoslavia collapsed into a civil war should remind us of the shockingly quick way that people can turn on each other and engage in extreme violence like mass murder.

Social syndrome as a cause of terrorism?

So, if personality is not a cause of terrorism, an alternative might be other root causes. One such cause might be poverty. However, there is no evidence that there are a disproportionate number of terrorists from poor and deprived backgrounds. Echoing arguments by the left realists, discussed in Chapter 4, there seems to be very little evidence to support the hypothesis that absolute poverty and associated social exclusions is a good predictor of terrorism. In a study by Robert Pape (2005) into suicide bombers, he found that only 17 per cent were either unemployed or from the lowest social class. Victoroff, in his review of the literature, found that many studies of terrorists revealed them to be aged between 23.2 and 31.3 and from middle-class backgrounds with some college education (2005). However, the demographic picture has changed over time and there are indications that more women are being recruited as suicide bombers.

It is also questionable that terrorists originate from politically repressed countries. The 7 July 2005 tube bombings in London and the failed attempt a fortnight later were committed by men from backgrounds that were not poor and they were not obviously repressed. Similarly, the argument that terrorists may be uneducated is also not borne out by the evidence. In research by Sageman (2004) the majority of his respondents had finished college, with 20 per cent having a doctoral degree. The failed bombings at Glasgow airport and in London were committed by terrorists who worked or trained as doctors; the leader of the 7 July tube bombs, Mohammad Sidique Kahn, was a teaching assistant.

In one study by Piazza (2006) it is suggested that absolute and relative deprivation has little effect on terrorist violence, and that 'social cleavage' may be to blame. Social cleavage is a political system with many small parties who represent special interest groups rather than a few larger parties that speak to a diverse constituency as in Britain. For example, the Labour, Conservative and Liberal Democrats all want to be inclusive of a wide range of different people, albeit with different core groups. However, this study has several methodological problems that detract from its findings. In demonstrating that countries with high levels of terrorist violence can also be either highly developed or mid-range economies (as opposed to being poor as the 'poverty causes terrorism' hypothesis would predict), Piazza does not take into account terrorists that might be acting on behalf of the deprivation of another country, such as Islamic Jihadists or the IRA, both of whom have attacked outside of the country that they feel is deprived. So looking at the target country does not tell us anything about the problems for which the terrorists are trying to gain recognition. The 11 September attacks are a case in point where the target country is the richest in the world, the purported reason for the attack is American Imperialism in Middle Eastern countries. In this case, terrorists from outside America were involved. In the case of the 7 July London bombings, the terrorists were from Britain but acting on behalf of those who were killed, injured or impoverished by attacks by Britain and its allies in places like Afghanistan and Iraq. Perhaps this suggests another important aspect of terrorism that makes the 'poverty causes terror' hypothesis more complex – you do not have to be impoverished yourself to fight against poverty. The legend of Robin Hood is a case in point, and the type of analysis carried out by social scientists like Piazza are rendered meaningless if this is not taken into account.

Since absolute poverty is not easily linked with terrorism, then perhaps relative poverty or deprivation is causing frustration and aggression. As noted in Chapter 4, relative deprivation has been put forward by T.R. Gurr (1970) as an explanation for why groups rebel. Terrorism is committed by marginalised groups and targeted at the majority so *does* conform to the idea of a rebellion. However, the idea that relative deprivation is the cause of all terrorism is too narrow and cannot explain the varied forms that terrorism takes. Yet, this is precisely the explanations given by politicians such as President George W. Bush shortly after the 11 September attacks. The attacks were described as an attack on the democratic way of life of the American people, an attack on freedom. Moreover, this is often expressed as hate towards the democratic way of life (Maikovich 2005). Hate is certainly a plausible explanation for terrorism, however, many of those who engage in terrorism have hitherto enjoyed seemingly positive relations with their future enemy. Osama Bin Laden was originally supported by training from the Americans when he was a member of the Mujahideen (freedom fighters resisting the Russian occupation of Afghanistan). However, Kruglanski and Fishman (2006) argue that these factors do not satisfy the criteria of being a necessary cause of terrorism, and in many cases do not reach the level of a sufficient cause, but they argue that these issues may be contributing factors.

Terrorism as gradual drift to violence

Maikovich (2005) has employed Festinger's Cognitive Dissonance theory (1957) to explain how terrorism develops slowly over time. Festinger posited that when two sources of information (cognitions) were in opposition in the same person (dissonance), that person will feel distress or discomfort and will need to find a way to relieve it. An example might be that eating fatty foods to excess will lead to weight gain and ill health. Three ways to reduce this discomfort were presented. The first is to remove dissonant feelings (avoid fatty food), the second to add consonant cognitions (increased exercise improves health), and the third is to reduce the importance of dissonant cognitions (everyone else eats fatty foods so it cannot be that harmful). Later, a fourth option was added by other researchers, which was to increase the importance of consonant cognitions (the more I exercise the healthier I am, so fatty foods are OK to eat) (Harmon-Jones and Mills 1999, cited in Maikovich 2005). Maikovich uses this to explain why the majority of terrorist groups do not appear as a fully functioning organisation willing to use violence. Instead, they develop over time, often starting out as non-violent protest groups. As groups become more involved in violence, Maikovich suggests that initial feelings of ambivalence to the use of violence need to be overcome. Ambivalence, or contradictory feelings towards some action, is exactly the feeling of cognitive dissonance that Festinger described. It is the inability to tolerate uncertainty in the world that marks out someone who needs to reduce dissonance. Dissonance can be reduced by reference to five commonly used attributes that act as justifications for terrorists to overcome their feelings of dissonance at the use of violence.

Just world bias

This is the idea that people deserve their fates. In a just world, if someone dies then they must have deserved this fate. This fate is deserved because of something they have done, or something their governments have done. The idea was one put forward by Lerner in 1980, but we can see how many actions by western countries have fed this belief amongst terrorist groups in recent years. The 'shock and awe' of the early part of the second Gulf War, the lack of any weapons of mass destruction that were the original justification for the War, Guantanamo Bay and the Abu Ghraib scandal where American soldiers humiliated the prisoners, and the various anti-terror laws that many Muslims feel are directed at them, have all contributed to a sense that any terrorist attacks against western countries and the deaths of many people are justified because it is deserved. A just world bias is a very common attribute of terrorists and which must prove a very powerful weapon against dissonant feelings.

Social support

Another measure to reduce dissonance is the strong social support reported for many terrorists both within an organisation and through family, friends and political support. Bandura (2000: 141) has argued that there is a 'worldwide network of people, including reputable, high-level members of society, who contribute to the deathly enterprise by insulating' those involved from responsibility. Social and political support was provided by the political party Sinn Fein for the IRA, and in the Middle East, Palestinian terrorism is supported by Hamas. The Americans and British governments have both suggested that Iran is supporting terrorism in Iraq.

Prioritising dream imagery over external reality

This is the idea that terrorists use dreams as a way to justify their actions. Maikovich (2005) notes that Osama Bin Laden had dreams that he used to justify his terrorist acts, as did Mullah Omar, the leader of the Taliban in Afghanistan in 1994.

Diffusion of responsibility and moral disengagement

Both diffusion of responsibility and moral disengagement are very similar to the techniques of neutralisation thesis of Cohen and Matza and used by Cohen to explain mass murder, discussed in the previous chapter. Terrorists find it easier to commit acts that kill people if a legitimate authority takes the responsibility for the actions. In Cohen's use of Sykes and Matza, this is an appeal to higher loyalties. Moral disengagement is the way that terrorists use intermediaries to provide them with the materials for terrorism allowing them to disengage from the ultimate act of killing. Of course, this is only applicable to those higher up the hierarchy who do not carry out the final act.

Of course, this argument is problematic since it suggests that terrorists are better able to reduce dissonance to enable them to commit acts of terrorism. This is achieved because terrorists tend to be less able to cope with uncertainty or dissonance, so seek ways to reduce uncertainty. But, how do we know that terrorists are more resistant to uncertainty than those not engaged in terrorism? This might also lead us back into the terrorist personality where the terrorist is more likely to be anxious, conservative or in need of reassurance. However, the gradualism of becoming a terrorist is in line with other research into acts of violence. In a series of interviews with a professional hit man, Levi noted that initial acts of murder were difficult emotionally and needed to be overcome before the hit man became accomplished (Levi 1981). What such research suggests is that doing violence is not the outcome of a pathology, but in many cases a process of desensitisation. In many ways, this shares the common feeling that most people feel throughout their lives. When we start a new job, or first go to a new school or university we might feel anxious but, over time, for the majority, this anxiety subsides. Of course, shooting someone and attending a new university are about as different as can be, yet the function of a gradual desensitisation is similar.

Nevertheless, it is perhaps possible to see in this a series of techniques that might be used to prevent the breaking down of dissonance. Engaging with terrorist groups and their supporters rather than always employing a military 'solution' would reduce the evidence for the 'just world bias'. It is perhaps no surprise that there have been no terror attacks by Jihadists on France or Russia, two countries that criticised the war on Iraq. Such approaches might help to reduce the 'social support' afforded to terrorists. However, many politicians suggest that such engagement is wrong. Engagement with someone who cold-bloodedly murdered someone in the street would not be engaged with in open dialogue to reach some form of agreement. Despite this, engagement in Northern Ireland with the IRA and Sinn Fein has led to the political terrorism ceasing and the emergence of a new politics. So, perhaps, it is the manner in which such discussions are conducted that matters. It is difficult to counter the use of dream imagery to justify terrorism. However, with religious fundamentalism, there is a need for those with more liberal religious attitudes to make themselves heard and the media has a role to play in this since many news outlets would prefer to present the latest video by Osama Bin Laden and the quest for the CIA to authenticate it than interview a Muslim cleric denouncing violence. The final two methods to reduce dissonance might be countered if influential people pointed out that the hierarchical structure is designed to protect the preachers of terrorism and the planners and organisers at the expense of the young and impressionable.

Taylor and Horgan (2006) have also put forward an argument that the route into terrorism should be seen as a process involving various choices to continue or desist from involvement. They use an approach called Rational Choice theory, originally developed by Cornish and Clarke (1986), and then combine it with an American idea called Routine Activities theory proposed by Marcus Felson (see for example Felson 1998). These theories became central to governmental responses to crime from the 1980s and they still form the basis of crime prevention strategies. The theory begins with the criminal as a rational calculator, able to conduct a means–end analysis to calculate whether or not committing a crime, perhaps stealing a wallet, is worth the potential downside (being caught and/or injured by members of the public, or being caught on CCTV cameras and captured later). The criminal essentially asks the question, 'is this worth it?' The criminal actor makes choices about whether or not to commit a crime based on the opportunities available to them. In order to prevent crime, it is necessary to lessen the opportunities and raise the likelihood of being caught. Such ideas are central to the proliferation of CCTV in the UK, and can be seen realised in adverts reminding people not to leave mobile phones unattended and to be wary of leaving their drinks in pubs or clubs in case they are spiked. Reduce the opportunity and the crime will be prevented.

The problem with these accounts is that they produce a criminal actor that is far more rational than the empirical evidence tends to suggest, and ignore the causes of criminal behaviour. If the idea that criminals make rational choices when choosing to steal a bag is problematic then the same is true of terrorists choosing to explode a bomb. The goal of the thief is immediate free money. The goal of many acts of terrorism is so unlikely to occur that any claims to rationality are rendered questionable (Crenshaw 2000). They also ignore factors that can influence choices. Although Taylor and Horgan refer to events that provide the setting for behaviour, such as socialisation, family, early experiences and culture, there is little discussion of more direct forms of persuasion by peers and charismatic mentors. They state that these setting events happen in the past, are unchangeable and form the basis of an individual's socialisation. This account is very individualistic and says very little about the effect of the political indoctrination and the qualities of those who do the indoctrination. For example, there are many examples of social systems that exhibit many of the stated grievances of terrorist groups. The repressive military Junta of Burma, or Zimbabwe under General Robert Mugabe, can both be seen as unjust and violently repressive, but neither has yet seen terrorism or freedom fighters mobilised to attempt an overthrow. In terms of religion, Islamic fundamentalism's desire for a restored Muslim Caliphate, in its extreme form the overthrow of all other religions around the world, can be compared to the Christian crusades against the Muslim world between the eleventh and thirteenth centuries. Consequently, the struggle for power is not specific to any one religion, and the struggle against injustice does not always lead to terrorism. So, although it is necessary to understand why some people become involved in terrorism and others do not, so it is also necessary to understand why terrorism arises in some places and not in others. Consequently, it is possible that the qualities of individual leaders is a more important focus than individual terrorists (Crenshaw 2000).

Terrorists as celebrities

Although not all terrorists claim responsibility for their actions, it is clear that a significant number of terrorist incidents are designed to affect an audience. For those involved, it has been argued they are craving a form of celebrity, in a similar way to that of serial killers:

> For the ARA (Aryan Republican Army) and Timothy McVeigh (the Oklahoma Bomber), this insatiable need to be famous was, in fact, so strong that it outweighed every other motivational factor. It trumped their ideology, their purpose and their mission. (Hamm 2004: 337)

Terrorism is seductive in the same way that other crimes might be seductive (Katz 1988).

The righteous anger of the terrorist is a powerful emotion that propels them into violence. Terrorists often see themselves as freedom fighters; in Islamic fundamentalism they are treated as Martyrs who died in the cause of their religion and so died for their God. The evolutionary theorist and critic of religion Richard Dawkins has argued that the search for causes to suicide bombings need go no further than to just listen to what they say. When people say they will go directly to paradise and be waited upon by nubile virgins, this is what they believe (Dawkins 2006). One social psychologist uses an interesting phrase that sums this up when she refers to the 'theatrical violence' of terrorism (Maikovich 2005). This can be linked to the definition of terrorism as put forward by the American government, where terrorism means 'premeditated, politically motivated violence perpetuated against non-combatant targets by sub national groups or clandestine agents, usually intended to influence an audience' (US Department of State 2001: 17, cited in Piazza 2006: 165).

Terrorism is an act designed for an audience to witness, in this sense it is a performance (see for example Goffman 1959). The more spectacular, the bigger the audience. The 11 September attacks on America were discussed in cinematic terms; for example, the collapsing World Trade Center, for so long the backdrop for television and film, was compared to a cinematic special effect. Comic book superheroes seemed redundant, their worth as escapism severely limited in the aftermath of such tragedy. Specially written and illustrated comics appeared which showed characters like Spiderman and Superman standing in solidarity alongside firemen and policemen. A similar juxtaposition of fantasy and reality occurred during the Second World War when children wondered why Superman did not just beat up the Nazis. Instead, the comic book writers made the decision to only show the character in a secondary role to the military, who were depicted as the real superheroes.

There has been a blurring of the boundaries between war, terrorism and fiction such that reality tends to be viewed through the lens of what the public understands, fictional representations in cinema and television. The so-called 'shock and awe' bombing campaign that began the invasion of Iraq in the second phase of the Gulf War was intended to be a visual representation of what the American-led invasion was capable of, to scare the Iraqi military into abandoning their allegiance to Saddam Hussein. Even the Iraqi regime's spokesperson, Mohammed Saeed al-Sahhaf, nicknamed 'Comical Ali'[1], became a minor celebrity when he passionately exclaimed that the American military were being slaughtered by the Iraqi Army and that they were nowhere near Baghdad as American tanks were patrolling the streets of Baghdad within sight of the press conference.

Terrorism and the media

The greater accessibility of the Internet has allowed those previously denied access to the media a platform to promote their ideas largely unregulated by agencies of the state. In Iraq, dissident groups such as Al Qaeda have used information technologies for political purposes. Perhaps the most shocking example of this was the kidnap and murder of the British man Kenneth Bigley. Shown wearing an orange jumpsuit, Bigley was used for propaganda and his clothing a clear symbol of the group's grievance with the American prison camp at Guantanamo Bay. Bigley was beheaded and his murder filmed and then posted on a website. The furore this caused was in stark contrast to the similar case of Margaret Hassan. This case was followed by the media, but not to the same extent as Kenneth Bigley. Perhaps this was a case of sympathy fatigue or a deliberate attempt to starve the terrorists of publicity by not showing as much about the case, or the lack of coverage was to do with the fact that Hassan had married an Iraqi and lived in the country. It is likely that a combination of factors contributed to this. What is clear is that the fight for control of a story, and of the manner of defining an incident by using the media, has become central to both terrorists and those seeking to control it. Furthermore, what we define as terrorism, and what is left out of the definition, fundamentally affects the role that psychology can have in understanding the phenomenon. But, this leads to another aspect of the explanations for terrorism, the power of propaganda to manipulate impressionable people into joining terrorist groups. The next section deals with this.

Propaganda, peer pressure and naivety

Many studies give little attention to the role of mentors, teachers and preachers in the formation of the terrorist. Although the individual's social environment, such as their sense of history or politics, might be important, as Taylor and Horgan maintain (2006), many more people grow up within such an environment than ever go on to become involved in terrorism. Indeed, one of the common factors with the recent spate of Jihadist attacks is that the family of those involved express disbelief that their relative could be involved. As also noted above, the idea of the pathological terrorist does not withstand scrutiny, many of those involved appeared perfectly well socialised and well educated. However, it is very easy to manipulate people into believing a story when no alternatives are provided. In the previous chapter, Stanley Milgram's study of obedience is a case in point that explains the worrying ease with which generally high functioning people can be manipulated into committing terrifying acts of violence against people they do not know. Many terrorist training camps seem to provide training for a variety of scenarios. The most common images are akin to weapons training in the military with men being drilled to use guns. But, as yet, few terrorist attacks outside of the Middle East, India or Pakistan have used guns. The preference is either a bomb, or in the case of 11 September, a proxy for a bomb in the use of a passenger plane. This anomaly is perhaps one that needs addressing because it suggests that with this form of Islamic fundamentalism the training is designed for open warfare. The attack on Mumbai in 2008 was perhaps the outcome of such training and a reminder of the ability of terrorist groups to adapt to policing strategies aimed at dealing with them.

The writing of Max Weber provides an interesting basis for this discussion as he discussed what he thought were the three main forms that authority can take. In the following quotation from Weber it is possible to see how each might be working in combination in Islamic fundamentalism, with Sharia law, the traditions of Islam and the charisma of some preachers combining to form a very powerful form of domination and influence in a context where all of this is seen as under threat from non-believers.

> There are three pure types of legitimate domination. The validity of the claims to legitimacy may be based on:
>
> 1 Rational grounds – resting on a belief in the legality of enacted rules and the rights of those elevated to authority under such rules to issue commands (legal authority)
> 2 Traditional grounds – resting on an established belief in the sanctity of immemorial traditions and the legitimacy of those exercising authority under them (traditional authority); or finally,
> 3 Charismatic grounds – resting on devotion to the exceptional sanctity, heroism or exemplary character of an individual person, and of the normative patterns or order revealed or ordained by him (charismatic authority).
>
> (Weber 1920, in Roth and Wittich 1978: 215)

Very little research has been conducted on this area with regard to terrorism and the role of charismatic leaders. This may be because of a debate in history which has moved away from focusing on the power of influential figures towards a more holistic account that includes wider social factors. Nevertheless, it would make an interesting contribution. One approach that does take this into account is outlined below.

Can dictators and terrorists be profiled?

Victoroff has provided a profile of terrorists based on his review of the literature. But, rather than being one that could be regarded as the finished tool, it should instead be seen as a hypothesis for further testing. After stating that terrorists are heterogeneous, four typical characteristics are presented.

> a High affective valence regarding an ideological issue.
> b A personal stake – such as strongly perceived oppression, humiliation, or persecution; an extraordinary need for identity, glory, or vengeance; or a drive for expression of intrinsic aggressivity – that distinguishes him or her from the vast majority of those who fulfil characteristic a.
> c Low cognitive flexibility, low tolerance for ambiguity, and elevated tendency toward attribution error.
> d A capacity to suppress both instinctive and learned moral constraints against harming innocents, whether due to intrinsic or acquired factors, individual or group forces – probably influenced by a, b, and c. (Victoroff 2005: 35)

The first characteristic essentially means that terrorists have a high emotional attraction to a social, religious or political idea. But what this profile does not include is suggestibility such as demonstrated by Milgram. However, Victoroff does suggest that involvement in terrorism might have more to do with the charisma of a leader. Other forms of profiling routinely used since the terror attacks on America is that of potential suicide bombers. This is a contentious issue that has done much to damage relations between Muslims and non-Muslims as people perceived as Muslim are increasingly suspected of being risky. Lester, Yang and Lindsay (2004) maintain that it is possible to profile suicide bombers and that contrary to much of the research already cited in this chapter, suicide bombers may share a similar personality. They argue that the two main assertions regarding suicide bombers may be wrong. It is generally argued that suicide bombers do not have the same characteristics as suicidal people and that profiles are not possible. This is challenged by Lester et al. who maintain that too few studies have actually looked at the backgrounds of terrorists in the same way that FBI profilers, for example, look at the background of serial murderers. They refer to one of the few studies where this has been carried out, the American terrorist Timothy McVeigh who bombed the federal building in Oklahoma in 1995 killing 168 people. McVeigh's biography suggests he was a man who hated women and this hatred developed to encompass all people including children. Lester et al. argue that he had been taught not to trust anyone and not to get close to people. Men characterised as a women-hater tend to be bachelors, have military backgrounds, enjoy male-centric sport activities such as hunting and see women as the weaker sex. All of which is interesting if it were not for the fact that such a profile is useless since firstly many men have similar backgrounds but do not proceed to detonate bombs, and secondly knowing this profile would not help the police pick up someone like McVeigh because these thoughts are internal and cannot be 'seen' by the police. Picking up every man who hunts and was in the military would infringe many innocent men's civil liberties. As noted in Chapter 2, profiles such as these can send the police in the wrong direction and waste time. Lester et al. also argue that interviewing terrorists is not sufficient to understand their motivations; only by looking at the childrearing practices can one hope to provide a profile. To what end such an insight should be put is not explained.

In an intriguing coincidence of timing an article that seeks to use psychological profiling to explore whether or not Saddam Hussein had weapons of mass destruction (WMD) was published a month before the US-led invasion of Iraq on 20 March 2003. Using content analysis of Hussein's speeches Shaw (2003) puts forward a profile of the Iraqi leader in the run up to the invasion. Crucially, Shaw argues that his research supported 'the conclusion that acquisition and continued possession of WMD remained a high priority for Iraq ... during Hussein's rule' (2003: 353). However, the study also suggests that Hussein probably overestimated his WMD resources and their capabilities in defeating an enemy, but that the likelihood was high that any WMD he had would be used. It is noted that the failure to use WMD as the invasion began may be due to his orders not being obeyed, or he overestimated his ability to use these weapons. Shaw notes that an explanation for why they were not used 'awaits further post-war investigation' (2003: 362). Of course, no WMD have been found. The war was fought on the basis that Hussein would not allow his weapons to be inspected and this was taken as a sign that he wanted to hide his capabilities, which could be used against coalition troops or his neighbours, such as Israel. No one seemed to consider the possibility that Saddam Hussein's delaying tactics were designed to make his enemies *think* he had WMD when he did not possess any. This is a clear illustration of the problems with profiling, especially the false conclusions that can be drawn from data. Such conclusions can send the police along the wrong lines of enquiry in a murder case, or contribute to the justification for war.

Suicide for political advantage

Silke has argued that only recently has suicide been seen as a response to an illness such as depression (2006). Before the 1960s suicide was considered to be a rational response to certain situations; afterwards it was regarded as a pathological condition that deviated from a normal response to stress or frustration. In other words, there was nothing positive or logical about it. When combined with terrorism the pathological quality of many studies of suicide are joined by those that regard terrorists as mentally ill. Whereas many studies have now demonstrated that the 'terrorist as mad' approach has little evidence in its favour, few studies in psychology and psychiatry have managed to concede that suicide could be anything other than a deviant response without advantage. However, as Silke points out, suicide has often been used as an effective means to gain political advantage where other methods have failed. Moreover, a historical imagination is necessary to remember that the current use of suicide terrorism is not a new phenomenon but has been used throughout history. For example, Japanese Kamikaze pilots who flew their airplanes into enemy ships can be compared to suicide bombers today. For many soldiers fighting in the trenches of the First World War 'going over the top' to confront the enemy was recognised as a form of suicide since the chances of success were often so small.

What's to be done about Terrorism?

Crenshaw (2000) notes that we should be cautious about attempting to create general categories that seek to lump together the varied motivations for terrorism within one psychological model. Similarly, more research attention should be directed to those cases where terrorism has been successfully dealt with. The negotiations with the IRA that eventually lead to the Good Friday Agreement and the cessation of terrorism should be studied for what can be learned about the use of negotiation as opposed to the avoidance of discussions such as when Hamas was elected to power in Palestine in 2006. Hamas is still regarded as a terrorist organisation, and many countries, including the United States and the European Union have made it their policy not to speak to terrorist groups. Consequently, any repetition of the Northern Ireland experience becomes severely hampered by such stubborn foreign policies. A non-communicative approach only makes state-sanctioned kidnap and torture, such as extraordinary rendition, more likely (Internet Reference 2). The election of Barack Obama as President of the USA in 2008 has ushered in a more conciliatory form of politics. It will be interesting to see what happens with regard to opening up a dialogue with terrorist groups. Victoroff also suggests that an emphasis on early prevention of impressionable young people is necessary. Victoroff concludes his review of the literature on terrorism by saying that a middle way needs to be taken between those who argue for a single cause of terrorism and those that say the quest for causes should be abandoned because there is not one all-encompassing cause of terrorism:

> The leading psychological theories of terrorism include a broad spectrum of sociological, psychological, and psychiatric approaches. Strikingly, virtually none of them has been tested in a systematic way. (Victoroff 2005: 33)

Summary

- In common with other topics in this book, the definition of terrorism is contentious and relies on a political and moral judgement.
- There is little evidence that terrorists have a distinct personality that allows them to commit murder. There are also many different forms of terrorism rendering the quest for causes problematic.
- Those who engage in terrorism come from a variety of backgrounds.
- The link between poverty and terrorism is not straightforward. Affluent people can engage in terrorism on behalf of those who are poor.
- Terrorism can only be understood if we take a holistic approach that engages with historical, sociological, psychological and political theories. The social context is crucial for understanding the problem.

STUDY QUESTIONS

1 How helpful are typologies for categorising terrorist behaviour?

2 What problems might they create?

3 Should people be profiled as potential terrorists at airports or train stations?

4 By doing this, what problems might there be in the face of terrorists using different tactics?

5 Is talking with terrorist groups the right strategy?

6 If the definition of terrorism is contentious, how can you deal with the problem?

FURTHER READING AND USEFUL WEBSITES

A good place to look at the way that globalisation is affecting crime, which includes chapters on terrorism is K.F. Aas (2007), *Globalization and Crime*, London: Sage.

Other useful works include:

Horgan, J. (2003) 'The search for the terrorist personality', in A. Silke (ed.), *Terrorists, Victims and Society: Psychological Perspectives on terrorism and its consequences*, Chichester: Wiley. [The source book is also a good general resource.]

Silke, A. (1998) 'Cheshire Cat logic: the recurring theme of terrorist abnormality in psychological research', *Psychology, Crime and Law*, 4(1): 51–70.

See also the following website:

http://www.homeoffice.gov.uk/counter-terrorism/

Note

1 This is a play on the nickname of Ali Hassan Abd al-Majid al-Tikritieth, who was known as 'Chemical Ali' because of his role in the chemical attack on Iraqi Kurds.

7

Psychology in the Criminal Justice System: Interviewing Witnesses, Suspects and Eyewitness Testimony

---

Chapter Contents

OVERVIEW

This chapter explores the role of psychology as used to improve the way police interview suspects and witnesses and psychological research on the validity of eyewitness testimony. The importance of eyewitness testimony cannot be underestimated. The accuracy of recalled information about a witnessed crime can mean the difference between conviction and being acquitted. Moreover, the accuracy of eyewitness testimony may also mean the difference between a correct verdict and a miscarriage of justice where an innocent person is convicted due to faulty memory. Interviews with witnesses and suspects form some of the most important evidence put to a jury. Research into these areas will be discussed and assessed.

KEY TERMS

cognitive interview eyewitness testimony interrogative suggestibility

When Jean Charles de Menezes was witnessed at Stockwell Underground Station in London he was described as running away from his pursuers, leaping over a ticket barrier wearing a bulky padded jacket and resisting arrest. This was held to justify the seven bullets unloaded into his head as part of Operation Krakos, the shoot to kill policy aimed at dealing with suicide bombers in Britain. The report that followed painted a different picture. Menezes walked through the barrier, stopping to pick up a free newspaper, walked down the escalator and only ran as his train approached, all the time wearing a light denim jacket. He was innocent and nothing in his demeanour could possibly justify the decision to shoot him. He just happened to live in the wrong place at the wrong time. Had it not been for the massive media focus the early eyewitness testimony may have stood to bias the investigation, indeed the Metropolitan Police's initial six-day resistance to the Independent Police Complaints Commission almost made that inevitable. What this shows is that much more investigation is needed before eyewitness testimony can be relied upon. There is also the suggestion that eyewitness testimony was deliberately distorted to fit the account the police wished to present. Either way, eyewitness testimony needs careful consideration.

The question that we need to consider is to what extent does the criminal justice system have unrealistic expectations of the reliability of eyewitness testimony? In particular, the question is to what extent is human memory fallible, malleable and subjective? We are not concerned in this section with deliberate lying on the witness stand, though clearly this does happen. What we are concerned with is the impact of unwitting mistakes when giving eyewitness testimony, for example falsely remembering the events of a crime or the misidentification of a suspect. This section will look at some of the techniques used to retrieve eyewitness information, some theories of memory which underpin them, and the problems associated with human memory and the impact this can have on jury decisions.

Eyewitnesses

Eyewitness testimony is a major tool of the Criminal Justice system and accounts for many convictions. However, it is also one of the most flawed forms of evidence upon which to base a case. Until recently, it was not possible to state with any accuracy the extent to which eyewitness testimony is unreliable. However, with advances in the use and reliability of forensic science, in particular DNA testing, many cases of innocent people convicted on the basis of eyewitness testimony have come to light after forensic tests proved their innocence (Wells, Memon and Penrod 2006). It was the work of Elizabeth Loftus in the 1970s that helped the study of eyewitness memory become an important object of study for psychology (see Loftus 1979). In the UK, the Devlin inquiry for the government into the reliability of eyewitness testimony highlighted the many problems and noted cases where eyewitness testimony led to a miscarriage of justice (Devlin 1976). Later a distinction was made between factors that the Criminal Justice system had control over, such as how the line up was arranged or how witnesses were questioned, and those factors that pertained to an individual's characteristics such as their ability to remember, for example, but which the police could not control. These were termed system variables and estimator variables respectively (Wells 1978). This important distinction allowed psychological research to become applied to the practice of police questioning. The first part of this chapter will focus on research into those aspects of the eyewitness process over which the Criminal Justice System has little control, the remainder of the chapter looks at system variables and how the Criminal Justice System can be improved to increase accuracy of recall.

Estimator variables

Several variables have been identified that can have an effect on the way we witness events. The following outlines some of the main variables.

Cross-race identification

Meissner and Brigham (2001) conducted a study that looked at research spanning 30 years on the effect of race on witness recall, in particular what has been termed own-race bias. They found what they term a 'mirror effect' where there are less errors in recalling a face and more positive identifications when the face is derived from the witness' own race. By looking at 39 studies and conducting a **meta-analysis** of the findings Meissner and Brigham found that participants were 1.4 times better able to identify a face from their own race and 1.56 times more likely to mistakenly identify a face if it was not their race. They further argue that there does not seem to be any correlation between a person's attitude to other races and their witnessing performance or that more interracial contact results in improved accuracy.

Stress

Deffenbacher et al. (2004) conducted a review of the effects that stress can have on the subsequent recall of a witness. They found that there was a significant link between high stress levels and the ability of a witness to recall information. Similarly, Morgan et al. (2004) conducted a study on military personnel who underwent survival training that required them to experience a realistic scenario of being a prisoner of war and being interrogated. Although the interrogations were conducted by instructors, the level of stress inflicted was high. It was found that exposure to someone who subjected them to intense pressure for a prolonged period did not lead to accurate recall. For a live line-up where the instructor was placed in a line-up of people not involved, only 30 per cent of those under the most stress could pick out their interrogator.

Weapons effect and memory for stressful events

One of the most important aspects of eyewitness memory is the effect that negative experiences have on memory recall. It might be common sense to assume that the more serious an incident the more likely it is to be remembered. However, if someone points a gun at your head you are more likely to focus on the gun than on the person who is holding it. This is called the weapon effect, where the witness focuses on the weapon to the neglect of other aspects of the scene such as the perpetrator (Loftus, Loftus and Messo 1987). You may well remember the day as long as you live, but you may not remember the day accurately. Although in the majority of studies into this effect the participants were not exposed to real violence and the event was an experiment, 80 per cent of psychologists in one study argued that the effect was real enough to warrant it being mentioned to a jury in court. In real life eyewitness events, the effect is less reliably shown (Valentine, Pickering and Darling 2003). It might be assumed that the effect would manifest differently for different age groups, however Davies, Smith and Blincoe (2008) and Pickel et al. (2008) have demonstrated the effect in children in an experimental study.

Memory and emotional arousal: the Yerkes Dodson law

The weapon effect demonstrates how emotional arousal effects memory recall. But, how much emotion is needed to have an effect? Christianson (1992), in a review of the literature, suggests that the much referenced Yerkes Dodson law (Yerkes and Dodson 1908) has very little evidence to support its contentions. This theory suggests that there is an optimum level of arousal that results in the best level of cognitive functioning, including the ability to remember an event. The hypothesis is that the more emotionally arousing an event is, after an optimum level, the less is remembered. So witnessing a violent act, for example, would be regarded as a highly arousing event, certainly more so than most situations where memory is called into use. However, Christianson reviews the literature to find little to support this. Many studies demonstrate that highly arousing events can lead to good recall. This is because the event tends to be more thoroughly rehearsed and replayed, activities that are crucial to 'fixing' an event in long-term memory (Alexander et al. 2005). For example, if we wish to remember the name of an author for an exam, then we need to repeat it in our minds many times. A highly arousing event like witnessing a crime causes us to do the same, especially for aspects central to the event, such as what was said by those involved, if a weapon was used and the actions that took place (Paz-Alonso and Goodman 2008). However, Paz-Alonso and Goodman (2008) argue that the research so far has not looked at arousal to a very high level, for example few studies look at the effect that witnessing a murder would have on memory recall. In their study, subjects watched a film depicting a murder. It was found that central aspects of the film were particularly well remembered, which adds weight to the weapons effect discussed above. However, if the respondents were presented with misleading information after watching the film they were twice as likely to report misleading information two weeks after the film was 'witnessed' and they were overly confident in their false memories. Findings such as these are highly important when we consider the way that the police interview witnesses and construct post-event narratives.

Exposure duration

As might be expected, the longer the witness observes an event the better is their ability to accurately recall the face of a perpetrator. Memon, Hope and Bull (2003) demonstrated in their study that recall was significantly better if the witness saw the face for 45 seconds as opposed to 12 seconds. Correct identifications were made in 90 per cent of the trials when the face was seen for 45 seconds as opposed to only 32 per cent correct identification when exposure was 12 seconds.

Use of a disguise

The nature of crime is such that those committing a planned crime may disguise their features in order to make later identification difficult. Shapiro and Penrod (1986) reviewed the literature and found that when an appearance changed after the event the level of accurate recall dropped from 75 per cent for non-changed appearance to 54 per cent for those who had changed. Pozzulo and Marciniak (2006) support this finding but add a note about how presentation of suspects in a live line-up might improve accurate witness recall. The traditional method is a simultaneous line-up where the suspect is placed in a line with other innocent people at the same time. This can be compared to the sequential line-up where each person is presented one after the other. It has been suggested that the sequential line-up is a better method because it results in less false identifications (Searcy, Bartlett and Memon 2000). Searcy et al. found, however, that the advantage of the sequential line-up did not improve witness recall appreciably when the line-up members, including the suspect, did not match the offender's appearance at the crime scene.

Retention interval

Shapiro and Penrod's meta-analysis also found that, as perhaps expected, the shorter the time between witnessing an event and recalling it, the more accurate the recall. Because this is a meta-analysis each study they looked at used a different period of delay, but the difference in accurate recall fell from 61 per cent to 51 per cent when long delay was compared to short delay.

Intoxication of the witness

Dysart, Lindsay, MacDonald and Wicke (2002) revealed that the more alcohol the witness consumed the more likelihood there was that they would make a false identification when the suspect was not in the show-up. A show-up is where the suspect is presented to the witness without any fillers, or volunteers used to check how accurate the witness is. This is a system that is used in North America by the police, according to Dysart et al., when the witness is intoxicated. However, no significant difference was found in the accuracy of a witness when the suspect was in the show-up and they had consumed different levels of alcohol. In England and Wales the show-up is not allowed under the Police and Criminal Evidence Act 1984 (PACE), although if a suspect is known to the police but not arrested the police can arrange a 'confrontation' between the witness and the suspect to see if an identification can be made. Identification line-ups should be video recorded as an ideal and the suspect must be shown with at least eight other people of similar age and ethnicity and if the suspect has an obvious characteristic like dyed hair, a piercing or a tattoo then it should be concealed or the fillers should also be presented with this characteristic. The suspect can also choose where they stand in the line-up.

In summary, Charmaine and Wells (2006) have estimated that 16 per cent of defendants who go to trial will be cases of mistaken identity, and Wells et al. (2006) state that eyewitnesses only pick out the suspect 50 per cent of the time. Clearly, the weight of evidence is that eyewitness evidence is deeply flawed and cases based solely on its use would be problematic. There are system variables that can improve the validity of eyewitness testimony, such as different techniques to interview witnesses. The following section of this chapter turns to these methods.

The police and investigative interviewing: current practice in England and Wales

The image of the highly trained police officer interrogating a suspect using an array of tried and tested techniques to elicit a confession is one commonplace in fictional depictions of police practice. In England and Wales, however, the training of police officers in investigative interviewing was introduced as recently as 1992. Although a series of manuals were developed prior to this, many were in contravention of the Police and Criminal Evidence Act 1984 (Gudjonsson 2007). PACE, as it became known, was introduced after a series of high profile miscarriages of justice. In particular, the Maxwell Confait murder case, where three teenage boys were convicted and institutionalised for three years after two pleaded guilty to the murder, and all to the arson that destroyed the house in which Confait's body was left. As McBarnet stated shortly after the Fisher Report in 1977 into the case, the police were able to convince the jury beyond reasonable doubt because police interviewing of suspects was based on an adversarial system where the police could use intimidation (McBarnet 1978). The three convictions were overturned when evidence emerged that the murder and the subsequent fire could not have occurred simultaneously, which was what the boys confessed to. This cast doubt on the timeline of events and brought a previous suspect back into the frame who had an alibi for when the events were originally said to occur. As McBarnet argued, the police try to support their version of events and any evidence found that might contradict this version, and so help the suspects, is ignored or repressed. PACE was introduced to remedy these problems through a series of measures such as the right to a solicitor. An appropriate adult needs to be present before an interview can take place with young people or adults with mental health problems. The interview also needs to be recorded, although there is no requirement that the interview be visually recorded.

Other legislative changes have meant the police must interview suspects, victims and witnesses more carefully. Prior to the introduction of the Crown Prosecution Service in 1986, the police made the decision to proceed to court after a suspect was charged with an offence. After the CPS, this function became independent of the police. The CPS essentially make the decision on whether or not there is sufficient evidence for a case to proceed to court when there is a realistic prospect of conviction, and where such conviction is in the public interest (Internet Reference 5). After changes in the law in 1994, the right to silence was abolished so that a court can make inferences from a silence during an interview when questions were asked. For example, failure to account for why you were in a particular place, why marks or objects were on your person or failure to mention a fact that it would be reasonable to mention can all be taken as evidence of guilt. However, you cannot be convicted solely on refusal to answer questions, other evidence must be presented. With these legislative changes, a new style of interviewing needed to be introduced. The police now need to take into account evidence that might reveal a suspect's innocence and the Crown Prosecution Service, and not the police, weighed up the evidence. The police also needed to take into account the way defence solicitors were more likely to find fault in the investigatory process. The ability to elicit a valid confession that withstands scrutiny has become crucially important.

Consequently, the PEACE model was introduced in England in 1992 and is based on a one-week training course for police officers (Gudjonsson 2007). The aim was to standardise the police interviewing of suspects. PEACE stands for:

- Preparation: officers are expected to know the case details and organise the legally required procedures such as arranging legal representation and a suitable interview room.
- Engage and explain: the interview needs to begin with the police explaining what will take place and reminding the suspect of their legal rights.
- Account: the interviewee is invited to tell their side of the event. The interviewer can challenge the interviewee on details of the account.
- Closure: the interviewer closes the interview by summarising the account given by the interviewee and asking if that summary reflected what the interviewee said. Any corrections in the detail of the account can be made.
- Evaluate: the interviewers evaluate the interview and the quality of the evidence obtained as well as their own performance.

The original training programme has been expanded so that there are more advanced training courses for different types of crime such as serious crime and volume crime. Gudjonsson (2007) explains that there are two types of interviewing techniques that are based on psychological principles. Conversation management is more useful for those suspects who are uncooperative (Mortimer and Shepherd 1999) and the cognitive interview (CI) is generally used for victims and witnesses to an offence, although it can be used for suspects who are willing to cooperate (Fisher and Geiselman 1992; see Table 7.1 for a summary of the technique). The effectiveness of this training and the role of the cognitive interview within it has been questioned in a couple of studies of the police (Kebbell, Milne and Wagstaff 1999; Clark and Milne 2001). They found that some aspects of the CI were not followed due to the length of time it took, especially when used to elicit eyewitness testimony for less serious volume crime. The focus of the training is also on suspects rather than witnesses. Of the five-day training course, only two days were spent on training for interviewing suspects using the CI. Similarly, Dando, Wilcock and Milne (2008) found from their survey of police officers that 71 per cent felt dissatisfied with their training and 63 per cent felt the training is too suspect-centred. Davis, McMahon and Greenwood (2005) conducted research on a shorter form of the CI that reduced the amount of time taken during the interview and found that it still produced reliable information. However, Walsh and Milne (2008) found evidence that training in CI techniques did not lead to a large improvement in interviewing technique. Despite the seeming complexity of the CI, at its core, the CI could be summarised by saying that it encourages free recall through the use of open-ended questions. Indeed, it is often argued that best practice in interviewing is the use of open-ended questions. Yet, when asked what constitutes a good interview with a child, police officers in one survey felt that their performance was dictated by the child's ability to talk openly. Rather than realising that the skill of the interviewer in eliciting these responses from well-chosen questions is important, these officers focused instead on the child. The utility of open-ended questions was not rated highly (Wright, Powell and Ridge 2007).

America has also had its share of miscarriages of justice where a suspect was interrogated in such a way that they were compelled to give false testimony or admit guilt when a later investigation found them to be innocent. In 1966 a court case became the basis for what later became known as the *Miranda* rights. Similar to the right to remain silent in the UK, the suspect must waive their right to silence in order for anything they say to be used against them in court. Many suspects are tricked into doing this, especially true of the young and vulnerable, and where the police put pressure on the suspect to waive their rights. There is, as yet, no requirement that the interrogation be recorded in the same way that there is a requirement under PACE in England and Wales. A survey in America of police officers' attitudes about their interviewing skills by Kassin et al. (2007) found that 77 per cent of them thought they were accurate in lie detection. As will be discussed later in this chapter this is a very optimistic figure with most people, including the police, little better than chance at picking out a liar. Police also overestimated the number of people who waive their *Miranda* rights. The police estimated this happens in as many as 81 per cent of the interrogations whereas several studies cited by Kassin et al. have suggested the range is from 46 to 68 per cent. However, contrary to what many commentators on American police interrogations argue, the majority (81 per cent) wanted the interrogation video recorded. It is often argued by the majority of police departments that this would lead to the police being unable to undertake certain interrogation techniques in case these methods would offend judges and juries.

The cognitive interview

The cognitive interview is a technique that incorporates cognitive retrieval techniques and context reinstatement. It begins with a period of free recall, after which the interviewer uses open-ended questions, often based on aspects of the free recall period as prompts. This is followed by an attempt to elicit the context in which the witnessed event occurred – that is attempting to evoke the environmental cues that existed at the time of the witnessed event, e.g. the location, the time, colours, smells etc. The attempt is to provide detailed reporting and multiple retrieval, e.g. starting recall at different temporal points in the witnessed event, such as starting in the middle, end and then beginning. And finally attempting to elicit imagery and emotion (Milne and Bull 1999). Fisher and Geiselman provide a guide to the procedures that need to be followed, in Table 7.1 opposite. The types of question asked are also important. The CI mainly uses open questions rather than closed questions. Rather than asking for concrete

Table 7.1   *Reference guide to conducting the cognitive interview*

I Introduction

    A   Control *E/W**'s anxiety.

    B   Develop rapport.

    C   Tell *E/W* to actively volunteer information, not passively wait for *INT** to ask questions.

    D   Explicitly request detailed information.

    E   Tell *E/W* not to edit her thoughts.

    F   Tell *E/W* not to fabricate or make up answers.

    G   Convey that *INT* expects *E/W* to concentrate intensely.

II Open-ended Narration

    A   Recreate the general context.

    B   Request narrative description.

    C   Do not interrupt.

    D   Long pause after *E/W* stops speaking before asking next question.

    E   Identify *E/W*'s images.

             1 Ask *E/W* to indicate clearest image.

             2 Ask or infer other images.

    F   Sketchy notes to indicate *E/W*'s images.

    G   Develop a tentative probing strategy (Principles of Detail and Momentum).

III Probing Memory Codes

    A   Re-emphasise importance of *E/W* concentration.

    B   Recreate context of specific event.

    C   Ask *E/W* to close her eyes.

    D   Ask open-ended, framed question.

    E   Request detailed description.

    F   Do not interrupt *E/W*'s narration.

    G   Take detailed notes.

    H   Long pause after *E/W* stops speaking before asking follow-up questions.

    I   Exhaust image for information not included in narration.

    J   Probe remaining images.

    K   Re-probe images activated earlier.

    L   Probe concept codes.

IV Review

    A   Review for *E/W* from *INT*'s memory or notes.

    B   Speak slowly and deliberately.

    C   Ask *E/W* to interrupt immediately if she remembers new information or if errors in *INT*'s review.

    D   If new leads develop, probe relevant information.

V Close

    A   Collect background.

    B   Remind *E/W* to call when she thinks of new information.

    C   Create a positive, last impression.

Source: Reproduced from Fisher and Geiselman (1992: 193–4.)

* *E/W* = Eyewitness; *INT* = Interviewer

facts through closed questioning, such as what weapon was used, the CI aims for a narrative. The status of the interviewer is also important. It has been found that if the witness regards the interviewer as a naïve third party they are more likely to volunteer information, even if they are not sure of its accuracy. An attempt is made to transfer control to the witness and away from the interviewer. Geiselman et al. (1985) in a study of different forms of interview demonstrated that the CI is better than the standard police interview and interviews that use hypnosis in gaining reliable recall of events from a staged crime viewed by the respondents, and better than standard interviews at eliciting reliable recall from children (Saywitz, Geiselman and Bornstein 1992). It has also been found that the CI reduces the likelihood of children reporting erroneous details when being asked misleading questions (Milne and Bull 2003). In a meta-analysis of 42 studies that tested the effect of the cognitive interview, Köhnken et al. (1999) found that the cognitive interview resulted in 41 per cent more correct details being remembered by respondents. Nevertheless, there was also a higher number of incorrect details reported with the CI than with a standard interview.

Arguably, the CI does nothing more than formalise and further encourage techniques of recall that people use anyway. It has been found, for example, that when using different interview techniques other than the CI, witnesses spontaneously recalled the context of the event and imagery surrounding it. However, it has been found that the specific **mnemonic** aspects of the CI increase recall by 60 per cent more than if the respondent is just asked to recall the event four times (Campos and Alonso-Qeucuty 1999). For example, the CI has specific techniques such as changing of the witness' perspective so that they recall the event as if from another person's perspective or recall the event in a different order. A further advantage is that the interviewer is encouraged to create a communicative rapport between witness and interviewer. Nevertheless, the utility of the CI in aiding recall is also closely linked to the skills of the interviewer (Memon and Higham 1999; Fisher, Mello and McCauley 1999). As noted, the police in the UK receive only five days of training, casting further doubt on the reliability of eliciting eyewitness evidence through interviews.

Interviewing children as victims and witnesses

Another problem that has been identified is that witnesses may feel uncomfortable with a detailed verbal re-enactment of a traumatic event in court. This is especially the case when victims of sexual violence are asked to recall the events. Such problems are magnified with children and the CI has been shown to have limited value for interviewing children, especially those under six years old (Geiselman 1999). Consequently, since 1991 in England and Wales children have been allowed to present their testimony on videotape. This system combines elements of both the police station interview and the need to present such testimony for the benefit of a jury in a court. The interviewer must interview the child in such a way to elicit testimony that is usable in court and makes logical sense. A form of CI is used in this interview. However, it has been found that such testimony, when played on a screen in court, requires the viewers to concentrate more carefully on what is being said as well as there being no opportunity for the child to elaborate or explain a point (Westcott and Kynan 2004). A further problem is that different methods of presenting testimony, for example, live in court, on CCTV, or on video, may have different effects on whether or not an observer, for example a jury, believes or remembers the testimony. Landström, Granhag and Hartwig (2007) conducted a study which suggested that children testifying in a live presentation were more positively perceived by observers than when testifying on video and these presentations were better remembered than were the recorded testimony. In a review of the literature on children as eyewitnesses, Goodman and Melinder (2007) note that there is more variability in children's responses to questioning than adults. Even children of the same age can respond in different ways, with some being very suggestible and others resistant to suggestion. Such research demonstrates the need for flexibility in interviewing techniques.

Conversation management (CM)

Milne and Bull (1999) review the work of Eric Shepherd who has written extensively on conversation management. This technique is designed to alert interviewers to their own biases and use of stereotypes in the interview scenario. The main difference with CM is that the interviewer takes more direct control over the direction of the interviewees responses. In the CI, it is the free recall of the interviewee that directs the interview. The CM technique attempts to overcome the accusatory approach of traditional police interviews where the interviewer has already made up their mind about the suspect's guilt and the interview is designed to extract a confession. As noted, the Maxwell Confait case led to a miscarriage of justice because evidence that contradicted the police's belief in the three boys' guilt was ignored. Traditional interview tactics are beset by the following three problems that the CM aims to eradicate.

- *Premature closure* is the process of pre-empting the answers before they are given. This happens when a police officer reads a case file and uses their experience to predict what the interviewee will say. This leads to:

- *Confirmation bias* where the interviewer attends to those aspects of the interviewee's answers that fit with their preconceived beliefs of what happened and ignores those elements that go against their beliefs. A similar problem is:
- *Defensive avoidance* where aspects of the case file that might weaken it are avoided or ignored.

CM is based on the ACCESS system. This stands for the process that needs to be followed.

- Assess: the investigator must begin the process by looking at the written testimony and form an action plan based on the investigation's objectives. It is here where they need to be aware of the potential for premature closure through defensive avoidance of evidence.
- Collect and Collate: through audio recording and good note-taking the investigator draws together data that is reliable, comprehensible and easily used through systematic collection.
- Evaluate: the integration and analysis of the data follows its collection and involves checking that details match and make logical sense both within one person's testimony and between one person and another.
- Survey: all the material needs to be looked at together so that a view can be taken on the weight of the evidence and to think about alternative hypotheses. This last issue is perhaps the most radical aspect as it tends to go against the way crime is investigated by the police. Innocent until proven guilty is not a phrase that describes police practices. The fact that the police look for suspects demonstrates that the police are looking for someone they suspect of committing the crime (Reiner 2000).
- Summary: this is the production of an overview of the case, where there have been new lines of inquiry and the recommendation for the future. Where this involves further investigation then a return to the Assess stage begins the process again.

Regardless of the utility of these systems, many studies have demonstrated the way that the police resort to techniques that their colleagues use or that they feel work. The limited training in these techniques is likely to result in police officers falling back on techniques that do not work, but involve less work (Reiner 2000).

What the CM aims to do is get a suspect to provide as much detail as they can so that the police can put together a case and look for anomalies in the story when compared to other pieces of information garnered from elsewhere. However, what the CM or the CI cannot do with any degree of surety is determine if what the suspect says is the truth. There are two main ways that an interviewee can provide information that does not reflect what actually happened. One is through what has become known as interrogative suggestibility where the interviewer asks questions or presents information that leads to the interviewee providing false information. The other is the deliberate lie where the interviewee is fully aware of their deception. The following section looks at some ways that this has been tackled.

Detecting deceit: the police as unreliable lie detector

Television and film has given the public the impression that the police officer and detective are uniquely trained to spot a deceitful suspect. Even if we are innocent, a conversation with a police officer can result in us becoming overly sensitive to our utterances and body language in case we are thought to be lying. Evidence from psychological studies, however, suggests that police officers are no better at spotting a deceitful person than the public (Vrij, Edwards and Bull 2001a, 2001b). Professional lie detectors, such as the police, are no better at detecting a liar than the usual source of psychological research, college students. Both groups detect liars between 45 and 60 per cent of the time. The average rate of accurately detecting when someone is lying or telling the truth with professional lie detectors was 55 per cent. With laypeople, the rate is actually higher at 57 per cent (Vrij 2004). Considering that the probability of catching a liar by chance alone is 50 per cent, this figure does not illustrate that people are good lie detectors. Similarly, police officers tend to hold stereotypical views of what to look for in a liar and are resistant to methods to improve their detection of deceit; even so such stereotypes are also widely held by the public (Vrij 2008). For example, Vrij notes that police officers often react in disbelief when told that liars do not usually look away or fidget. Instead, the opposite has been observed; liars tend to decrease their movements (2008). Nevertheless, as Vrij notes, this does not mean that all liars do this, only the majority. In the studies carried out by Vrij, 64 per cent of 181 respondents decreased the movement of their hands, fingers and arms during deception, and 35 per cent showed an increase. Therefore, basing lie detection on body movement alone would have limited success. Of course, for such observations to be meaningful, the observer would need to watch the person behaving when not lying in order to have honest behaviour against which to judge dishonest behaviour. Consequently, the stereotypical liar who fidgets and looks nervous is not borne out by the evidence, nor are such actions as masking the mouth with the hand. There is no evidence that liars look up to the left either as is sometimes suggested. Vrij suggests that the act of lying may take up cognitive energy and so liars do not attend to their body language meaning that fidgeting is less likely.

Granhag and Strömwall (2001) reported a study that aimed to determine if repeated interrogations would lead to better detection of liars. The study also wanted to see if interrogators who interviewed a witness in person were better at detection than someone who watched the interrogation on video. The study found that interrogators were poor at detecting deceit. But, also that the inter- rogators were more likely to believe the interviewee was telling the truth than the video observer. This finding prompted the authors to state that 'interroga- tors should be careful not to hold a too lenient attitude towards suspects' (Granhag and Strömwall 2001: 85). Perhaps a good strategy for the police in Sweden, where this research took place. In England and Wales under the requirements of PACE this advice might jeopardise the case. What this research suggests is that humans from whatever profession are not good at detecting liars.

Nevertheless, the strategic use of such evidence that is collected has also been studied to see how it might best be presented to a suspect (Hartwig, Granhag and Strömwall 2007). Hartwig et al. have shown that guilty suspects employ a less detailed testimony than innocent suspects when asked to recall an event where they are not sure of what evidence there is against them. It is argued that this verbal difference is due to guilty suspects not wishing to give anything away by potentially providing contradictory testimony. An example they provide is that a suspect may deny being at the crime scene when asked directly about their whereabouts at a particular time. When the police have direct evidence that the person was at the crime scene it is possible to spot the differences in the way a guilty person and innocent person responds to this direct question. Innocent suspects tend to believe that by telling the truth this will be sufficient to set them free. This results in a different form of testimony than the more vague testimony of the guilty suspect. Although this technique shows some promise, it potentially runs contrary to the PACE rules in England and Wales, although it is a technique that might be used in the USA. Moreover, it does not take into account the strength of the evidence. Just because someone was at the scene of a crime does not mean that they committed the crime. As always, such strategies are no replacement for methodical police work for the collection of evidence.

The polygraph lie detector

A further example of the way that science is being put forward as a time- saving system for detecting lies is the polygraph system of comparing physiolog- ical changes when people tell lies, such as increased heart rate or perspiration on the hands and now a growing body of research around the potential of scanning brain activity called functional magnetic resonance imaging (fMRI) (Langleben 2008; Spence 2008). Of course, where the slow and meticulous collection of evidence is deemed too slow these methods may become much more widespread. Yet, the controversy around the use of torture such as waterboarding, which is the simulation of drowning, on terrorist suspects in

America, alerts us to the more barbaric methods to which people can resort. As much as anything else, it is this use of torture and the tacit approval of the techniques by the American government, that should alert us to the low reliability of other forms of lie detection such as the polygraph or the potential that some would argue lies in the fMRI (Langleben 2008). In a review of the evidence for polygraph lie detection the National Research Council of the National Academies in America (2004) found that there was little evidence to support the polygraph as a lie detector. Although in laboratory experiments the polygraph is better than chance at picking a liar, it is by no means perfect. It is argued that in the real world, where there are many more variables than can be controlled in the lab, the validity is much less. However, Honts and Amato (2007) have noted that much of the problem with the polygraph is the effect of the examiner. Poorly trained and a high turnover of staff due to high stress levels associated with the job are to blame for this problem. Honts and Amato have presented research that utilised an automated polygraph procedure that makes the human examiner less central to the outcome. Rather than the human examiner asking the questions, in this version the questions are audio recorded. Therefore, any examiner stress or potentially leading manner in their asking of a question is eliminated. The results were significantly better than with the human examiner conducting the test. At present, such tests are not used as evidence in criminal trials in the UK or the USA, but they are used in the USA for testing the credibility of employees for security sensitive jobs such as the Central Intelligence Agency and the Department of Defence. What is clear is that the polygraph is not sufficiently precise to detect deception to base a criminal case around. Mistakes are made in not detecting deceit where deceit is present and falsely detecting deceit in an innocent person (Vrij 2008).

Interrogating 'terrorists'

The previous chapter looked at terrorism and showed how psychology has been applied to understanding this phenomena. Psychology has also been used to work on the best methods of interrogating terrorist suspects in detention camps such as Guantanamo Bay (Internet Reference 6). The interrogation of terrorist suspects is regarded as a potentially more serious and time-sensitive form of interviewing than that carried out with criminal suspects and witnesses because it is assumed that such activity can result in such a massive loss of life as happened on 11 September 2001. Nevertheless, the involvement of psychologists in this field has caused much debate and controversy since the techniques that have been used and approved by the American government are potentially in conflict with the Geneva Convention, the rules set up after the Second World War to protect prisoners of war from harsh treatment. After the invasions of Afghanistan and Iraq those prisoners detained by the Americans were reassigned as 'enemy combatants', a term which allowed the rules of Geneva to be circumvented. Consequently, the methods of interrogation have been extremely harsh. Sleep deprivation through the playing of loud music, prolonged periods of being made to walk around naked and waterboarding where the prisoner has a cloth put over their face and water poured onto it which simulates drowning have all been reported as techniques that are used. Psychologists have been present during these interrogations. Until September 2008, The American Psychological Association (APA) had refused to condemn those members who take part in this torture. This is in contrast to the American Medical Association and the American Psychiatric Association who have banned their members from this activity (Internet Reference 6). Although some restrictions on involvement were made, use of techniques like sleep deprivation in certain circumstances were permitted. It has been noted, however, that the psychologist has an important role to play in military interrogations because they are able to make sure the prisoner is treated fairly. However, an organisation called Psychologists for the Ethical Treatment of Prisoners argue that the involvement of psychologists in such techniques in any capacity provides tacit approval of the techniques (Internet Reference 7). The next section looks at more subtle forms of questioning, but it serves as a powerful reminder that if the asking of a leading question can result in flawed testimony, then the use of techniques that would qualify as torture under the Geneva Conventions would also lead to unreliable testimony.

Interrogative suggestibility

A more subtle form of deceit is where the interviewee alters their testimony in response to questioning. Misleading questions have been shown to lead to post-event alterations to memory. Erroneous information contained in a question has a powerful effect. A variety of studies by Loftus and colleagues have consistently shown the powerful effects of misleading information (Loftus 1975, 1979) and other studies have revealed the varied suggestibility of different people, with particular problems associated with children and people with learning difficulties (Gudjonsson 1984, 2003; McFarlane, Powell and Dudgeon 2002). Misleading post-event information can lead to errors in the recall of the original event. Interviewers can facilitate this in a number of ways, which are termed non-neutral questions (Milne and Bull 1999). They tend to occur when the interviewer already has knowledge of an event and seeks to have it confirmed by the interviewee. In one study by Loftus (1975) it was found that simply swapping the definite article 'the' with the indefinite article 'a' results in different testimony. 'Did you see *the* shotgun?' suggests that a shotgun was present, whereas 'Did you see *a* shotgun?' suggests only the possibility of its presence. The former question results in more affirmative responses than the latter even if no shotgun was present. In a review of a real case of suspected child abuse, Garven et al. (1998, cited in Milne and Bull 1999: 98) identified five ways that the children's testimony may be affected by suggestive questioning other than by leading questions.

1 The interviewer claims to have knowledge about the case from other people.
2 Praising the child when they say something.
3 Criticising the child or suggesting that their testimony is inadequate.
4 Repeating a question that has already been answered.
5 Asking for speculation about aspects of the case that were not directly witnessed.

The Gudjonsson Suggestibility Scale

The test to determine the extent to which someone is suggestible during an interrogation was designed by Gudjonsson and is called the Gudjonsson Suggestibility Scale, or GSS (Gudjonsson 1984). The test involves the subject being played a short piece of recorded narration. They are then required to recall what they heard in as much detail as possible. The interviewer then asks 20 questions, 15 of which are leading questions and suggest an inaccurate answer. This results in a score, called Yield 1, which is the number of leading questions the subject agreed with. This is followed by a negative feedback condition that aims to further test the suggestibility of the subject. The interviewer says, 'You have made a number of errors. It is therefore necessary to go through the questions once more, and this time try to be more accurate.' The same list of questions is asked again and the 'Shift' score is calculated. This is the number of leading questions where a different answer is given. Yield 2 is the number of leading questions agreed with on the second round of questioning. Finally, there is the total suggestibility score, which is Yield 1 + Shift. A version of the Gudjonsson Suggestibility Scale has been used with children between the ages of 3 and 5 years old (McFarlane et al. 2002). The researchers wanted to see if there were differences in the level of suggestibility between the different ages, between boys and girls, children with high and low IQ scores and social economic status. It was found that all the variables had an effect but that IQ was the main variable that predicts suggestibility. Children with high IQs were less susceptible to suggestion. Girls were more suggestible than boys and low social economic position resulted in a greater level of suggestibility. Nevertheless, the study found that the level of suggestibility that results from these variables is quite small. All variables combined only accounted for 27 per cent of the increase in suggestibility.

Another example of this is a study carried out by Crombag, Wagenaar and Van Koppen (1996). This was a study of a real plane crash and the memory of those who saw it. An Israeli cargo airplane crashed into a block of flats in the Netherlands destroying the homes and killing 43 people. The study involved asking subjects a misleading question that implied that the moment the plane crashed was filmed. The study found that people reported seeing the event unfold on television. The recall included the moment the plane hit the building, yet this was never filmed, only the aftermath of the incident. The study demonstrates how post-event **confabulations** can occur due to the way that a witness is asked questions.

Another method to determine the extent to which someone is amenable to suggestion is a computer program designed by Kassin and Kiechel (1996). A subject is asked to sit at a computer and is told they are taking part in a typing test. They are told not to press the 'ALT' key on the keyboard as this will cause the computer to crash and the data to be erased. After 45 seconds the experimenter secretly turns off the computer and accuses the subject of hitting the 'ALT' key. They found that 65 per cent of the subjects signed a written confession to say they did hit the prohibited key and 12 per cent internalised the belief meaning they came to believe they had actually touched the key. In another condition, the same instruction was given to the candidates and the computer switched off. This time a confederate of the experimenter claimed to have seen the subject hit the 'ALT' key: 100 per cent of the subjects confessed and 65 per cent came to believe they were responsible. Although this test has been criticised for its lack of authenticity with real situations where people are pressured to confess to crimes they did not commit, it is still illustrative of the ease with which people will falsely confess. Research to see if certain personality types are more prone to confessing has proved inconclusive. Forrest, Wadkins and Larson (2006) suggested that their research using the Kassin and Kieshel method on students did not show any variation due to personality differences because the subjects were too homogeneous (Forrest et al. 2006). But, Gudjonsson et al. (2004) suggested males were more likely than females to falsely confess, and those scoring highly on the Eysenck Personality Questionnaire Psychoticism scale also falsely confessed more. However, this research was again conducted on students in Iceland and the numbers who admitted to being interrogated by the police was 25 per cent, of whom only 3.7 per cent (or 1 per cent of the total sample of 1080 respondents) admitted to falsely confessing to a crime. Despite these significant problems, Gudjonsson et al. conclude that personality is a significant predictor of who will falsely confess to a crime.

Research into interviewee suggestibility of witnesses and suspects has important implications for interviewers and the Criminal Justice System. Police officers are often pressured to build a case and get a conviction. There is also the more subtle peer pressure that is evident in the police where getting convictions can lead to promotion. Such pressures can result in police officers pushing witnesses and suspects too far. As already noted, the Conversation Management system of interviewing suspects is designed to sensitise interviewers to the effects that their own biased interpretation of the case file can have on the subsequent interview, thus leading to distortions where important information can be missed. This research suggests another way that the interviewer can alter the testimony of the witness to support their perceived version of the events. For example, if a red car was seen at the location of a crime and was thought to be used by the perpetrator, a suggestive question to a witness who saw a car at the scene might be, 'When you saw the red car making its getaway, how fast was it going?' The witness may or may not have seen a red car or did not attend to the car's colour, but such a question can result in the witness' memory of the event being altered, or at the least providing testimony to which they may feel compelled to agree in court (Milne and Bull 1999). It has been suggested that the CI might prove to be a useful technique to overcome post-event misinformation. However, in one study it was found that there was not a significant difference between the CI and a standard interview in preventing misleading information leading to errors in witness recall (Centofanti and Reece 2006). One suggestion for reducing interviewer suggestibility has been presented by Boon and Baxter (2000, 2004). By informing an interviewee that there may be misleading questions in an interview or by telling children that the questions might be 'tricky' has the effect of reducing suggestibility. In summary, how the police interview witnesses and suspects is an essential aspect of criminal investigations. Clearly, more time spent in training for this activity could have profound results for social justice.

The decision making of juries

One of the least understood aspects of the Criminal Justice System is the decision making of juries. For example, what effect do different social and personal variables have on the perceived reliability of the witness or suspect? For example, are higher status witnesses held to be more reliable than low status witnesses? This can be broken down further by including other demographic variables, such as age, race and gender. Add to this personal characteristics such as whether or not the witness has been accused of a crime previously, or if their character is perceived as untrustworthy, and the result can have an important impact upon the result of a jury's deliberations. It has also been argued that despite all the work on the psychological accuracy of eyewitnesses and human memory in general, an overriding effect is subjective expectations, not objective conditions. Attractive defendants can lead to a favourable outcome for the defendant. Although conversely an attractive defendant who provides no justification is often treated more severely. Devine et al. (2001: 699–701) in an exhaustive literature review of studies on jury decision making over 45 years between 1955 and 1999 summarised the research on the decision making of juries around four themes as follows.

Theme 1: Jurors often do not make decisions in the manner intended by the courts, regardless of how they are instructed. Consequently, it matters little what evidence the judge instructs the jury to focus on or the warnings given that the jury should not take a certain piece of evidence into account. Jurors tend to make their mind up quickly and the evidence tends to change this opinion only minimally.

Theme 2: Dispositional characteristics may predict jury outcomes better than juror verdict preferences. Various studies have shown that knowing the demographic characteristics of a jury only helps researchers to increase their prediction of the verdict by 5–15 per cent. However, even though it may be the case that we cannot reliably predict a verdict from an individual's characteristics, at the group level the situation is more complex. At the jury level of decision making, there is good evidence of favouritism when the defendant shares social demographic characteristics with the jury. Devine et al. point out, however, that this finding pertains to mock jury experiments and such homogeneity of jury composition is less likely to occur in real trials. Furthermore, evidence suggests that it is the weight of evidence that influences a jury more than composition bias.

Theme 3: Kalven and Zeisel's (1966) 'liberation' hypothesis is alive and well. The last point above was put forward by Kalven and Zeisel in 1966. They argued that bias was more likely to occur when the evidence against a defendant was weak or ambiguous. This 'liberated' the jury from the evidence, which takes on less importance and allows bias to impact the deliberation process.

Theme 4: Deliberation processes do influence jury outcomes in some situations. Kalven and Zeisel (1966) found that the best indicator of a jury's final verdict is to ask their opinion before they go into the deliberation stage where they are required to discuss the evidence. In other words, jurors make up their mind before they begin to discuss the case (Kalven and Zeisel 1966; also Sandys and Dillehay 1995). The proportion of verdicts that changed after deliberation is one in ten, or 10 per cent. The Justice System is based on a deliberation of the evidence; however, deliberation tends to focus on the possible verdict and its implications for the defendant, rather than the balance of strength in the evidence.

The effect of race on juries

Where research looks at decision making of black juries, Skolnick and Shaw (1997) found that black members were harsher in their sentencing when the defendant was white than vice versa. However, the authors note the problem with this study is that it was explicitly intended to mimic the former American Football player and actor O.J. Simpson's murder trial and so might not be generalisable elsewhere since it was carried out in the same place and at the same time as this much-publicised trial. However, this same effect has been shown by Sommers and Ellsworth (2000) who showed how harsher judgments were passed by black jurors on white defendants than when the roles were reversed. One possible explanation was put forward for why this might occur. When questioned, black jurors had a more negative perception of the jury system than whites. On a scale of 1 to 7 with 7 being the most unfair, black jurors rated the system as 6.9, whereas whites rated the fairness of the jury system as 4.7. These authors argue, therefore, that the harsher judgments of black jurors may be due to this perception of unfairness in the system resulting in a rebalancing effect. Nevertheless, in reviewing the scant literature on the overall racial composition of the jury, Sommers (2007) found that the more whites in a jury than blacks the more likely a defendant was to be found guilty, and this was especially strong when the defendant was black. This finding holds true in studies with whites and Latinos. Essentially, this suggests that the more socially powerful group tends to judge more harshly a defendant from the more powerless group. Why this occurs is less clear. It has been argued that a diverse jury allows for different opinions to be expressed during deliberation. However, the finding that a jury's first impression before deliberation tends to be the one that eventually gets given is important here (Kalven and Zeisel 1966; also Sandys and Dillehay 1995). In a study by Sommers (2006), however, it was found that all white juries were more likely to convict a black defendant than a mixed race jury (four whites and two blacks). However, white jurors were less likely to give a guilty verdict at the predeliberation stage when the jury was mixed race than when all members were white. Sommers suggests that this shows that the idea that mixed juries results in a simple exchange of information during deliberation is not borne out by this study. Nevertheless, there was a difference in the way all white and mixed race juries analysed the evidence. The tendency in mixed juries was for a more thorough analysis suggesting that the advantage of mixed race juries were useful in ways other than fulfilling a democratic ideal to reflect the social composition of society. As noted, there are many factors that influence a decision in a case as complex as a crime, for example, the weight of evidence against the suspect and how it is presented can also have an effect. Devine et al. summarised the research on the racial composition of juries as follows:

Jury–defendant similarity bias has thus been observed across a number of studies and contexts and appears to be a robust phenomenon. When the evidence against the defendant is weak or ambiguous, juries that are demographically similar to the defendant tend to be lenient; however, when the defendant's culpability is clear, juries tend to be harsher. (2001: 674)

Strength of evidence is a difficult variable to quantify leading to variations in its definition from one study to another, but overall this is the most important variable in determining a jury's verdict (Devine et al. 2001). Summers points out that there are many questions still to be answered. In defence of mock jury experiments he argues that they are better able to show why juries make certain decisions than can be found through looking at archival data from real jury decisions. However, one issue that is interesting is that the conclusion that few studies show a clear relationship between the race of the defendant and the race of the jury is made without any reference to the statistics on differential arrest and sentencing of people from different races. Few of them critically analyse what they mean by black, Asian or white. The complexity of race relations means that two individuals termed Asian could be of Pakistani and Indian origin. Although both countries used to be part of the same country before 1947, since then there has been high tension and war. Consequently, psychological research must be aware of such complexity.

Evaluation of psychology in the Criminal Justice System

Many suggestions have been advanced to overcome some of the problems associated with the unwitting inaccuracy of eyewitness testimony and the effect of prejudice and preconceptions of the jury. One such example is replacing the jury with a mixture of experts and laymen, making more use of psychologists to provide expert testimony on the problems associated with eyewitness accounts, better and increased training for police officers in their interviewing of witnesses as well as in the interrogation of suspects to avoid errors in witness recall and the intimidation and possible elicitation of false confession from suspects. However, criminological studies of the way that the Police and Criminal Justice System are organised suggests that whatever psychological innovation is put forward, unless the culture of the organisation can be changed then the innovation will fail. One suggestion might be to integrate the research on cop culture, for example, with the design of psychological research. It is pointless, at present, to suggest changing police interview practice if the working rules presently followed by the police mitigate against change (see Reiner 2000, for a full review of this literature). Moreover, the Criminal Justice System is complex and is affected by numerous bureaucratic rules that make research difficult. For example, one area of interest which remains closed to investigators is the jury room itself where a jury deliberates its verdict. The only form of research that can be undertaken is with mock jury scenarios. Consequently all such research stands accused of bias and inapplicability when compared to real life situations. Nevertheless, psychology has made inroads into our understanding of some of the problems of the Criminal Justice System. The remedies for such problems, however, often reach into the very core of the meaning of justice and democracy in western industrialised countries. This is the topic of the final chapter.

Summary

- Eyewitness testimony is a very unreliable form of evidence with a very high error rate.
- The reliability of eyewitness testimony can be split into those variables that the Criminal Justice System has no control over (estimator variables) and those that can be affected by better techniques of interviewing or presentation of line-ups (system variables).
- The way that the police interview witnesses and suspects is an essential aspect of criminal investigations. Clearly, more time spent in training for this activity could have profound results for social justice.
- The culture of organisations involved in criminal justice can have an effect on the successful implementation of better techniques for eliciting information from suspects and witnesses. Sociological criminology has studied 'cop culture' for many years and pointed out the entrenched reluctance to embrace organisational change (Reiner 2000). Psychological research would have more success in promoting change if such research was incorporated into the study.

STUDY QUESTIONS

1 If we were to replace the jury with experts, what would prevent them from being any less prejudiced than a jury made up from the public?

2 If eyewitness testimony is so flawed, why do we still place so much weight on it in court?

3 Should psychologists be involved with interrogation tactics such as waterboarding? Assess the arguments for and against.

4 Should there be a specially trained interrogation section in the police to overcome the problems discussed in this chapter? Or is one week's training sufficient?

5 Psychological research has raised several potentially useful innovations for improving the interviewing technique of the police. Use the Cognitive Interview guide in Table 7.1 to guide you through an interview with a friend or another student. Pick a topic to ask questions about. How easy is it to follow? Did you find the guide useful? How might it be improved?

FURTHER READING

Christianson, S.Å. (1992) 'Emotional stress and eye-witness memory: a critical review', *Psychological Bulletin*, 112(2): 284–309.

Devine, D.J., Clayton, L.D., Dunford, B.B., Seying, R. and Pryce, J. (2001) 'Jury decision making: 45 years of empirical research on deliberating groups', *Psychology, Public Policy, and Law*, 7(3): 622–727.

McAuliff, B. and Kovera, M. (2007) 'Estimating the effects of misleading information on witness accuracy: can experts tell jurors something they don't already know?', *Applied Cognitive Psychology*, 21: 849–70.

Vrij, A. (2008) *Detecting Lies and Deceit: Pitfalls and Opportunities*. Chichester, West Sussex: John Wiley.

8

Brave New World? Psychology as a System of Governance

Chapter Contents

OVERVIEW

The chapter will situate the psychology of crime within a broader understanding of developments in criminal justice and social theory in the last three decades in western developed countries. The chapter will draw on the concepts of governmentality and risk to outline an argument that places psychology among a number of disciplines that some social theorists argue form a system of control and governance. This critical approach will be contrasted by attempts to synthesise psychology and sociology in order to overcome the problems with each subject and so create a more robust approach to the study of crime that is able to account for both the social, individual and political elements of what is a very complex phenomena. The chapter will argue that it is necessary for psychology to be more fully aware of the social, political and historical aspects of crime and deviance and to become more fully aware of the effect of some of the uses to which psychological research can be put.

KEY TERMS

governmentality psychosocial criminology

Psychology as governmentality:
Michel Foucault and Nikolas Rose

As risk becomes dominant in the arrangement of society, so science comes to play a central, defining role in the way that society is governed (Beck 1992). Yet, governance is never anything other than political and if science is to be a medium of governance, so it will become political in its practices. (Hebenton and Seddon 2009: 353)

This chapter represents a companion to the first chapter in that it begins where that one ended. It was noted that new ideas have emerged from late modern theorising to do with risk, identity and emotion. Throughout this book, I have noted the way that psychology needs to become more fully aware of the politics of its science. The quotation that begins this chapter makes this point clear and also suggests that science, and one can read here psychology, will become more political. It remains to be seen if this will happen, although one of the main themes of this book is that psychology needs to become aware of the political implications of its research. The work of Michel Foucault has radically altered our understanding of the way that different forms of knowledge develop and the reasons for their development. For example, what makes us look to psychology for the answers about the way humans behave? And, when a psychologist tells us something about humans, why do we listen? What gives the psychologist the power and authority that means we listen? Foucault's work moves us beyond simple ideas about power. The concept of **governmentality** in Foucault's work is useful here because it refers to the way that problems are created, and how they are then dealt with. It moves beyond Marxist perspectives that seek to situate the responses to problems within the state. Foucault's work highlighted how modes of control are created and how they become accepted as useful. So, for example, he was interested in how madness was defined and how those designated mad were treated. He was also interested in how sciences of the mind, such as psychology, developed and gained their authority, their right to speak the truth (Foucault 1972). Foucault's book *Discipline and Punish* on the way that various societies turned away from execution towards imprisonment is perhaps best known in criminology (1977). However, his ideas have been developed by other writers such as Nikolas Rose who focused on the way that psychology developed (1985, 1999).

Rose's book *Governing the Soul* (1999) sets out to study how human identity is created in the practices of psychology. Specifically, Rose looks at how the human subject understands itself through the language created within psychology. In other words, in the language specific to psychology a picture of humans emerges. This forms a narrative which becomes part of our own everyday language. We compare our lives to this narrative to see if we match it. This has resulted in excessive individualism where we focus on our sense of self to the detriment of any focus on community. In other words, there is an overemphasis on the 'I' and a neglect of the 'us'. Words from psychology have become words we use every day to understand ourselves. We talk of being stressed, or that our self-esteem is low, we feel depressed or we talk of how intelligent we are. Furthermore, Rose argues against theories that suggest that the state is the key architect of power. Rose notes that the sciences of the mind, what he calls the 'psy sciences', actively create and shape government. They are not merely instruments of power. Moreover, the psy sciences have provided us with a way to express ourselves and a way to gain self-realisation. There has been a movement away from the state as the all powerful authority towards the autonomous individual able to make decisions and strive for a better life. In this regard, Rose presents the positive side of the psy sciences. Rose rejects the simplistic argument that psychology, for example, is a system of power over individuals that seeks to manipulate and control them. Psychology also allows people to become more autonomous of the state, not more dependent on it. Rose is undoubtedly right to point out the complexity of our relationship to psychology. However, Rose is still concerned with what exactly we are meant to aspire to and the way that we are meant to constantly strive for some vague form of happiness based on shallow changes to our lifestyles. Moreover, psychology is forged on the assumption of a norm and then a deviation from the norm. Consequently, psychology was the science of those who differed from the norm, who were pathological. Psychology developed, according to Rose, as a science offering to show how abnormal people could be dealt with.

> Psychology's role as an administrative technology cannot be understood as the application of a psychological knowledge of normality, gained through theoretical reflection or laboratory investigation, to a domain of practical problems. On the contrary, it was through attempts to diagnose, conceptualise and regulate pathologies of conduct that psychological knowledge and expertise first began to establish its claims for scientific credibility, professional status and social importance. (Rose 1985: 226)

Essentially, psychology did not develop to find out how normal people operated, but how abnormal people operated. Psychology developed, in much the same way as criminology, to respond to deviance.

This is one of the reasons for a split between the psychological and sociological variants of criminology. Some sociologically minded criminologists distrust psychology because it seems to be a throw-back to earlier forms of criminology where the focus was on the individual (Garland 2001). As criminology moved into the 1970s and drew on a more critical and radical set of discourses (see for example Taylor et al. 1973) the wider social context of crime became more important, at least in this radical form of the subject. When this is linked to the move towards a risk society, the focus on the individual becomes less tenable. Yet, this fails to note the tendency of psychology to categorise and create typologies. The irony of a subject that focuses on the individual is that it tends towards an essentialist understanding of the human and so presents an all-encompassing set of practices. So, for example, the categorisations and typologies that are commonplace throughout psychology imply that humans fit into a few groups and behave in similar ways – less like individuals and more like the categories that we are all meant to fit into if we believe our horoscopes. However, key questions are rarely asked about the people who are fitted into the boxes. The majority of all crimes are committed by men, yet why one sex should have such a massive impact rarely gets asked (Cowburn 2005). The majority of all crime is also committed by young people. However, psychological and psychiatric explanations tend to fall back on their individualistic focus, as the following section will discuss.

Psychology, ADHD and the need for caution

Attention Deficit Hyperactivity Disorder (ADHD) is a phenomenon that was only recognised in 1980 in the USA. Debates are fierce concerning whether or not the condition is as widespread as the diagnoses suggest, if the condition exists at all or whether or not the condition says more about a society that is intolerant of children doing what children tend to do, which is be hyperactive or dreamy, the two polar extremes described by Selikowitz (2004). The bell curve, the statistical device that describes the normal distribution of a phenomena, has an optimum point where the majority of people's behaviour can be placed. According to some authors, to describe the condition of ADHD as being concerned with inattentiveness that manifests in either hyperactive or dreamy behaviour demonstrates our desire to produce homogeneous children (Timimi 2005). Unnever, Cullen and Pratt (2003) make the point that there are few studies on the effect of ADHD on juvenile delinquency from a criminological perspective; they are mostly from psychology and psychiatry. In their study, they found that low self-control was a major factor in children with ADHD, but that parental management and monitoring can have an effect on self-control. They argue that there is a strong social element to ADHD that is often ignored by the medical model usually employed by psychologists.

Consequently, this research should be seen as a cautionary one for those psychiatrists who insist on using drugs as the sole treatment for ADHD. It could be argued that the current interest in this area has less to do with the problem being perceived as one worthy of the attention of psychologists and psychiatrists, as it is the huge amount of money that pharmaceutical companies can make out of the invention of drugs, such as Ritalin, to control children diagnosed as having the condition (Timimi 2005). In 2008, a study showed that many commonly prescribed drugs for depression only work on those with severe forms of the illness and that pharmaceutical companies systematically withhold data that might prove their product less beneficial than it is (Kirsch et al. 2008). A short while later, the drug company Smith Kline Beecham were found by the UK government's Medicine and Healthcare products Regulatory Agency to have withheld research that showed the anti-depressant drug Seroxat may contribute to suicidal feelings when given to teenagers (Internet References 8 and 9). In addition to this, psychological research can have profound and disturbing implications, even if the researchers themselves never intended for such an outcome. Awareness of the history of an idea and how it has been applied can raise our awareness of both mistakes and useful lessons that may have been forgotten. For example, it would be very dangerous indeed for psychologists to forget the application of seemingly altruistic research into race and intelligence. Studies into Intelligence Quotients (IQ) became the theories that formed one of the justifications for the Nazi genocide during the Second World War (Gould 1997). To forget this would mean that more recent attempts to highlight the role of intelligence and race in crime, such as Hernnstein and Murray's *The Bell Curve* (1994), could go uncriticised without an awareness of the uses to which it could be put. With a change in emphasis away from studying the causes of crime towards predicting crime, we are seeing another moment when awareness of the political and historical background to these debates is essential. The risk society thesis suggests that more and more people will become caught up in a disciplinary net that seeks to categorise and control those deemed to be risky before any crime has been committed. Psychology will be at the centre of this and will need to respond appropriately (Cohen 1985). It is hoped that this response takes heed of the history and politics of civil and human rights.

Psychosocial criminology and gender

One recent approach that seeks to combine the individual focus of psychology with the social aspect of sociology is psychosocial criminology. This approach has used gender as a way to demonstrate the utility of its approach. Psychosocial criminology is an attempt to answer the question of 'Why did they do it?' and 'Why, given the same set of circumstances does one person commit a crime and another does not?' (Gadd and Jefferson 2007). This can only be answered, they claim, by a psychosocial approach that seeks to address the complexity of the subject. A synthesis between the sociological and the psychological is sought through looking at case studies to understand the process of becoming criminal. Jefferson has argued that analysis of the offender is inadequate within criminology. Criminology of all persuasions has not been able to account for the role of both psychological emotions and the culture within which they are enacted (Jefferson 2002). Another way to say this is that criminology is rather strange in that it seems to ignore the one aspect of a crime that interests people the most: the motivation. Psychosocial criminology, at least that version of it discussed by Jefferson, also aims to explore ambiguity and ambivalence. Discussing stories in film or literature that depict different outcomes for two related people, such as the sibling cop and thief, Jefferson says:

> The dramatic potential of such stories is obvious, but their power to pull in audiences suggests an interest in exploring and understanding why and how similar circumstances produce dissimilar outcomes: how conformity and deviance are reproduced and/or resisted. This appears to exceed the curiosity of most criminologists. (Jefferson 2002: 149)

Psychosocial criminology seeks to redress the paucity of discussion of emotion. Criminology, Jefferson contends, is a 'peculiarly passionless subject' (Jefferson 2002: 152). This criticism is one shared by another recent approach: cultural criminology (Webber 2007b). The reconciliation of emotion (the individual response usually the preserve of psychology) with the social and cultural factors (the reserve of sociology) is the task of psychosocial criminology. As Gadd and Jefferson maintain:

> In place of messily complex human subjects shot through with anxiety and self-doubt, conflictual feelings and unruly desires we are offered depleted

caricatures: individuals shorn of their social context, or who act, we are told, purely on the basis of reason or 'choice', interested only in the maximisation of utility. Or, we are presented with individuals who are nothing but the products of their social circumstances who are not beset by any conflicts either in their inner or their outer worlds: pure social constructions, to use the fashionable jargon. (2007: 1)

Using a psychosocial framework, which combines the emotional with the cultural, Gadd and Jefferson outline their approach to the question of gender as a key variable in our understanding of crime. They initially take issue with Messerschmidt's argument that gender differences are enacted by what we do, and that what we do reproduces the social structure (1997, 1994, 1993). Another way to put this is that social structure is reproduced by social practices. So gender is reproduced by what we do. When a man performs masculinity appropriately in social situations then gender is reproduced. Violence and crime is one way that men reproduce their gender. Put simply, for some, being a man means being violent or committing crime. In contrast, wearing a skirt or kissing other men in public can threaten social order. Messerschmidt puts this as follows:

Young men situationally accomplish public forms of masculinity in response to their socially structured circumstances ... varieties of youth crime serve as a suitable resource for doing masculinity when other resources are unavailable. (1994: 82)

Where access to sport or work is blocked then masculinity is accomplished in other ways such as violence. According to Gadd and Jefferson, this account is too rational and purposive and does not fully account for those times when people 'choose' to act in ways that are contrary to notions of hegemonic masculinity. The argument is that this approach is too social and does not fully account for why one person chooses one form of masculinity over another. It is the conscious decision-making that is not included in the social approach. The contribution of psychosocial criminology is that it combines the two approaches, the individual and the social. With regard to gender, Gadd and Jefferson draw on a variety of psychoanalytic approaches to look at how gender is both chosen and reproduced so that gender difference has some predictability, but also how identity can be flexible. One of the problems with much of the psychological research on crime is that is posits a too static impression of the individual. Typologies and personality trait theories are all inflexible. Late modern and postmodern ideas have challenged this concept of the fixed identity and so presented a significant challenge for psychology, and all forms of science, to confront.

The following looks at some other new areas of crime that psychology and criminology will need to take more seriously. Already this book has looked at areas that criminology has not dealt adequately with, such as war and terrorism.

These areas have arguably been better served by psychology. However, the following issues pose various problems.

Psychology of rare crime and psychology of volume crime

From murder to rape, psychology has much to say. Consequently, this book has mainly focused on the role of psychology in the study of serious crime. Moreover, this is how the media depict the role of psychology in the study and investigation of crime. The majority of research in this area also focuses on these topics. However, that is not to say that psychology and crime need only focus on this. The psychology of volume crime, e.g. theft, burglary or street crime, is an area of increasing interest to some psychologists. David Canter in particular has argued that volume crime should be amenable to investigative psychology as much as topics like serial murder (Canter 2004). Bennell and Jones (2005) have shown how burglary can be linked by looking at the space between one burglary site and another. They found that the closer the two locations were the more likely that the same burglar carried out the crime. They explain that the utility of this finding is that choice of crime location is the aspect of the offence over which the burglar has most control.

In Chapter 2, Canter argued that themes rather than idiosyncrasies are the best focus for serial murder investigations. In a similar way, spatial mapping is useful for the police in this crime. What a burglar steals depends on many factors, not least of which is the availability of the item in the location. If the police linked crimes based on the type of items that were stolen the investigation would be dependent on a certain amount of chance. Furthermore, location is a more dependable piece of data than the items stolen. The former is more likely to be recorded accurately than what is stolen. Choice of location is more consistent than the type of item stolen. A further reason why volume crime is an important area for future research is that there are more opportunities to conduct research. Murder is rare, serial murder even rarer, so the chance that an individual psychologist may be called upon to profile a case of serial murder is equally rare. There are simply too many psychologists for them all to be called upon to profile a crime. By contrast, volume crime such as burglary is common.

Psychology and the problem of desistance

Psychology tends to be deterministic and positivistic and as such struggles to adapt its theories of crime causation to people whose behaviour changes. For example, Eysenck's personality trait theory posits traits as a stable construct that is mostly unchanged over the life course. However, a significant criminological finding is that the majority of all people who get involved in crime grow out of it, and a minority of all those who engage in crime go on to engage in crime throughout their lives (Rutherford 1986/2002; Matza 1995/1964). Furthermore, the majority of all crimes are committed by a minority of all those who engage in crime (Graham and Bowling 1995; Smith and McVie 2003). This means that a small number of people engage in multiple acts of crime, and the vast majority commit one or only a few crimes before desisting. Studying why people stop committing crime is a relatively recent topic for criminology with much being done in the last 20 years and linking this to effective social policy more recent still (Farrall and Maruna 2004; Burnett and Maruna 2004). This might be because the traditional purpose of criminology was the study of the cause of crime, not the study of what makes people stop. However, Travis Hirschi's theory of self-control in 1969 looked at the development of crime prevention factors over the life course. The more powerful are our social bonds to significant others, work, family and friends, the less likely we are to commit crime due to our desire not to break these bonds through being caught and convicted of a crime. Hirschi effectively reversed the common criminological and psychological question and posited the opposite, not why do we commit crime, but why do we not commit crime? He put forward four aspects of our social bonds: attachment, commitment, involvement and belief. Taken together these four elements act as factors that help people avoid crime or to desist from crime. Control theory has been criticised for several problems, but the main contribution to this discussion is that it redirected the focus of some criminologists away from the search for causes to the search for preventive measures. It also put forward an account that depathologised deviance, since without the social bonds, and if we could get away with it, we would all be involved in deviance. However, Hirschi went on to develop his themes further and in a book co-authored with Gottfredson it was suggested that lack of self-control was a more hardwired trait (Gottfredson and Hirschi 1990). They went on to claim that such lack of self-control and impulsivity was hard to change as the child got older (Gottfredson and Hirschi 1990, 1995). In the work of just one scholar we can see the two sides of this debate, one where the emphasis is on the social bonds a person has and not on the cause of crime, and in the other where social bonds are less important as a child gets older and their impulsivity becomes more entrenched.

Following the critiques of the stable psychological trait theory by people such as Matza, more contemporary research into desistance has sought to see it as a process. The problem of maturation, where ageing seems to somehow magically transform the majority of people (mostly heterosexual men) into law-abiding citizens is not an explanation but an observation. There are a number of approaches that have been put forward recently; one is cultural criminology where crime is not seen as pathological and where understanding the background cause is less important than the foreground emotions. Another is that crime is seen as sensually exciting and seductive (Katz 1988; Ferrell 1999; Webber 2007b). And, finally, narrative psychology, which similarly aims to overcome the reliance on trait theory but does so by accepting the existence of traits whilst allowing some scope for personality change. One way it does this is to allow people to present a self-narrative that makes sense of new experiences and allows personality and identity to change. It is based on the work of, amongst others, McAdams and argues for a three tier model of personality, which includes personality traits, personal strategies and identity narratives or self-stories (McAdams 1994; Maruna 2000). To this might be added a fourth her; the narratives that are created by others about us. For example, family, friends, teachers and even the police on criminal records (Webber 2007b). These three approaches present a significant challenge to traditional psychological and criminological theories that seek unitary causes of crime and stability in identity and personality.

Harm, green criminology and zemiology

One area that will need to be considered that has hitherto been neglected is that of actions which have more widespread and extreme consequences but which society has become accustomed not to think of as crime. Climate change and the reluctance of large corporations to move away from a reliance on fossil fuels is one such area that might become more fully accepted as a crime now that there is a scientific consensus as to the existence of climate change. Climate change might begin to take on the appearance of crime the more the effects become evident in rising seas and the resulting loss of land (see for example Beirne and South 2007 on green criminology). Crop failures and biological threats will increase leading to food shortage and disease. Conflict between one country and another over scarce resources will also increase and has lead to what some have termed green criminology. Indeed, the word harm becomes central to Hillyard and Tombs' argument about the future direction that criminology should take. This is sometimes referred to as **zemiology**, or the study of harms (Hillyard and Tombs 2007). They argue that there are many forms of activity that cause harm but are not held to be crime and so not caught in the narrow lens of criminology (Young 2007). Moreover, the harms that are not caught by criminology tend to be those with most far-reaching consequences. Certainly, these emerging issues present significant challenges to a discipline that has set itself on a course of understanding crime and justice at the level of the individual. How, for example, should psychology respond to the concerns of these debates? Or indeed, the burgeoning interest in green criminology? These clearly present questions that are not just drawing on groups, but on global factors far beyond the control of individuals. They also raise issues of history and culture (Ferrell et al. 2008).

The need for cross-disciplinary research

What this book set out to do was tackle the tricky subject of a discipline that sets out to help, but can often hinder, especially when it focuses on crime. Psychology and sociology have a long, interconnected history that has only recently diverged. This has left psychology without a social input, and sociology with a limited conception of the individual. Psychosocial criminology has been one way to bring the two elements together and cultural criminology at least suggests that the role of emotion and culture are important. Ultimately, however, the tension between the two sides can only be reduced if more people research across disciplinary boundaries. The ability to search journals from within and outside one's discipline may overcome this, and both students and established academics need to practise such searches in order to break through the narrowness of the creation of academic knowledge.

For example, many contemporary studies draw on a variety of different subjects, breaking through and merging disciplinary boundaries. Many of the psychological accounts discussed in this book are good examples of this. In the UK, Canter and Alison refer to criminologists and sociologists such as Marcus Felson and Anthony Giddens (Canter 2000; Alison and Stein 2001). It is interesting to see the unself-conscious way that these psychologists are able to draw on the knowledge accrued in other disciplines to add to their own. Criminology, and by this I am referring to the more sociological approach to crime, seems to have forgotten its own history of reflecting on psychology and has become almost ashamed of referring to any insight developed by psychologists. By the same token, psychology needs more awareness of social context and the way that political change can affect the way we see human behaviour.

Final words

It has been noted by many authors that psychology is unaware or unconcerned with the power that the discipline wields. For example, Hegarty argues that 'psychology's power and psychologists' awareness of it appear to repel each other like polarized magnets' (2007: 77). Hegarty talks about the invention of

IQ during the First World War as a property common to all humans but notes that white psychologists seemed unaware that the administering of an IQ test was perceived differently by black and white people. IQ testing was a cultural creation experienced differently by people from different cultural backgrounds. As Hegarty argues:

> Those people who are rendered 'impure' because their lives sit at the blurry boundaries of existing categories often experience violence from psychology as a result of their position on the nature versus nurture battleground. (Hegarty 2007: 84)

Because of this, criminology has moved further from psychology. Psychology's overemphasis on the individual and its use of positivistic methodologies has meant that criminology, by way of contrast, has ignored the individual offender (Gadd and Jefferson 2007). The psychosocial approach to criminology, suggested by Gadd and Jefferson, is one way to overcome this problem. Cultural criminology has also offered new and interesting avenues for researching culture and emotion (Ferrell et al. 2008). Ultimately, the best way to overcome the insularity of disciplinary boundaries is an awareness of the advantages and disadvantages of each discipline, coupled with a sense of creativity in how ideas often presented as disparate can be combined.

Summary

- When psychology is directed towards the study of crime it becomes a system of governance and control. This is an inherently political position.
- For example, the uses to which psychology is put can have negative consequences for civil liberties and human rights. The same is true of some forms of sociological criminology.
- It has been argued that psychology is too focused on the individual and sociological criminology on the social construction of crime. Missing from these accounts is an integration of the social, individual and emotional. Crucially sociological criminology has neglected questions of motivation. Psychosocial criminology attempts to overcome this.
- Psychological profiling is increasingly being directed towards volume crime.
- The individual focus of psychology has not dealt effectively with crimes that have a social, historical and political dimension such as terrorism and war. Similarly, the increasing interest in the notion of harm is bringing into criminology topics that hitherto were ignored, such as pollution. Psychology will need to take a more integrative approach to deal with these developments.

STUDY QUESTIONS

1 What are the ethical issues with seeking to intervene in someone's life before they commit an offence if they have been identified as a potential criminal?

2 Should we be more concerned with protecting the innocent than protecting the human rights of potential criminals?

3 Is a psychology of crime possible?

4 To what extent might we lose the unique qualities of an individual discipline, such as psychology and sociology, by arguing for more integration?

FURTHER READING

Gadd, D. and Jefferson, T. (2007) *Psychosocial Criminology: An Introduction*. London: Sage.

Glossary

Aetiology/etiology These two words mean the same thing, the former tends to be more common in American publications, the latter in English. The word means the study of causes. It originates in the field of medicine and referred to the search for the cause of disease. Consequently, its use in criminology or psychology is a reflection of the traditional approach to crime where it was seen as pathological, or a disease to be cured.

Anomie Anomie literally translates as without norms. Made famous in the book *Suicide* by Durkheim (1897/1951), but used later by Robert Merton in 1938, and with links to the British left realist tradition where it became relative deprivation. For Durkheim, anomie developed during times of social upheaval such as an economic boom or a recession. Our social bonds become strained and this leads to a sense of dislocation resulting in suicide in Durkheim's study, but in Merton's version it described the way that the goal of a good job and financial stability was not available to all and so resulted in frustration. This situation was deemed anomic. Some people responded by trying to attain the goals by innovating and committing crime to achieve the goal.

Anti-social behaviour *see* **Deviance**

Atavism A reversion to an earlier form; in evolutionary theory an atavism is a throwback to an earlier form of evolution.

Classicism A system for organising the criminal justice system in a more equitable way originating in the late eighteenth and early nineteenth century by philosophers such as Cesare Becarria and Jeremy Bentham. Humans freely chose to commit crime and should be punished in proportion to the severity of the offence. Punishment should act as a deterrent. Bentham's design for a prison, the Panopticon, derives from these ideas and hypothesised that the potential for constant surveillance in the prison cell would lead to self-regulation. The theory contrasts with positivism because it presents the human as rational calculator and not at the mercy of causes outside of their control. Neo-classicism describes a similar approach that came to prominence in the 1980s and was associated with Rational Choice Theory and Routine Activities Theory.

Confabulation The creation of imaginary events, behaviours or experiences to fill a gap in memory, or due to the suggestibility of the subject.

Dark figure of crime The dark figure of crime refers to the number of crimes that do not come to the attention of the police. Police-recorded crime figures based on crimes known to the police are an underestimate of the actual number of offences that take place. This is due to the fact that not all crimes are reported to the police or are not recorded as a crime (no-crimed). The response to this is the use of victim surveys that ask people about their own experiences of crime. The figures from such victim surveys as the British Crime Survey or the local victim crime surveys conducted by the left realist school of criminology report higher rates of victimisation. Consequently, they are said to uncover some of the dark figure of crime.

Determinism Determinism suggests that human behaviour is caused by factors over which they have little or no control. It can be seen in sociology and psychology. One of the main points of contrast between psychology and sociology is that the latter group of scholars regard the majority of the former as deterministic. David Matza (1995/1964) sought to distinguish between what he called hard and soft determinism. Hard determinism can be seen in the work of Lombroso where human behaviour is akin to a chemical property that has little reason or choice. Human freedom, Matza maintained, was illusory for this approach. Soft determinism still has the search for causes as its primary function but has more room for choice. Choice is constrained by structural forces, it is limited but it is there.

Deviance Deviance is a more inclusive category than the term 'crime' since it can include behaviour that would not be legally prohibited. It is behaviour that deviates from the norms as they stand at that point in time. Before criminology was widely taught in universities students could study the sociology of deviance. However, the term can be compared to 'antisocial behaviour' which equally describes activity that does not satisfy the legal criteria of a crime in that it can potentially include any activity that is not wanted. The Antisocial Behaviour Order in the UK (ASBO) is not a crime prevention measure, but a measure to prevent deviance. Sensitivity to deviant or anti-social activity can change socially and historically.

Due process This is a model of law which stipulates that the law should be followed in a clear and open manner so as to ensure fairness. The Criminal Justice System is seen as an impartial authority which does not take sides or be unfairly influenced.

Enlightenment Sometimes referred to as the age of enlightenment, this term describes a period in history leading up to the French Revolution in 1789. Associated with thinkers such as Voltaire, Montesquieu, Diderot and Rousseau, Enlightenment thought posited human reason as superior to superstition and so it is seen as the start of the modern era.

Epistemology   This is the study of how we know what we know. When someone asks you a question and you answer it, how did you come to know that the answer you gave was correct? If you read it in a newspaper, how do you know the accuracy of that source? In social sciences, it is assumed that the level of epistemology is higher than journalism because social scientists need to cite their sources. When reading this book you can see that I have provided references to research that has been published. You can look this up in the References, find it in a library and read the work in more detail. You might even disagree that my interpretation is the right one. In consequence, you might write an essay that disagrees with my point and adds to it by drawing on other studies. This is the slow build up of knowledge and the way social scientists demonstrate their entitlement to create knowledge. Closely linked to epistemology is **methodology**.

Etiology   *see* **Aetiology**

Ethnography   This is a research method originally derived from anthropology. It is a mainly qualitative approach that draws on close observation of a group or culture. Observers can take many different roles, but are usually either participants, living with the group under study and taking an active role in their daily lives, or non-participants, where the observer takes a more objective stance. Researchers tend to spend a long time undertaking such studies. Ethnographic research has been used in sociology and criminology, as well as some forms of social psychology.

Forensic psychology   A branch of psychology that deals with the legal system and the courts, it has come to mean a branch of psychology that is specifically concerned with crime.

Functionalism   An approach that describes the work of a number of different theorists such as Talcott Parsons, Emile Durkheim and R.K. Merton who regarded society as being organised as if it were an interrelated whole. When each part worked and the relationship to the other parts functioned smoothly society worked well as a whole. This is a consensus approach that suggests that the majority of people accepted that the organisation of society was the correct one. The theorists themselves also took this view.

Governmentality   A term that derives from the French social theorist Michel Foucault and describes the way that problems are created and how they become governable. It also describes the organisations that become part of the governing elite, as such psychology and criminology have been described as being part of this.

Intergroup   Refers to the relationship between one group and another, for example if we were to study traditional social class stratification we might refer to the differences between the working class and the middle class. This can be compared to **intra-group**.

Interrogative suggestibility   This is the extent to which someone's recall of an observation, such as a crime taking place, can alter during questioning. Questions can mislead in a number of ways, the most common being leading questions, where the interviewer leads the witness to say something that the interviewer already knows. The Gudjonsson Suggestibility Scale (GSS) is used in psychological experiments to determine an individual's level of suggestibility.

Intra-group   Refers to the relationships within one group. So, if we were to look at traditional forms of social stratification, we might notice that there are a huge range of differences *within* the working-class. This might make us question the utility of using differences between classes in a simple way since differences within groups are likely to be as large as those between groups.

Left realism   *see* **Realism**

Meta-analysis   A meta-analysis means that a researcher looks at a number of studies and analyses all of the results to arrive at one combined result. The term 'meta' can be added to many other words to demonstrate a macro-level of focus. So a meta-theory is a theory that includes many subtheories. An example is positivism which contains theories as diverse as Eysenck's personality theory and those forms of Marxism that posit the capitalist economy as the cause of crime after conducting statistical analyses of crime data.

Methodology   When writing up a research study it is necessary to tell the reader the process that the researchers went through to collect the data. If the study was based on interviews then the researchers will say how many there were, with whom and how long they took. If each interviewee was asked the same questions then these might be reproduced in an appendix. This is the method used, like a recipe. However, a methodology goes further to justify why the methods used were the best way to obtain the data necessary to answer the study's questions or objectives. A methodology combines a discussion of methods used and an epistemological discussion to demonstrate how the methods help to create valid data.

Mnemonic   A technique to help memory based upon word associations. For example, 'Richard Of York Gained Battle In Vain' is a mnemonic to help remember the correct sequence of the colours of the rainbow. Red, Orange, Yellow, Green, Blue, Indigo, Violet.

Neo-classicism   *see* **Classicism**

Pathological   Theories that treat crime and its cause as an illness tend to be referred to as pathological. Lombroso regarded crime as being caused by internal physical features and so was a naturally occurring problem such as an illness. Consequently, Lombroso's theory and others like it treat crime as a pathology. Sociological positivism also treats crime as a pathology to be cured, but sees the cause of the illness as social, such as poverty.

Positivism   Positivism is the application of the natural scientific method to the study of human behaviour. Positivism can be seen in both psychology and sociology. David Matza maintained that all criminology was positivistic since it tried to understand the criminal as different from the non-criminal (1995/1964). This distinction and categorisation of people into criminal and non-criminal is similar to the natural sciences when chemicals are demarcated due to their various properties and animals are categorised in terms of their differences and similarities into warm-blooded and cold-blooded animals and so on. The criticism of scientific studies are that they tend to be **deterministic** and do not allow for human creativity and the way we make sense and add meaning to our lives.

Profiling   The tool for providing the police with a guide to the type of person they are looking for. There are a number of ways that this can be done, but the main two are those of the FBI in America and David Canter's investigative psychology in the UK.

Psychiatry   A branch of medicine that deals with mental health problems. Unlike psychologists, psychiatrists can prescribe medication.

Realism   There are two forms of realism in criminology. They differ in their political bias. The terms left and right realism were coined by Jock Young, one of the leading writers in the left realist school. Both forms take crime seriously, and contrast with criminological theories that suggest crime is socially constructed. Left realism suggests crime is caused by relative deprivation and political marginality, whereas right realism tends to suggest crime is due to a moral failure.

Relative deprivation   Relative deprivation is the idea that deprivation is relative and based on social comparisons with other individuals or groups. It is a subjective interpretation and not based on objective reality. It can be contrasted with absolute deprivation or poverty. Relative deprivation can therefore effect anyone regardless of where they are placed in the social system or if they are rich or poor. It is most famously employed by the left realists as a cause of crime.

Right realism   *see* **Realism**

Risk   Risk and risk society are related concepts that derive from the idea that there has been a shift towards taking precautionary measures to deal with crime (Beck 1992; Ericson and Haggerty 1997). Related to this is the suggestion that we have moved towards actuarial justice (Feeley and Simon 1994), the use of statistical methods to determine the best ways to deal with offenders based upon calculations of their risk to the public. One criticism of these ideas is that there is an exaggeration of the focus on risk and that there is not much difference in this focus over time.

Structuralism   This is a theoretical approach that seeks to understand the social world by focusing on the structures that comprise it. For example, the economy is a structure that shapes the way we live our lives. We have very little control over it, yet the economy can have an effect on what we do. So if the economy is weak we may not want to spend so much money in case we lose our job. Consequently, structuralism is criticised as being too **deterministic** since humans have very little control over their own destinies.

Structure/agency debate   In sociology, the structure and agency debate revolves around whether we see humans as having control over their lives, so they are agents of their own destiny, or humans are controlled and manipulated by structural forces outside their control and that pre-existed them, such as the economy. In psychology, the nature/nurture debate is a version of this distinction, although rarely will the agency approach be as strong as in sociology. Most contemporary theorists of both sociological and psychological persuasions tend to see behaviour as a reflection of both structural influences and an agent's own choices.

Welfare or justice model   A model of criminal justice that is often juxtaposed with a justice model. A welfare model suggests that crime is caused by social deprivation rather than moral failings and so the best way to deal with such people is to provide welfare in the form of treatment, if they have an addiction, for example, or through help with getting back to work through education programmes. This is in contrast to the justice model which is based on the belief that crime is a conscious decision and moral failing and so needs to be punished with sanctions such as imprisonment. In reality, neither of these models has ever been the sole position taken by the criminal justice system, although there have been times when one or the other has been dominant.

Zemiology   Zemiology is the study of harm. Some academics have argued that we should abandon criminology in favour of zemiology because it is a more inclusive way to study human activity. Zemiology may be interested in topics like violence, but also pollution or the way that fashion can lead to anorexia.

References

Aas, K.F. (2007) *Globalization and Crime*. London: Sage.

Abarbanal, G. (2001) 'The victim', in M. LeBeau and A. Mozayani (eds), *Drug-facilitated Sexual Assault: A Forensic Handbook*. London: Academic Press.

Abrams, D. and Hogg, M.A. (1990) *Social Identity Theory: Constructive and Critical Advances*. Hemel Hempstead, Hertfordshire: Harvester Wheatsheaf.

Adorno, T., Frenkel-Brunswick, E., Levinson, D.J. and Sanford, R.N. (1950/1982) *The Authoritarian Personality*. New York: W.W. Norton.

Ainsworth, P.B. (2001) *Offender Profiling and Crime Scene Analysis*. Cullompton, Devon: Willan.

Alexander, K.W., Quas, J.A., Goodman, G.S., Ghetti, S., Edelstein, R.S., Redlich, A.D., Cordon, I.M. and Jones, D.P.H. (2005) 'Traumatic impact predicts long term memory for documented child sexual abuse', *Psychological Science*, 16(1): 33–40.

Alison, L., McLean, C. and Almond, L. (2007) 'Profiling suspects', in T. Newburn, T. Williamson and A. Wright (eds), *Handbook of Criminal Investigation*. Cullompton, Devon: Willan. pp. 493–516.

Alison, L., Smith, M.D., Eastman, O. and Rainbow, L. (2003a) 'Toulmin's Philosophy of Argument and its relevance to offender profiling', *Psychology, Crime and Law*, 9(2): 173–83.

Alison, L., Smith, M.D. and Morgan, K. (2003b) 'Interpreting the accuracy of offender profiles', *Psychology, Crime and Law*, 9(2): 185–95.

Alison, L. and Stein, K. (2001) 'Vicious circles: accounts of stranger sexual assault reflect abusive variants of conventional interactions', *Journal of Forensic Psychiatry*, 12(3): 515–38.

Allport, F.H. (1920) 'The influence of the group upon association and thought', *Journal of Experimental Psychology*, 3: 159–82.

American Psychological Association (1994) *DSM-IV: Diagnostic and Statistical Manual of Mental Disorders*. Washington, DC: American Psychological Association.

Amir, M. (1967) 'Victim precipitated forcible rape', *Journal of Criminal Law, Criminology and Police Science*, 58: 493–502.

Amir, M. (1971) *Patterns in Forcible Rape*. Chicago, IL: University of Chicago Press.

Archer, J. and Vaughn, E.A. (2001) 'Evolutionary theories of rape', *Psychology, Evolution and Gender*, 3(1): 95–101.

Arendt, H. (1964) *Eichman in Jerusalem: A Report on the Banality of Evil*. New York: Penguin.

Association of Chief Police Officers (ACPO) (2006) *Operation Matisse: Investigating Drug Facilitated Sexual Assault*. London: ACPO.

Badey, T.J. (1998) 'Defining international terrorism: a pragmatic approach', *Terrorism and Political Violence*, 10: 90–107.

Bandura, A. (2004) 'The role of selective moral disengagement in terrorism and counter-terrorism', in F.M. Moghaddam and A.J. Marsella (eds), *Understanding Terrorism: Psychosocial Roots, Consequences and Interactions*. Washington, DC: American Psychological Association. pp. 121–50.

Barak, G. (1998) *Integrating Criminologies*. Needham Heights, MA: Allyn and Bacon.

Barak, G. (2001) 'Integrative criminology', in E. McLaughlin and J. Muncie (eds), *The Sage Dictionary of Criminology*. London: Sage. pp. 153–54.

Baudrillard, J. (1983) *Simulacra and Simulations*, trans. P. Foss, P. Patton and P. Beitchman. New York: Semiotext(e).

Bauman, Z. (1997) *Postmodernity and its Discontents*. New York: New York University Press.

Beck, U. (1992) *Risk Society: Towards a New Modernism*. London: Sage.

Becker, H.S. (1963) *Outsiders: Studies in the Sociology of Deviance*. New York: Free Press of Glencoe.

Beirne, P. and South, N. (eds) (2007) *Issues in Green Criminology: Confronting Harms Against Environments, Humanity and Other Animals*. Cullompton, Devon: Willan.

Bennell, C. and Jones, N.I. (2005) 'Between a ROC and a hard place: a method for linking serial burglaries by *modus operandi*', *Journal of Investigative Psychology and Offender Profiling*, 2(1): 23–42.

Blackman, S. (2005) 'Youth subcultural theory: a critical engagement with the concept, its origins and politics, from the Chicago School to postmodernism', *Journal of Youth Studies*, 8(1): 1–20.

Blair, J., Mitchell, D. and Blair, K. (2005) *The Psychopath: Emotion and the Brain*. Oxford: Blackwell Publishing.

Bohner, G., Jarvis, C.I., Eyssel, F. and Siebler, F. (2005) 'The causal impact of rape myth acceptance on men's rape proclivity: comparing sexually coercive and noncoercive men', *European Journal of Social Psychology*, 35: 819–28.

Boon, J.C. and Baxter, J.S. (2000) 'Minimizing interrogative suggestibility', *Legal and Criminological Psychology*, 5(2): 273–84.

Boon, J.C. and Baxter, J.S. (2004) 'Minimizing extraneous, interviewer-based interrogative suggestibility', *Legal and Criminological Psychology*, 9(2): 229–38.

Bosworth, K., Espelage, D. and Simon, T. (1999) 'Factors associated with bullying behaviour in middle school students', *Journal of Early Adolescence*, 19(3): 341–62.

Bottoms, A.E. (1994) 'Environmental criminology', in M. Maguire, R. Morgan and R. Reiner (eds), *The Oxford Handbook of Criminology*. Oxford: Oxford University Press. pp. 585–658.

Bourgois, P. (1995) *In Search of Respect: Selling Crack in El Barrio*. New York: Cambridge University Press.

Box, S. (1983) *Power, Crime and Mystification*. London: Tavistock.

Boyle, K. (2005) *Media and Violence*. London: Sage.

Bradley, A.R. and Wood, J.M. (1996) 'How do children tell? The disclosure process in child sexual abuse', *Child Abuse and Neglect*, 20(9): 881–91.

Brady, I. (2001) *The Gates of Janus: Serial Killing and its Analysis*. Los Angeles, CA: Feral House.

Brittain, R.P. (1970) 'The sadistic murderer', *Medicine, Science and the Law*, 10: 198–207.

Britton, P. (1997) *The Jigsaw Man: The Remarkable Career of Britain's Foremost Criminal Psychologist*. London: Bantam Press.

Browne, A. and Finkelhor, D. (1986) 'Impact of child sexual abuse: review of the research', *Psychological Bulletin*, 99: 66–77.

Brownmiller, S. (1975) *Against our Will: Men, Women and Rape*. Harmondsworth, Middlesex: Penguin.

Brush, S.T. (1996) 'Dynamics of theory change in the social sciences: relative deprivation and collective violence', *Journal of Conflict Resolution*, 40(4): 523–45.

Bulmer, M. (1984) *The Chicago School of Sociology: Institutionalization, Diversity and the Rise of Sociological Research*. Chicago, IL: University of Chicago Press.

Burgess, J., Douglas, J. and Ressler, R. (1985a) 'Classifying sexual homicide crime scenes', *FBI Bulletin*, 54: 12–17.

Burgess, J., Douglas, J. and Ressler, R. (1985b) 'Crime scene and profile characteristics of organized and disorganized murders', *FBI Bulletin*, 54: 18–25.

Burnett, R. and Maruna, S. (2004) 'So "prison works", does it? The criminal careers of 130 men released from prison under Home Secretary, Michael Howard', *The Howard Journal*, 43(4): 390–404.

Burr, J. (2001) 'Women have it. Men want it. What is it?: Constructions of sexuality in rape discourse', *Psychology, Evolution & Gender*, 3(1): 103–5.

Campos, L. and Alonso-Quecuty, M.L. (1999) 'The cognitive interview: much more than simply "try again"', *Psychology, Crime and Law*, 5(1): 47–59.

Canter, D.V. (1984) 'Vandalism: overview and prospect', in C. Levy-Leboyer (ed.), *Vandalism: Behaviour and Modifications*. Amsterdam: North Holland. pp. 343–55.

Canter, D.V. (1995) *Criminal Shadows: Inside the Mind of the Serial Killer*. London: HarperCollins.

Canter, D.V. (2000) 'Offender profiling and criminal differentiation', *Legal and Criminological Psychology*, 5(1): 23–46.

Canter, D.V. (2004) 'Offender profiling and investigative psychology', *Investigative Psychology and Offender Profiling*, 1(1): 1–16.

Canter, D. and Alison, L. (2000) 'The social psychology of crime: groups, teams and networks', in D. Canter and L. Alison (eds), *The Social Psychology of Crime: Groups, Teams and Networks*. Aldershot, Hampshire: Ashgate.

Canter, D.V., Bennell, C., Alison, L.J. and Reddy, S. (2003) 'Differentiating sex offences: a behaviourally based thematic classification of stranger rapes', *Behavioural Sciences and the Law*, 21: 157–74.

Canter, D. and Heritage, R. (1990) 'A multivariate model of sexual offence behaviour: developments in offender profiling', *Journal of Forensic Psychiatry*, 1: 185–212.

Canter, D., Reddy, S. and Alison, L. (2000) 'Levels and variations of violation in rape', in D. Canter and L. Alison (eds), *Profiling Rape and Murder* (Vol. 5). Aldershot, Hampshire: Ashgate.

Carr, E.H. (1987) *What is History?* London: Penguin.

Centofanti, A.T. and Reece, J. (2006) 'The cognitive interview and its effect on misleading postevent information', *Psychology, Crime and Law*, 12(6): 669–83.

Charmaine, S.D. and Wells, G.L. (2006) 'Applied lineup theory', in R.C.L. Lindsay, D.F. Ross, J.D. Read and M.P. Toglia (eds), *Handbook of Eyewitness Psychology: Memory for People*. Mahwah, NJ: Erlbaum. pp. 219–54.

Christianson, S.Å. (1992) 'Emotional stress and eye-witness memory: a critical review', *Psychological Bulletin*, 112(2): 284–309.

Christie, N. (1977) 'Conflicts as property', *British Journal of Criminology*, 17(1): 1–15, cited in E. McLaughlin, R. Fergusson, G. Hughes and L. Westmarland (eds) (2004), *Restorative Justice: Critical Issues*. Milton Keynes: Open University Press. pp. 21–39.

Clarke, C. and Milne, R. (2001) *National Evaluation of the PEACE Investigative Interviewing Course*. London: Home Office.

Clarke, J. (1976) 'Style', in S. Hall and T. Jefferson (eds), *Resistance Through Ritual*. London: Unwin Hyman. pp. 175–85.

Cleckley, H.M. (1941) *The Mask of Sanity*, 4th edn. St Louis, MO: Mosby.

Cloward, R. and Ohlin, L. (1960) *Delinquency and Opportunity*. London: Collier-Macmillan.

Cohen, A.K. (1955) *Delinquent Boys: The Culture of the Gang*. New York: Free Press.

Cohen, L.E. and Felson, M. (1979) 'Social change and crime rate trends; a routine activity approach', *American Sociological Review*, 44: 588–608.

Cohen, P. (1972) 'Sub-cultural conflict and working class community', in *Working Papers in Cultural Studies*, No. 2 (Spring). CCCS: University of Birmingham.

Cohen, S. (1972/2002) *Folk Devils and Moral Panics: The Creation of Mods and Rockers.* London: MacGibbon and Kee. (3rd edn with revised Introduction, London: Routledge.)

Cohen, S. (1980) *Folk Devils and Moral Panics: The Creation of Mods and Rockers*, 2nd edn. Oxford: Blackwell.

Cohen, S. (1985) *Visions of Social Control.* Cambridge: Polity Press.

Cohen, S. (2001) *States of Denial: Knowing About Atrocities and Suffering.* Cambridge: Polity Press.

Coleman, L. (2004) *The Copycat Effect.* New York: Paraview Pocket-Simon and Shuster.

Comte, A. (1830–1842/1969) *Cours de philosophie positive.* 4 vols. Paris: Anthropos.

Connell, R. (1995) *Masculinities.* Cambridge: Polity Press.

Copson, G. (1995) *Coals to Newcastle? Part 1: A Study of Offender Profiling* (Paper 7). London: Police Research Group Special Interest Series, Home Office.

Cornish, D. and Clarke, R. (eds) (1986) *The Reasoning Criminal.* New York: Springer.

Cowburn, M. (2005) 'Hegemony and discourse: reconstructing the male sex offender and sexual coercion by men', *Sexualities, Evolution and Gender*, 7(3): 215–31.

Cowburn, M. and Dominelli, L. (2001) 'Masking hegemonic masculinity: reconstructing the paedophile and the dangerous stranger', *British Journal of Social Work*, 31: 399–415.

Crenshaw, M. (2000) 'The psychology of terrorism: an agenda for the 21st century', *Political Psychology*, 21(2): 405–20.

Crime Operational Support (2008) *The Role of a Behavioural Advisor.* London: National Policing Improvement Agency.

Crombag, H.F.M., Wagenaar, W.A. and Van Koppen, P.J. (1996) 'Crash memories and the problem of "source monitoring"', *Applied Cognitive Psychology*, 10(2): 95–104.

Cullen, F.T. and Messner, S.T. (2007) 'The making of criminology revisited: an oral history of Merton's anomie paradigm', *Theoretical Criminology*, 11(1): 5–37.

Dando, C., Wilcock, R. and Milne, R. (2008) 'The cognitive interview: inexperienced police officers' perceptions of their witness/victim interviewing practices', *Legal and Criminological Psychology*, 13(1): 59–70.

Danziger, K. (1990) *Constructing the Subject: Historical Origins of Psychological Research.* Cambridge: Cambridge University Press.

Darwin, C. (1859) *On the Origin of the Species.* London: Murray.

Davies, G.M. (2001) 'Is it possible to discriminate true from false memories?', in G.M. Davies and T. Dalgleish (eds), *Recovered Memories: Seeking the Middle Ground.* London: John Wiley. pp. 153–74.

Davies, G.M., Smith, S. and Blincoe, C. (2008) 'A "weapon focus" effect in children', *Psychology, Crime and Law*, 14(1): 19–28.

Davies, M. and McCartney, S. (2003) 'Judgement of victim blame and rape myth acceptance in a depicted male rape', *Journal of Community and Applied Social Psychology*, 13: 391–8.

Davis, M.R., McMahon, M. and Greenwood, K.M. (2005) 'The efficacy of mnemonic components of the cognitive interview: towards a shortened variant for time-critical investigations', *Applied Cognitive Psychology*, 19(1): 75–93.

Dawkins, R. (2006) *The God Delusion.* London: Transworld Publishers.

Day, L.E. and Vandiver, M. (2000) 'Criminology and genocide studies: notes on what might have been and what still could be', *Crime, Law and Social Change*, 43: 43–59.

Deffenbacher, K.A., Bornstein, B.H., Penrod, S.D. and McGorty, E.K. (2004) 'A meta-analysis review of the effects of high stress on eyewitness memory', *Law and Human Behavior*, 28(6): 687–706.

De Lint, W. (2003) 'Keeping open windows: police as access brokers', *The British Journal of Criminology*, 43(2): 379–98.

Devine, D.J., Clayton, L.D., Dunford, B.B., Seying, R. and Pryce, J. (2001) 'Jury decision making: 45 years of empirical research on deliberating groups', *Psychology, Public Policy, and Law*, 7(3): 622–727.

Devlin, L. (1976) *Report to the Secretary of State for the Home Department of the Departmental Committee on Evidence of Identification in Criminal Cases*. London: Her Majesty's Stationery Office.

Diener, E. (1979) 'Deindividuation, self-awareness and disinhibition', *Journal of Personality and Social Psychology*, 37(7): 1160–71.

Dietz, P.E. (1986) 'Mass, serial and sensational homicides', *Bulletin of the New York Academy of Medicine*, 62: 477–91.

Doherty, K. and Anderson, I. (2004) 'Making sense of male rape: constructions of gender, sexuality and experience', *Journal of Community and Applied Social Psychology*, 14: 85–103.

Dollard, J., Doob, L.W., Miller, N.E., Mowrer, O.H. and Sears, R.R. (1939) *Frustration and Aggression*. New Haven, CT: Yale University Press.

Douglas, J., Ressler, R., Burgess, A. and Hartman, C. (1986) 'Criminal profiling from crime scene analysis', *Behavioral Sciences and the Law*, 4(4): 401–21.

Downes, D. (1966) *The Delinquent Solution*. London: Routledge and Kegan Paul.

Downes, D. (1988) 'The sociology of crime and social control in Britain, 1960–1987', *The British Journal of Criminology*, 28(2): 45–57.

Durkheim, E. (1893/1984) *The Division of Labor in Society*. New York: Macmillan.

Durkheim, E. (1895/1938) *The Rules of Sociological Method*. Chicago, IL: University of Chicago Press.

Durkheim, E. (1897/1951) *Suicide: A Study in Sociology*. Glencoe, IL: Free Press.

Dysart, J.E., Lindsay, R.C.L., MacDonald, T.K. and Wicke, C. (2002) 'The intoxicated witness: effects of alcohol on identification accuracy from showups', *Journal of Applied Psychology*, 87(1): 170–5.

Echebarria-Echabe, A. and Fernández-Guede, E. (2006) 'Effects of terrorism on attitudes and ideological orientation', *European Journal of Social Psychology*, 36: 259–65.

Edward Day, L. and Vandiver, M. (2000) 'Criminology and genocide studies: notes on what might have been and what still could be', *Crime, Law and Social Change*, 34: 43–59.

Egan, V. (2004) 'The status of sensational interests as indicators of possible risk', in J.R. Adler (ed.) (2004) *Forensic Psychology: Concepts, Debates and Practices*. Cullompton, Devon: Willan. pp. 115–39.

Egger, S. (1998) *The Killers Among Us*. New York: Praeger.

Ericson, R. and Haggerty, K. (1997) *Policing the Risk Society*. Toronto, Ontario: Toronto University Press.

Erikson, E. (1964) *Insight and Responsibility*. New York: Norton.

Eysenck, H.J. (1964/1977) *Crime and Personality*. St Albans, Hertfordshire: Paladin.

Fadiman, J. and Frager, R. (2004) *Personality and Personal Growth*, 6th edn. London: Prentice Hall.

Farrall, S. and Maruna, S. (2004) 'Desistance-focused criminal justice policy research: introduction to a special issue on desistance from crime and public policy', *The Howard Journal*, 43(4): 358–67.

Feeley, M. and Simon, J. (1992) 'The new penology: notes on the emerging strategy of communications and its implications', *Criminology*, 30: 449–74.

Felson, M. (1998) *Crime and Everyday Life: Insights and Implications for Society*, 2nd edn. London: Pine Forge Press.

Ferrell, J. (1999) 'Cultural criminology', *Annual Review of Sociology*, 25: 396–418.

Ferrell, J., Hayward, K. and Young, J. (2008) *Cultural Criminology: An Invitation*. London: Sage.

Festinger, L. (1957) *A Theory of Cognitive Dissonance*. Evanston, IL: Row, Peterson.

Festinger, L., Pepitone, A. and Newcomb, T.M. (1952) 'Some consequences of deindividuation in a group', *Journal of Abnormal and Social Psychology*, 47: 383–9.

Fisher, Sir H. (1977) *The Confait Case: Report*. London: Her Majesty's Stationery Office.

Fisher, R.P. and Geiselman, R.E. (1992) *Memory-enhancing Techniques for Investigative Interviewing: The Cognitive Interview*. Springfield, IL: Charles Thomas.

Fisher, R.P., Mello, E.W. and McCauley, M.R. (1999) 'Are jurors' perceptions of eyewitness credibility affected by the cognitive interview?', *Psychology Crime and Law*, 5(1): 167–76.

Forrest, K.D., Wadkins, T.A. and Larson, B.A. (2006) 'Suspect personality, police interrogations, and false confessions: maybe it is not just the situation', *Personality and Individual Differences*, 40: 621–8.

Forth, A.E. and Hare, R.D. (1989) 'The contingent negative variation in psychopaths', *Psychophysiology*, 26: 676–82.

Foucault, M. (1971) *Madness and Civilisation*. London: Tavistock.

Foucault, M. (1972) *The Archeology of Knowledge*. London: Routledge.

Foucault, M. (1977) *Discipline and Punish: The Birth of the Prison*. London: Penguin.

Fox, J.A. and Levin, J. (2002) 'Mass murder: an analysis of extreme violence', *Journal of Applied Psychoanalytic Studies*, 5(1): 47–64.

Fox, J.A. and Levin, J. (2005) *Extreme Killing: Understanding Serial and Mass Murder*. Thousand Oaks, CA: Sage.

Freedman, L. (2007) 'Terrorism as strategy', *Government and Opposition*, 43(2): 314–39.

Freud, S. (1896/1962) 'The aetiology of hysteria', *The Complete Psychological Works of Sigmund Freud* (Vol. 3; trans. J. Strachey). London: Hogarth Press.

Frick, P.J. and Hare, R.D. (2001) *The Antisocial Screening Device*. Toronto, Ontario: Multi-Health Systems.

Friedrichs, D.O. (2000) 'The crime of the century? The case for the Holocaust', *Crime, Law and Social Change*, 34: 21–41.

Fritzon, K. and Brun, A. (2005) 'Beyond Columbine: a faceted model of school-associated homicide', *Psychology, Crime and Law*, 11(1): 53–71.

Frosh, S. (1999) *The Politics of Psychoanalysis: An Introduction to Freudian and Post-Freudian theory*, 2nd edn. Basingstoke: Macmillan.

Furnham, A. and Schofield, S. (1987) 'Accepting personality test feedback: a review of the Barnum effect', *Current Psychological Research and Review*, 6: 162–78.

Gadd, D. and Jefferson, T. (2007) *Psychosocial Criminology: An Introduction*. London: Sage.

Gallagher, B. (2000) 'The extent and nature of known cases of institutional child sexual abuse', *British Journal of Social Work*, 30: 795–817.

Gard, M. and Bradley, B.S. (2000) 'Getting away with rape: erasure of the psyche in evolutionary psychology', *Psychology, Evolution and Gender*, 2(3): 313–19.

Garland, D. (2001) *The Culture of Control: Crime and Social Order in Contemporary Society*. Oxford: Oxford University Press.

Garland, D. (2002) 'Of crime and criminals: the development of criminology in Britain', in M. Maguire, R. Morgan and R. Reiner (eds), *The Oxford Handbook of Criminology*, 3rd edn. Oxford: Oxford University Press.

Geiselman, R.E. (1999) 'Commentary on recent research with the cognitive interview', *Psychology, Crime and Law*, 5(1): 197–202.

Geiselman, R.E., Fisher, R.P., MacKinnon, D.P. and Holland, H.L. (1985) 'Eyewitness memory enhancement in the police interview: cognitive retrieval mnemonics versus hypnosis', *Journal of Applied Psychology*, 70(2): 401–12.

George, W.H. and Martinez, L.J. (2002) 'Victim blaming in rape: effects of victim and perpetrator race, type of rape and participant racism', *Psychology of Women Quarterly*, 26: 110–19.

Giddens, A. (1978) *Durkheim*. London: Fontana Press.

Giddens, A. (1984) *The Constitution of Society*. Oxford: Polity Press.

Giddens, A. (1990) *The Consequences of Modernity*. Stanford, CA: Stanford University Press.

Gill, O. (1977) *Luke Street: Housing Policy, Conflict and the Creation of the Delinquent Area*. London: Macmillan.

Gilligan, C. (1982) *In a Different Voice*. Cambridge, MA: Harvard University Press.

Glass, J.M. (1997) 'Against the indifference hypothesis: the holocaust and the enthusiasts for murder', *Political Psychology*, 18(1): 129–45.

Glueck, B.H. (1917a) 'Psychiatric clinic', in Sing Sing Prison, *Annual Report, for the Fiscal Year Ending June 30*, 1917: 95–104.

Glueck, B.H. (1917b) 'Types of delinquent careers', *Mental Hygiene*, 1: 171–95.

Glueck, B.H. (1918a) 'Concerning prisoners', *Mental Hygiene*, 2: 177–218.

Glueck, B.H. (1918b) 'A Study of 608 admissions to Sing Sing Prison', *Mental Hygiene*, 2: 85–151.

Glueck, B.H. (1919) Review of *Die Psychopathischen Verbrecher (The Psychopathic Criminal)* by Karl Birnbaum, in *Mental Hygiene*, 3: 157–66.

Godfrey, B.S., Lawrence, P. and Williams, C.A. (2007) *History and Crime*. London: Sage.

Goffman, E. (1959) *The Presentation of Self in Everyday Life*. London: Penguin.

Goodman, G.S. and Melinder, A. (2007) 'Child witness research and forensic interviews of young children: a review', *Legal and Criminological Psychology*, 12(1): 1–19.

Goodwill, A.M. and Alison, L.J. (2005) 'Sequential angulation, spatial dispersion and of distance attack patterns from home in serial rape and burglary', *Psychology, Crime & Law*, 11(2): 161–76.

Gottfredson, M. and Hirschi, T. (1990) *A General Theory of Crime*. Stanford, CA: Stanford University Press.

Gottfredson, M. and Hirschi, T. (1995) 'National crime control policies', *Society*, 32(2): 30–6.

Gould, S.J. (1997) *The Mismeasure of Man*, revised and expanded edn. London: Penguin.

Graham, J. and Bowling, B. (1995) *Young People and Crime*. Home Office Research Study No. 145. London: Her Majesty's Stationery Office.

Granhag, P.A. and Strömwall, L.A. (2001) 'Deception detection based on repeated interrogations', *Legal and Criminological Psychology*, 6(1): 85–101.

Green, L. and Masson, H. (2002) 'Adolescents who sexually abuse and residential accommodation: issues of risk and vulnerability', *British Journal of Social Work*, 32: 149–68.

Groth, A.N. (1979) *Men who Rape: The Psychology of the Offender*. New York: Plenum Press.

Grubin, D. (1998) *Sex Offending against Children: Understanding the Risk*, Police Research Series Paper 99, London: Home Office.

Gudjonsson, G.H. (1984) 'A new scale of interrogative suggestibility', *Personality and Individual Differences*, 5(3): 303–14.

Gudjonsson, G.H. (2003) *The Psychology of Confessions and Denials: A Handbook*. Chichester: Wiley.

Gudjonsson, G.H. (2007) 'Investigative interviewing', in T. Newburn, T. Williamson and A. Wright (eds), *Handbook of Criminal Investigation*. Cullompton, Devon: Willan. pp. 466–92.

Gudjonsson, G.H. and Copson, G. (1997) 'The role of the expert in criminal investigation', in J.L. Jackson and D. Bekerian (eds), *Offender Profiling: Theory, Research and Practice*. Chichester: Wiley. pp. 61–76.

Gudjonsson, G.H., Sigurdsson, J.F., Bragason, O.O., Einarsson, E. and Valdimarsdottir, E.B. (2004) 'Confessions and denials and the relationship with personality', *Legal and Criminological Psychology*, 9(1): 121–33.

Gurr, T.R. (1970) *Why Men Rebel*. Princeton, NJ: Princeton University Press.

Hagan, J., Hirschfield, P. and Shedd, C. (2002) 'First and last words: apprehending the social and legal facts of an urban high school shooting', *Sociological Methods Research*, 31(2): 218–54.

Hale, R. (1997) 'Motives of reward among men who rape', *American Journal of Criminal Justice*, 22: 101–19.

Hall, S., Critcher, C., Jefferson, T., Clarke, J. and Roberts, B. (1978) *Policing the Crisis*. London: Macmillan.

Hall, S. and Jefferson, T. (eds) (1976) *Resistance Through Rituals: Youth Subcultures in Postwar Britain*. London: Unwin Hyman.

Hamm, M.S. (2004) '"Apocalyptic violence" the seduction of terrorist subcultures', *Theoretical Criminology*, 8(3): 323–39.

Haney, C., Banks, W.C. and Zimbardo, P.G. (1973) 'Interpersonal dynamics in a simulated prison', *International Journal of Criminology and Penology*, 1: 69–97.

Harding, D.J., Fox, C. and Mehta, J.D. (2002) 'Studying rare events: lessons from a study of rampage school shootings', *Sociological Methods and Research*, 31(2): 174–217.

Hare, R.D. (1980) 'A research scale for the assessment of psychopathy in criminal populations', *Personality and Individual Differences*, 1: 111–19.

Hartwig, M., Granhag, P.A. and Strömwall, L.A. (2007) 'Guilty and innocent suspects' strategies during police interrogations', *Psychology, Crime and Law*, 13(2): 213–27.

Healy, W. (1915) *The Individual Delinquent*. Boston, MA: Little, Brown.

Hebdidge, D. (1976) 'The meaning of mod', S. Hall and T. Jefferson (eds), *Resistance through Ritual*. London: Unwin Hyman. pp. 87–96.

Hebenton, B. and Seddon, T. (2009) 'From dangerousness to precaution: managing sexual and violent offenders in an insecure and uncertain age', *British Journal of Criminology*, 49(3): 343–62.

Hegarty, P. (2007) 'Getting dirty: psychology's history of power', *History of Psychology*, 10(2): 75–91.

Her Majesty's Inspector of Constabulary (2007) *Without Consent: A Report on the Joint Review of the Investigation and Prosecution of Rape Offences*. London: HMIC.

Herman, J.L. (1992) *Trauma and Recovery: From Domestic Abuse to Political Terror*. London: Pandora.

Herrnstein, R. and Murray, C. (1994) *The Bell Curve*. New York: The Free Press.

Hillbrand, M. (2001) 'Homicide-suicide and other forms of co-occurring aggression against self and others', *Professional Psychology: Research and Practice*, 32(6): 626–35.

Hillyard, P. and Tombs, S. (2007) 'From "crime" to social harm?', *Crime, Law and Social Change*, 48(1–2): 9–25.

Hirschi, T. (1969) *Causes of Delinquency*. Berkeley: University of California Press.

Hobbs, D. (1997) 'Criminal collaboration: youth gangs, subcultures, professional criminals, and organised crime', in M. Maguire, R. Morgan and R. Reiner (eds), *The Oxford Handbook of Criminology*, 2nd edn. Oxford: Oxford University Press.

Hobsbawm, E.J. (1987) *The Age of Empire: 1875–1914*. London: Weidenfeld and Nicholson.

Hobsbawm, E.J. (1994) *Age of Extremes: The Short Twentieth Century 1914–1991*. Harmondsworth, Middlesex: Penguin.

Hogg, M.A. and Abrams, D. (1988) *Social Identifications: A Social Psychology of Intergroup Relations and Group Processes*. London: Routledge.

Hogg, M.A. and Abrams, D. (1999) 'Social identity and social cognition: historical background and current trends', in D. Abrams and M.A. Hogg (eds), *Social Identity and Social Cognition*. Oxford: Blackwell Publishers. pp. 1–25.

Hollin, C. (1989) *Psychology and Crime: An Introduction to Criminological Psychology*. London: Routledge.

Hollin, C. (2002) 'Criminological psychology', in M. Maguire, R. Morgan and R. Reiner (eds), *The Oxford Handbook of Criminology*. London: Oxford University Press. pp. 144–74.

Holmes, R.M. and Holmes, S.T. (1998) *Serial Murder*, 2nd edn. Thousand Oaks, CA: Sage.

Holmes, R.M. and Holmes, S.T. (2001a) *Sex Crimes*, 2nd edn. Thousand Oaks, CA: Sage.

Holmes, R.M. and Holmes, S.T. (2001b) *Mass Murder in the United States*. Upper Saddle River, NJ: Prentice Hall.

Holmes, R.M. and Holmes, S.T. (2002) *Profiling Violent Crimes*, 3rd edn. Thousand Oaks, CA: Sage.

Honts, C.R. and Amato, S. (2007) 'Automation of a screening polygraph test increases accuracy', *Psychology, Crime and Law*, 13(2): 187–99.

Hooper, C. and Koprowska, J. (2004) 'The vulnerabilities of children whose parents have been sexually abused in childhood: towards a new framework', *British Journal of Social Work*, 34(2): 165–80.

Horgan, J. (2003a) 'Leaving terrorism behind: an individual perspective', in A. Silke (ed.), *Terrorists, Victims and Society: Psychological Perspectives on Terrorism and its Consequences*. Chichester, West Sussex: John Wiley. pp. 109–30.

Horgan, J. (2003b) 'The search for the terrorist personality', in A. Silke (ed.), *Terrorists, Victims and Society: Psychological Perspectives on Terrorism and its Consequences*. Chichester, West Sussex: John Wiley. pp. 3–27.

Horn, D.G. (2003) *The Criminal Body: Lombroso and the Anatomy of Deviance*. London: Routledge.

Horvath, M. and Brown, J. (2005) 'Drug-assisted rape and sexual assault: definitional, conceptual and methodological developments', *Journal of Investigative Psychology and Offender Profiling*, 2: 203–10.

Horvath, M. and Brown, J. (2007) 'Alcohol as drug of choice: is drug-assisted rape a misnomer?', *Psychology, Crime and Law*, 13(5): 417–29.

Hudson, B. (2003) *Justice in the Risk Society*. London: Sage

Hyman, H.H. (1942) 'The psychology of status', *Archives of Psychology*, 269.

Jamieson, R. (1998) 'Towards a criminology of war in Europe', in V. Ruggiero, N. South and I. Taylor (eds), *The New Criminology*. London: Routledge. pp. 480–506.

Janz, J. (2004) 'Psychology and society: an overview', in J. Janz and P. van Drunen (eds), *A Social History of psychology*. Oxford: Blackwell Publishing. pp. 12–44.

Jefferson, T. (1987) 'Beyond paramilitarism', *The British Journal of Criminology*, 27(1): 47–53.

Jefferson, T. (1997) 'Masculinities and crime', in M. Maguire, R. Morgan and R. Reiner (eds), *The Oxford Handbook of Criminology*, 2nd edn. Oxford: Oxford University Press. pp. 535–57.

Jefferson, T. (2002) 'For a psychosocial criminology', in K. Carrington and R. Hogg (eds), *Critical Criminology: Issues, Debates, Challenges*. Cullompton, Devon: Willan. pp. 145–67.

Jefferson, T. (2004) 'From cultural studies to psychosocial criminology: an intellectual journey', in J. Ferrell, K. Hayward, W. Morrison and M. Presdee (eds), *Cultural Criminology Unleashed*. London: Glasshouse Press. pp. 29–39.

Jenks, C. (2003) *Transgression*. London: Routledge.

Jewkes, Y. (2004) *Media and Crime*. London: Sage.

Jones, T., MacLean, B. and Young, J. (1986) *The Islington Crime Survey*. Aldershot, Hampshire: Gower.

Kahn, A.S., Jackson, J., Kully, C., Badger, K. and Halvorsen, J. (2003) 'Calling it rape: difference in experiences of women who do and do not label their sexual assault as rape', *Psychology of Women Quarterly*, 27: 233–42.

Kalven, H., Jr. and Zeisel, H. (1966) *The American Jury*. Boston, MA: Little, Brown.

Kassin, S.M. and Keischel, K.L. (1996) 'The social psychology of false confessions: compliance, internalization and confabulation', 7(3): 125–8.

Kassin, S.M., Leo, R.A., Meissner, C.A., Richman, K.D., Colwell, L.H., Leach, A. and La Fon, D. (2007) 'Police interviewing and interrogation: a self-report survey of police practice and beliefs', *Law and Human Behaviour*, 31: 381–400.

Katz, J. (1988) *Seductions of Crime: Moral and Sensual Attractions in Doing Evil*. New York: Basic Books.

Kawakami, K. and Dion, K.L. (1993) 'The impact of salient self-identities on relative deprivation and action intentions', *European Journal of Social Psychology*, 23(5): 525–40.

Kebbell, M.R., Milne, R. and Wagstaff, G.F. (1999) 'The cognitive interview: a survey of its forensic effectiveness', *Psychology, Crime and Law*, 5(1): 101–15.

Kelman, H.C. and Hamilton, V.L. (1989) *Crimes of Obedience*. New Haven, CT: Yale University Press.

Kirsch, I., Deacon, B.J., Huedo-Medina, T.B., Scoboria, A., Moore, T.J. and Johnson, B.T. (2008) 'Initial severity and anti-depressant benefits: a meta-analysis of data submitted to the Food and Drug Administration', *Public Library of Science Medicine*, 5(2): e45 doi:10.1371/journal.pmed.0050045.

Kitzinger, J. (1999) 'The ultimate neighbour from hell: media framing of paedophiles', in B. Franklin (ed.), *Social Policy, the Media and Misrepresentation*. London: Routledge. pp. 707–21.

Köhnken, G., Milne, R., Memon, A. and Bull, R. (1999) 'The cognitive interview: a meta-analysis', *Psychology, Crime and Law*, 5(1): 3–27.

Koss, M.P. and Oro, C.J. (1982) 'Sexual experiences survey: a research instrument investigation into sexual aggression and victimization', *Journal of Consulting and Clinical Psychology*, 50: 455–7.

Kraepelin, E. (1917) *Lectures on Clinical Psychiatry*, revised and edited by T. Johnstone, 3rd English edn. New York: William Wood.

Krafft-Ebing, R. (1886/1965) *Psycopathia Sexualis*. New York: Stein and Day.

Kruglanski, A.W. and Fishman, S. (2006) 'The psychology of terrorism: "syndrome" versus "tool" perspectives', *Terrorism and Political Violence*, 18(2): 193–215.

Lacquer, W. (1999) *The New Terrorism: Fanaticism and the Arms of Mass Destruction*. New York: Oxford University Press.

Laing, R.D. and Esterson, A. (1964/1990) *Sanity, Madness and the Family: Families of Schizophrenics*. New York: Basic Books. (First published 1964.)

Landström, S., Granhag, P.A. and Hartwig, M. (2007) 'Children's live and videotaped testimonies: how presentation mode affects observers' perception, assessment and memory', *Legal and Criminological Psychology*, 12(2): 333–47.

Langleben, D.D. (2008) 'Detection and deception with fMRI: are we there yet?', *Legal and Criminological Psychology*, 13(1): 1–9.

Lea, J. (1992) 'The analysis of crime', in J. Young and R. Matthews (eds), *Rethinking Criminology: The Realist Debate*. London: Sage. pp. 67–94.

Lea, J. (1998) 'Criminology and postmodernity', in P. Walton and J. Young (eds), *The New Criminology Revisited*. London: Macmillan.

Lea, J. and Young, J. (1993/1984) *What Is To Be Done About Law and Order?* London: Pluto Press. (First Published 1984.)

Leary, M.R., Kowalski, R.M. and L. Smith and Philips (2003) 'Teasing, rejection, and violence: case studies of the school shootings', *Aggressive Behaviour*, 29(3): 202–14.

Le Bon, G. (1908/1896) *The Crowd: A Study of the Popular Mind*. London: Unwin. (First published in French in 1896.)

Lee, M.R. and DeHart, E. (2007) 'The influence of a serial killer on changes in fear of crime and the use of protective measures: a survey-based case study of Baton Rouge', *Deviant Behaviour*, 28(1): 1–28.

Lemert, E.M. (1967) *Human Deviance, Social Problems and Social Control*. Englewood Cliffs, NJ: Prentice Hall.

Lerner, M.J. (1980) The Belief in a Just World: A Fundamental Delusion. New York: Plenum Press.

Lester, D., Yang, B. and Lindsay, M. (2004) 'Suicide bombers: are psychological profiles possible?', *Studies in Conflict and Terrorism*, 27(4): 283–95.

Levi, K. (1981) 'Becoming a hit man: neutralization in a very deviant career', *Journal of Contemporary Ethnography*, 10(1): 47–63.

Levi-Strauss, C. (1966) *The Savage Mind*. London: Wiedenfeld and Nicholson.

Levi-Strauss, C. (1973) *Tristes Tropiques*. London: Merlin Press.

Loftus, E.F. (1975) 'Leading questions and the eyewitness report', *Cognitive Psychology*, 7(4): 560–72.

Loftus, E.F. (1979) *Eyewitness Testimony*. Cambridge, MA: Harvard University Press.

Loftus, E.F., Loftus, G.R. and Messo, J. (1987) 'Some facts about "weapon focus"', *Law and Human Behaviour*, 11(1): 55–62.

Lombroso, C. (1876) *L'Uomo Delinquente*. Milan: Hoepli.

London, K., Bruck, M., Wright, D.B. and Ceci, S.J. (2008) 'Review of the contemporary literature on how children report sexual abuse to others: findings, methodological issues, and implications for forensic interviewers', *Memory*, 16(1): 29–47.

Lyotard, J.-F. (1984) *The Postmodern Condition: A Report on Knowledge*, trans. G. Bennington and B. Massouri. Minneapolis: University of Minnesota Press.

MacKenzie, D. (1976) 'Eugenics in Britain', *Social Studies of Science*, 6: 499–532.

Maguire, M. (1997) 'Crime statistics, patterns, and trends: changing perceptions and their implications', in M. Maguire, R. Morgan and R. Reiner (eds), *The Oxford Handbook of Criminology*, 2nd edn. Oxford: Oxford University Press. pp. 135–88.

Maikovich, A.K. (2005) 'A new understanding of terrorism using cognitive dissonance principles', *Journal for the Theory of Social Behaviour*, 35(4): 373–97.

Maruna, S. (2000) 'Criminology, desistance and the psychology of the stranger', in D. Canter and L. Alison (eds), *The Social Psychology of Crime: Groups, Teams and Networks*. Aldershot, Hampshire: Ashgate. pp. 287–320.

Marzuk, P.M., Tardiff, K. and Hirsch, C.S. (1992) 'The epidemiology of murder-suicide', *Journal of the American Medical Association*, 267: 3179–83.

Matza, D. (1995; 1964) *Delinquency and Drift*. New Brunswick, NJ: Transaction Publishers.

McAdams, D.P. (1994) *The Person: An Introduction to Personality Psychology*. Fort Worth, TX: Sage.

McBarnet, D. (1978) 'The Fisher Report on the Confait Case: four issues', *The Modern Law Review*, 41(4): pp. 455–63.

McCauley, C. (2002) 'Psychological issues in understanding terrorism and the response to terrorism', in C.E. Stout (ed.), *The Psychology of Terrorism: Theoretical Understandings and Perspectives*, Vol. III. Psychological Dimensions to War and Peace. Westport, CT: Praeger Publishers/Greenwood Publishing Group. pp. 3–29.

McFarlane, F., Powell, M.B. and Dudgeon, P. (2002) 'An examination of the degree to which IQ, memory performance, socio-economic status and gender predict young children's suggestibility', *Legal and Criminological Psychology*, 7(2): 227–39.

McGrath, J.E., Arrow, H. and Berdahl, J.L. (2000) 'The study of groups: past, present and future', *Personality and Social Psychology Review*, 4(1): 95–105.

McGregor, J. (2005) Is it Rape?: *On Acquaintance Rape and Taking Women's Consent Seriously*. Aldershot, Hampshire: Ashgate.

Mead, G.H. (1934) *Mind, Self and Society*. Chicago, IL: University of Chicago Press.

Meissner, C.A. and Brigham, J.C. (2001) 'Thirty years of investigating the own-race bias in memory for faces: a meta-analytic review', *Psychology, Public Policy and Law*, 7(1): 3–35.

Meloy, J.R., Hempel, A., Mohandie, K., Shiva, A. and Gray, B. (2001) 'Offender and offense characteristics of a nonrandom sample of adolescent mass murderers', *Journal of the American Academy of Child and Adolescent Psychiatry*, 40(6): 719–28.

Memon, A. and Higham, P.A. (1999) 'A review of the cognitive interview', *Psychology, Crime and Law*, 5(1): 177–96.

Memon, A., Hope, L. and Bull, R. (2003) 'Exposure duration: effects on eyewitness accuracy and confidence', *British Journal of Psychology*, 94(3): 339–54.

Merton, R.K. (1938) 'Social structure and anomie', *American Sociological Review*, 3(5): 672–82.

Merton, R.K. (1957) *Social Theory and Social Structure*, revised edn. New York: Free Press.

Merton, R.K. (1995) 'Opportunity structure: the emergence, diffusion and differentiation of a sociological concept, 1930's–1950's', in F. Adler and W.S. Laufer (eds), *The Legacy of Anomie Theory*. London: Transaction Publishers. pp. 3–78.

Messerschmidt, J.W. (1993) *Masculinities and Crime*. Maryland: Rowman and Littlefield.

Messerschmidt, J.W. (1994) 'Schooling, masculinities and youth crime by white boys', in T. Newburn and E.A. Stanko (eds), *Just Boys Doing Business: Men, Masculinities and Crime*. London: Routledge. pp. 81–99.

Messerschmidt, J.W. (1997) *Crime as Structured Action*. London: Sage.

Milgram, S. (1963) 'Behavioural study of obedience', *Journal of Abnormal and Social Psychology*, 67(4): 371–8.

Milne, R. and Bull, R. (1999) *Investigative Interviewing: Psychology and Practice*. Chichester, West Sussex: John Wiley.

Milne, R. and Bull, R. (2003) 'Does the cognitive interview help children to resist the effects of suggestive questioning?', *Legal and Criminological Psychology*, 8(1): 21–38.

Morgan III, C.A., Hazlett, G., Doran, A., Garrett, S., Hoyt, G., Thomas, P., Baranoski, M. and Southwick, S.M. (2004) 'Accuracy of eyewitness memory for persons encountered during exposure to highly intense stress', *International Journal of Law and Psychiatry*, 27(3): 265–79.

Morris, T. (1957) *The Criminal Area: A Study in Social Ecology*. London: Routledge.

Mortimer, A. and Shepherd, E. (1999) 'Frames of mind: schemata guiding cognition and conduct in the interviewing of suspected offenders', in A. Memon and R. Bull (eds), *Handbook of the Psychology of Interviewing*. Chichester, West Sussex: John Wiley. pp. 293–315.

Muggleton, D. (2000) *Inside Subcultures: The Postmodern Meaning of Style*. Oxford: Berg.

Mulvey, E.P. and Cauffman, E. (2001) 'The inherent limits of predicting school violence', *American Psychologist*, 56(10): 797–802.

National Research Council of the National Academies in America (2004) *The Polygraph and Lie Detection*. Washington, DC: National Academies Press.

Nye, R.A. (1995) 'Introduction to the Transaction Edition', in G. Le Bon (1896), *The Crowd: A Study of the Popular Mind*. London: Transaction Publishers. pp. 1–26.

Oakes, P.J., Haslam, S.A. and Turner, J.C. (1994) *Stereotyping and Social Reality*. Oxford: Blackwell Publishers.

O'Malley, P. (2001) 'Risk, crime and prudentialism revisited', in K. Stenson and R. Sullivan (eds), *Crime, Risk and Justice: The Politics of Crime Control in Liberal Democracies*. Cullompton, Devon: Willan. pp. 89–103.

Painter, K., Lea, J., Woodhouse, T. and Young, J. (1989) *The Hammersmith and Fulham Crime and Policing Survey*. London: The Centre for Criminology, Middlesex Polytechnic.

Palermo, G.B. (1994) 'Murder-suicide: an extended suicide', *International Journal of Offender Therapy and Comparative Criminology*, 38: 205–16.

Palermo, G.B. (1997) 'The Berserk Syndrome: a review of mass murder', *Aggression and Behavior*, 2(1): 1–8.

Pape, R. (2005) *Dying to Win: The Strategic Logic of Suicide Terrorism*. New York: Random House.

Park, R.E. (1952) *Human Communities: The City and Human Ecology*. New York: Free Press.

Parker, A.D. and Brown, J. (2000) 'Detection of deception: statement validity analysis as a means of determining truthfulness or falsity of rape allegations', *Legal and Criminological Psychology*, 5(2): 237–59.

Parker, H.J. (1974) *View From The Boys: A Sociology of Down-Town Adolescents*. London: David and Charles.

Paz-Alonso, P.M. and Goodman, G.S. (2008) 'Trauma and memory: effects of post-event misinformation, retrieval order, and retention interval', *Memory*, 16(1): 58–75.

Pearson, G. (1975) *Deviant Imagination: Psychiatry, Social Work and Social Change*. London: Macmillan.

Pearson, G. (1983) *Hooligan: A History of Respectable Fears*. London: Macmillan.

Pearson, G. (1994) 'Youth, crime and society', in M. Maguire, M. Morgan and R. Reiner (eds), *The Oxford Handbook of Criminology*. Oxford: Oxford University Press. pp. 1161–206.

Perls, F.S. (1947/1969) *Ego, Hunger and Aggression*. New York: Random House.

Piazza, J.A. (2006) 'Rooted in poverty?: Terrorism, poor economic development, and social change', *Terrorism and Political Violence*, 18(1): 159–77.

Pickel, K.L., Narter, D.B., Jameson, M.M. and Lenhardt, T.T. (2008) 'The weapon focus effect in child eyewitnesses', *Psychology, Crime and Law*, 14(1): 61–72.

Post, J.M. (2005) 'When hatred is bred in the bone: psycho-cultural foundations of contemporary terrorism', *Political Psychology*, 26(4): 615–36.

Post, J.M., Sprinzak, E. and Denny, L.M. (2003) 'The terrorists in their own words: interviews with twenty-five incarcerated Middle Eastern terrorists', *Terrorism and Political Violence*, 15: 171–84.

Pozzulo, J.D. and Marciniak, S. (2006) 'Comparing identification procedures when the perpetrator has changed appearance', *Psychology, Crime and Law*, 12(1): 429–38.

Pratt, J. (2005) 'Child sexual abuse: purity and danger in an age of anxiety', *Crime, Law and Social Change*, 43: 263–87.

Rafter, N. (1997) 'Psychopathy and the evolution of criminological knowledge', *Theoretical Criminology*, 1(2): 235–59.

Rafter, N. (2005) 'The murderous Dutch fiddler: criminology, history and the problem of phrenology', *Theoretical Criminology*, 9(1): 65–96.

Ramos, L.R., Koss, M.P. and Russo, N.F. (1999) 'Mexican-American women's definition of rape and sexual abuse', *Hispanic Journal of Behavioural Sciences*, 21: 236–65.

Reicher, S. (1987) 'Crowd behaviour as social Action', in J.C. Turner, M.A. Hogg, P.J. Oakes, S.D. Reicher and M.S. Wetherall, *Rediscovering The Social Group: A Self-Categorisation Theory*. Oxford: Blackwell. pp. 171–202.

Reicher, S. (1996) '"The Battle of Westminster": developing the social identity model of crowd behaviour in order to explain the initiation and development of collective conflict', *European Journal of Social Psychology*, 26: 115–34.

Reiner, R. (2000) *The Politics of the Police*, 3rd edn. Oxford: Oxford University Press.

Ressler, R.K., Burgess, A.W. and Douglas, J.E. (1988) *Sexual Homicide: Patterns and Motives*. Lexington, MA: Lexington Books.

Robinson, L. (2004) 'Black adolescent identity and the inadequacies of western psychology', in J. Roche, S. Tucker, R. Thomson and R. Flynn (eds), *Youth in Society*, 2nd edn. London: Sage. pp. 153–9.

Rock, P. (1978) 'Reviews', *British Journal of Criminology*, 18(2): 201–03.

Rose, N. (1985) *The Psychological Complex: Psychology, Politics and Society in England 1869–1931*. London: Routledge and Kegan Paul.

Rose, N. (1999) *Governing the Soul: The Shaping of the Private Self*, 2nd edn. London: Free Association Books. (First edition published 1989).

Rossmo, D.K. (2000) *Geographic Profiling*. Boca Raton, FL: CRC Press.

Roth, G. and Wittich, C. (eds) (1978) *Max Weber: Economy and Society*, Vol. 1. Berkeley: University of California Press.

Rozee, P.D. and Koss, M.P. (2001) 'Rape: a century of resistance', *Psychology of Women Quarterly*, 25: 295–311.

Rumney, P.N.S. (2006) 'False allegations of rape', *Cambridge Law Journal*, 65(1): 128–58.

Runciman, W.G. (1966) *Relative Deprivation and Social Justice*. London: Routledge and Kegan Paul.

Runciman, W.G. (1989) *Confession of a Reluctant Theorist: Selected Essays of W.G. Runciman*. Hemel Hempstead, Hertfordshire: Harvester Wheatsheaf.

Rutherford, A. (2002) *Growing out of Crime: The New Era*. Winchester: Waterside Press. (Originally published 1986.)

Sageman, M. (2004) *Understanding Terror Networks*. Philadelphia: University of Pennsylvania Press.

Salfati, C.G. and Canter, D. (1999) 'Differentiating stranger murders: profiling offender characteristics from behavioural styles', *Journal of Behavioural Sciences and the Law*, 17: 391–406.

Sandys, M. and Dillehay, R.C. (1995) 'First-ballot votes, prediliberation dispositions, and final verdicts in jury trials', *Law and Human Behaviour*, 19(2): 175–95.

Santilla, P., Junkkila, J. and Sandnabba, N.K. (2005) 'Behavioural linking of stranger rape', *Journal of Investigative Psychology and Offender Profiling*, 2: 87–103.

Saywitz, K.J., Geiselman, R.E. and Bornstein, G.K. (1992) 'Effects of cognitive interviewing and practice on children's recall and performance', *Journal of Applied Psychology*, 77(5): 744–56.

Searcy, J., Bartlett, J.C. and Memon, A. (2000) 'Influence of post-event narratives, line-up conditions and individual differences on false identification by young and older witnesses', *Legal and Criminological Psychology*, 5(2): 219–35.

Segal, L. (2001) 'Nature's way?: Inventing the natural history of rape', *Psychology, Evolution & Gender*, 3(1): 87–93.

Selikowitz, M. (2004) *ADHD: the Facts*. Oxford: Oxford University Press.

Seltzer, M. (1998) *Serial Killers: Death and Life in America's Wounded Culture*. London: Routledge.

Shah, J.Y., Kruglanski, A.W. and Friedman, R. (2003) 'Goal systems theory: integrating the cognitive and motivational aspects of self-regulation', in S. Spencer and S. Fein (eds), *Motivated Social Perception: The Ontario Symposium* 9. Mahwah, NJ: Lawrence Earlbaum Associates. pp. 243–75.

Shapiro, P.N. and Penrod, S. (1986) 'Meta-analysis of facial identification studies', *Psychological Bulletin*, 100(2): 139–56.

Shaw, C. and McKay, H. (1942) *Juvenile Delinquency in Urban Areas*. Chicago, IL: University of Chicago Press.

Shaw, E.D. (2003) 'Saddam Hussein: political psychological profiling results relevant to his possession, use, and possible transfer of weapons of mass destruction (WMD) to Terrorist Groups', *Studies in Conflict and Terrorism*, 26(5): 347–64.

Sherif, M., Harvey, O.J., White, B.J., Hood, W. and Sherif, C. (1961) *Intergroup Conflict and Cooperation: The Robbers' Cave Experiment*. Norman: University of Oklahoma Institute of Intergroup Relations.

Shildrick, T. and MacDonald, R. (2005) 'In defence of subculture: people, leisure and social divisions', *Journal of Youth Studies*, 9(2): 125–40.

Showalter, E. (1997) *Hystories*. London: Picador.

Shye, S. (1985) 'Nonmetric multivariate models for behavioural action systems', in D. Canter (ed.), *Facet Theory Approaches to Social Research*. New York: Springer. pp. 97–148.

Siegal, J.A. and Williams, L.M. (2003) 'The relationship between child sexual abuse and female delinquency and crime: a prospective study', *Journal of Research in Crime and Delinquency*, 40(1): 71–94.

Silke, A. (1998) 'Cheshire Cat Logic: the recurring theme of terrorist abnormality in psychological research', *Psychology, Crime and Law*, 4(1): 51–70.

Silke, A. (2003) 'Becoming a terrorist', in A. Silke (ed.), *Terrorist, Victims and Society: Psychological Perspectives on Terrorism and its Consequences*. Chichester, West Sussex: John Wiley. pp. 29–53.

Silke, A. (2006) 'The role of suicide in politics, conflict, and terrorism', *Terrorism and Political Violence*, 18: 35–46.

Silvestri, M. and Crowther-Dowey, C. (2008) *Gender and Crime*. London: Sage.

Sjöberg, R.L. and Lindblad, F. (2002) 'Limited disclosure of sexual abuse in children whose experiences were documented by videotape', *American Journal of Psychiatry*, 159(2): 312–14.

Skolnick, J. (1966) *Justice without Trial*. New York: Wiley.

Skolnick, P. and Shaw, J.I. (1997) 'The O.J. Simpson criminal trial verdict: racism or status shield?', *Journal of Social Issues*, 53(3): 503–16.

Smith, D.J. and McVie, S. (2003) 'Theory and method in the Edinburgh study of youth transitions and crime', *The British Journal of Criminology*, 43(1): 169–95.

Snook, B. (2004) 'Individual differences in distance travelled by serial burglars', *Investigative Psychology and Offender Profiling*, 1(1): 53–66.

Snook, B., Cullen, R.M., Mokros, A. and Harbort, S. (2005) 'Serial murderers' spatial decisions: factors that influence crime location choice', *Investigative Psychology and Offender Profiling*, 2(3): 147–64.

Sommers, S.R. (2006) 'On racial diversity and group decision-making: identifying multiple effects of racial composition on jury deliberations', *Journal of Personality and Social Psychology*, 90(4): 597–612.

Sommers, S.R. (2007) 'Race and decision making of juries', *Legal and Criminological Psychology*, 12(2): 171–87.

Sommers, S.R. and Ellsworth, P.C. (2000) 'Race in the courtroom: perceptions of guilt and dispositional attributions', *Personality and Social Psychology Bulletin*, 26(11): 1367–79.

Sorenson, T. and Snow, B. (1991) 'How children tell: the process of disclosure in child sexual abuse', *Child Welfare*, 70(1): 13–15.

Spaulding, E.R. (1923/1969) *An Experimental Study of Psychopathic Delinquent Women*. Montclair, NJ: Paterson Smith.

Spence, S.A. (2008) 'Playing Devil's advocate: the case *against* fMRI lie detection', *Legal and Criminological Psychology*, 13(1): 11–25.

Staub, E. (1989) *The Roots of Evil: The Psychological and Cultural Origins of Genocide and Other Forms of Group Violence*. Cambridge: Cambridge University Press.

Staub, E. (1996) 'Cultural–societal roots of violence: the examples of genocidal violence and of contemporary youth violence in the United States', *American Psychologist*, 51(2): 117–32.

Staub, E. (1999) 'The roots of evil: social conditions, culture, personality, and basic human needs', in A.G. Miller (guest ed.), *Special Issue: Perspectives on Evil and Violence, Personality and Social Psychology Review*, 35: 627–66.

Stouffer, S.A., DeVinney, L.C., Suchman, E.A., Star, S.A and Williams, R.M. (1949) *The American Soldier: Adjustment During Army Life*. Princeton, NJ: Princeton University Press.

Strangeland, P. (2005) 'Catching a serial rapist: hits and misses in criminal profiling', *Police Practice and Research*, 6(5): 453–69.

Strauss, A. (ed.) (1964) *George Herbert Mead on Social Psychology*. Chicago, IL: University of Chicago Press.

Sturman, P.A. (2000) *Drug–assisted Sexual Assault: A Study for the Home Office*. London: Police Research Scheme.

Summit, R. (1983) 'The child sexual abuse accommodation syndrome', *Child Abuse and Neglect*, 7(2): 179–92.

Sutherland, E.H. (1949) *Principles of Criminology*. Chicago, IL: Lippincott.

Sutherland, E.H. and Cressey, D. (1974) *Criminology*. New York: Lippincott.

Swanson, H.Y., Parkinson, P.N., O'Toole, B.I., Plunkett, A.M., Shrimpton, S. and Oates, R.K. (2003) 'Juvenile crime, aggression and delinquency after sexual abuse: a longitudinal study', *The British Journal of Criminology*, 43(4): 729–49.

Sykes, G. and Matza, D. (1957) 'Techniques of neutralisation: a theory of delinquency', *American Sociological Review*, 22: 664–70.

Tajfel, H. and Turner, J.C. (1979) 'An integrative theory of intergroup conflict', in W.G. Austin and S.Worschel (eds), *The Social Psychology of Intergroup Relations*. Monterey, CA: Brooks/Cole.

Tajfel, H. and Wilkes, A.L. (1963) 'Classification and quantitative judgement', *British Journal of Psychology*, 54(1): 101–14.

Taylor, I., Walton, P. and Young, J. (1973) *The New Criminology: For A Social Theory of Deviance*. London: Routledge and Kegan Paul.

Taylor, M. and Horgan, J. (2001) 'The psychological and behavioural bases of Islamic fundamentalism', *Terrorism and Political Violence*, 13(4): 37–71.

Taylor, M. and Horgan, J. (2006) 'A conceptual framework for addressing psychological process in the development of the terrorist', *Terrorism and Political Violence*, 18(4): 585–601.

Thornhill, R. and Palmer, C. (2000) *A Natural History of Rape: Biological Bases for Sexual Coercion*. London: MIT Press.

Timimi, S. (2005) *Naughty Boys: Anti-social Behaviour, ADHD and the Role of Culture*. Basingstoke, Hampshire: Palgrave Macmillan.

Turner, J.C. (1988) 'Foreword', in M.A. Hogg and D. Abrams, *Social Identifications: A Social Psychology of Intergroup Relations and Group Processes*. London: Routledge. pp. x–xii.

Turner, J.C., Hogg, M.A., Oakes, P.J., Reicher, S.D. and Wetherall, M.S. (1987) *Rediscovering the Social Group: A Self-Categorisation Theory*. Oxford: Blackwell.

Undeutsch, U. (1982) 'Statement reality analysis', in A. Trankell (ed.), *Reconstructing the Past: The Role of Psychologists in Criminal Trials*. Stockholm: P.A. Norstedt and Soners. pp. 27–56.

Unnever, J.D., Cullen, F.T. and Pratt, T.C. (2003) 'Parental management, ADHD, and delinquest involvement: reassessing Gottfredson and Hirschi's general theory', *Justice Quarterly*, 23(3): 471–500.

Valentine, T., Pickering, A. and Darling, S. (2003) 'Characteristics of eyewitness identification that predict the outcome of real lineups', *Applied Cognitive Psychology*, 17(8): 969–93.

Vega, J.V.A. (2001) 'Naturalism and feminism: conflicting explanations of rape in a wider context', *Psychology, Evolution & Gender*, 3(1): 47–85.

Victoroff, J. (2005) 'The mind of the terrorist: a review and critique of psychological approaches', *Journal of Conflict Resolution*, 49(3): 3–42.

Vrij, A. (2004) 'Why professionals fail to catch liars and how they can improve', *Legal and Criminological Psychology*, 9(2): 159–81.

Vrij, A. (2008) *Detecting Lies and Deceit: Pitfalls and Opportunities*. Chichester, West Sussex: John Wiley.

Vrij, A., Edwards, K. and Bull, R. (2001a) 'Police officers', social workers', teachers' and the general public's beliefs about deception in children, adolescents and adults', *Legal and Criminological Psychology*, 11(2): 297–312.

Vrij, A., Edwards, K. and Bull, R. (2001b) 'Police officers' ability to detect deceit: the benefit of indirect deception detection measures', *Legal and Criminological Psychology*, 6(2): 185–96.

Vrij, A., Kneller, W. and Mann, S. (2000) 'The effect of informing liars about criteria-based content analysis on their ability to deceive CBCA-raters', *Legal and Criminological Psychology*, 5(1): 57–70.

Walsh, D.W. and Milne, R. (2008) 'Keeping the PEACE? A study of investigative interviewing practices in the public sector', *Legal and Criminological Psychology*, 13(1): 39–57.

Webber, C. (2007a) 'Revaluating relative deprivation theory', *Theoretical Criminology*, 11(1): 97–120.

Webber, C. (2007b) 'Background, foreground, foresight: the third dimension of cultural criminology?', *Crime Media Culture*, 3(2): 139–57.

Weber, M. (1904) '"Objectivity" in social science', from E.A. Shils and H.A. Finch (eds and trans) (1949), *Max Weber: The Methodology of the Social Sciences*. New York: Simon and Shuster, The Free Press.

Weber, M. (1922) 'Bureaucracy', from H.H. Gerth and C. Wright Mills (eds and trans) (1946), *From Max Weber: Essays in Sociology*. New York: Oxford University Press.

Wells, G.I. (1978) 'Applied eyewitness testimony research: system variables and estimator variable', *Journal of Personality and Social Psychology*, 36(12): 1546–57.

Wells, G.L., Memon, A. and Penrod, S.D. (2006) 'Eyewitness evidence: improving its probative value', *Psychological Science in the Public Interest*, 7(2): 45–75.

Westcott, H.L. and Kynan, S. (2004) 'The application of a "story-telling" framework to investigative interviews for suspected child sexual abuse', *Legal and Criminological Psychology*, 9(1): 37–56.

Whyte, W.F. (1993/1943) *Street Corner Society: The Social Structure of an Italian Slum*, 4th edn. London: University of Chicago Press.

Willis, P. (1977) *Learning to Labour: How Working-Class Kids Get Working-Class Jobs*. London: Saxon House.

Woodhams, J., Hollin, C.R. and Bull, R. (2007) 'The psychology of linking crimes: a review of the evidence', *Legal and Criminological Psychology*, 12(2): 233–49.

Wright, R., Powell, M.B. and Ridge, D. (2007) 'What criteria do police officers use to measure the success of an interview with a child?', *Psychology, Crime and Law*, 13(4): 395–404.

Yacoubian, G.S. (2000) 'The (in)significance of genocidal behaviour to the discipline of criminology', *Crime, Law and Social Change*, 34: 7–19.

Yerkes, R.M. and Dodson, J.D. (1908) 'The relation of strength of stimulus to rapidity of habit-information', *Journal of Comparative Neurology of Psychology*, 18: 459–82.

Young, J. (1992) 'Ten points of realism', in J. Young and R. Matthews (eds), *Rethinking Criminology: The Realist Debate*. London: Sage. pp. 24–68.

Young, J. (1994) 'Incessant chatter: recent paradigms in criminology', in M. Maguire, R. Morgan and R. Reiner (eds), *The Oxford Handbook of Criminology*. Oxford: Oxford University Press. pp. 69–124.

Young, J. (1997) 'Left Realist criminology: radical in its analysis, realist in its policy', in M. Maguire, R. Morgan and R. Reiner (eds), *The Oxford Handbook of Criminology*, 2nd edn. Oxford: Oxford University Press. pp. 473–98.

Young, J. (1999) *The Exclusive Society*. London: Sage.

Young, J. (2007) *The Vertigo of Late Modernity*. London: Sage.

Zimbardo, P.G. (1970) 'The human choice: individuation, reason, and order versus deindividuation, impulse, and chaos', in W.J. Arnold and D. Levine (eds), *1969 Nebraska Symposium on Motivation*. Lincoln: University of Nebraska Press. pp. 237–307.

Internet references

(1) The National Police Improvement Agency: Research protocols: http://www.npia.police.uk/en/docs/Research_Protocols.pdf (accessed 6 August 2009)

(2) Outsourcing Torture: The secret history of America's 'extraordinary rendition' program: http://www.newyorker.com/archive/2005/02/14/050214fa_fact6 (accessed 4 October 2007)

(3) School massacre plots hatched on internet: http://www.guardian.co.uk/germany/article/0,,2214416,00.html (accessed 21 November 2007)

(4) Report on the Virginia Tech Massacre: http://news.bbc.co.uk/1/shared/bsp/hi/pdfs/30_08_07_virgtech_report.pdf (accessed 30 August 2007)

(5) The role of the Crown Prosecution Service: http://www.cps.gov.uk/about/role.html (accessed 21 February 2008)

(6) The psychology industry's long and shameful history with torture: http://www.motherjones.com/news/feature/2008/03/the-enablers.html (accessed 2 December 2008)

(7) American Psychological Association's ethical guidelines for psychologists involved in the interrogation of prisoners: http://www.ethicalapa.com/ (accessed 2 December 2008)

(8) GSK escapes prosecution over drug trial data: http://www.newscientist.com/article/mg19726473.600-gsk-escapes-prosecution-over-drug-trial-data.html (accessed 23 December 2008; originally published 14 March 2008)

(9) Questions on the effectiveness of Seroxat for depression: http://www.mhra.gov.uk/Howweregulate/Medicines/Medicinesregulatorynews/CON014153 (accessed 11 March 2008)

Index